# A DICTIONARY OF RHYMING SLANG

Titles of related interest published by Routledge:

*by Eric Partridge*

*A Concise Dictionary of Slang and Unconventional English*
edited by Paul Beale

*A Dictionary of Catch Phrases*

*A Dictionary of Clichés*
edited by Paul Beale

*A Dictionary of Slang and Unconventional English*
edited by Paul Beale

*Origins: an etymological dictionary of Modern English*

*The Routledge Dictionary of Historical Slang*
edited by Jacqueline Simpson

*Shorter Slang Dictionary*
by Eric Partridge and Paul Beale; edited by Rosalind Fergusson

*Shakespeare's Bawdy*
foreword by Stanley Wells

*You Have a Point There: a guide to punctuation and its allies*

# A DICTIONARY OF RHYMING SLANG

*by*

JULIAN FRANKLYN

LONDON AND NEW YORK

*Second edition with an Appendix, 1961*
*Reprinted 1969*
*Reprinted with illustrations and*
*first issued as a paperback 1975*
*Reprinted 1977, 1979, 1981, 1984, 1986 and 1987*

*Reprinted 1989, 1991, 1996, 2001 by Routledge*
*11 New Fetter Lane, London, EC4P 4EE*

*Routledge is an imprint of the Taylor & Francis Group*





*Printed and Bound in Great Britain by*
*St Edmundsbury Press, Bury St Edmunds, Suffolk*





*ISBN 0 4150 4602 5*

To

ERIC PARTRIDGE

with respect for his learning, admiration of his industriousness, and appreciation of his human qualities

# PREFACE

A PREFACE is—or ought to be—an ambivalent item of literary output, inasmuch as being written last it is meant to be read first. That it runs a grave risk of not being read at all is unfortunate, but it stands a better chance of catching the eye than does a page headed 'Acknowledgements'.

Hence I find it reasonable to apply the suspense technique employed by writers of thrillers and here record my thanks to Eric Partridge, first for the abstract quantity of his having set an example, secondly for the moral favour of his support and encouragement and thirdly for the practical value of not only his two vast works, *A Dictionary of Slang and Unconventional English*, and *A Dictionary of the Underworld*, both of which contain a great deal of expertly defined and annotated rhyming slang, but also for the enlightenment gained from his numerous, and at once masterly, scholarly and entertaining essays and articles on the subject.

I have to thank him, too, for his having introduced me, some few years ago, to Sidney J. Baker, the acknowledged authority on rhyming slang in Australia, and on all other forms of Australian speech.

I distinctly remember how Mr Baker and I paced up and down the Colonnade of the British Museum, discussing the Cockney dialect, and slang, and speech habits of individuals. Among my own contributions to the last aspect of slovenly affectedness was the story of how I had once abandoned, because of it, the chance of securing a job (which I greatly needed).

I had been introduced to an executive of the Metro-Goldwyn-Mayer Organization who had asked me to ring him up and make an appointment to call at his office and conclude the arrangements.

At the appointed time I made the call and a feminine voice, very ladylike, drawled or moaned 'ham jam'. I tried again. 'Ham jam' was again the reply at which I insisted that I wanted the Metro-Goldwyn-Mayer Organization. 'Hearts awry', moaned the voice, and at that moment the missing link fell into place. 'Ham jam' meant the initial letters MGM; 'hearts awry' meant 'that's right'. I rang off. When telling the yarn to Baker I did not dream a time would come, as it now has, when I would be publicly thanking him for permission to quote from his work.

He collaborated with Professor David W. Maurer of Louisville University in the production of an important article entitled 'Australian Rhyming Argot in the American Underworld', published in *American Speech, a Quarterly of Linguistic Usage*, from which both he and Professor Maurer have generously granted me permission to quote. The latter goes further, saying, 'If I can supply you with any additional information by letter, I shall be glad to do so. . . . I believe the situation has not changed much since 1944.' Indeed, it has not changed much in the United States, but there has been post-war growth in Australia.

Such developments as there may have been in U.S.A. are more likely to be in New York than in Chicago: Sydney, Australia has most assuredly evolved some new expressions.

Nearer home, and known to all, is Mr Lupino Lane, who lent both the Lord Chamberlain's Certified Copy of *Me and My Girl*, which happens to be the only copy in existence, and a private note-book, with permission to quote the relevant passages from both. The latter contained the fruits of many years of observation of rhyming slang used by actors and others connected with the world of the theatre.

The authors and the publishers whose names appear in conjunction with the examples used have all earned thanks and gratitude by their generous permission to re-print in this volume; and finally, the informants—so kind, tolerant and helpful—should be publicly acknowledged. That they remain anonymous is from no wish of the author to suppress the names of his helpers, but in deference to the wishes of the majority of them. As one of them put it, 'What! thay ain't no taste in nuffink, china! yeh git sorted aht boi every berk what finks 'e knows berra an what you do, who'll pump yeh brains aht o' yeh fer the proice of a pint.'

So much for suspense technique—the moment has now come when the task of forewording must be faced. In the introductory essay it will be observed that the theory of origin that has been universally accepted by scholars is here rejected and that in analysing the Victorian viewpoint of 'underworld', indication is given of one of the reasons for this rejection. After demolition and excavation comes the rebuilding and the architect of the new edifice (if no one else) is convinced of its superiority.

In the Glossary will be found a number of terms not hitherto placed upon record and which cannot therefore be dated within a decade: other terms which may have found their way into print have not been discovered, and again their dating is vague.

The present author is himself responsible for annotation and comment. To give a concrete example—Mr Lupino Lane should not be criticized for any notes or comments on terms gleaned from his private note-book, for it contained none.

Errors there may be: omissions there are. The author humbly invites corrections and enlightenment, but begs for extensive definitions with (if possible) chronological information. For example, 'Hen and hog= bog' will be welcome in order to plug a gap in knowledge, but 'Hen and hog=bog (a muddy patch, with no reference to slang for W.C.) first heard in Maidstone, Kent, in 1910. A term used by cattle-drovers. Now obsolete,' will be far more useful, and, by the way, 'hen and hog' does not mean *bog*, is not (and never was) used by anyone; it is just an example of how to fill the back of a post-card.

Finally, although the predominant rhythm is either iambic or trochaic (see page 18) a term that is of another rhythm, or of none at all, must, in spite of its violation of the rules, be admitted. In the glossary will be found a number of single words devoid of rhythm and in some examples rhyming but weakly with their meanings, hence it should not be assumed that a term of this kind, known to the reader, but omitted from the glossary, is also known to the author who has rejected it.

## PREFACE to the SECOND EDITION

FROM time to time a newspaper will print an article declaring that London's costers are no longer Cockney, that dialect is dying, that rhyming slang is dead.

These laments are superfluous, these obituaries premature; as attested by the call for a second edition of this dictionary and confirmed by there being—in round figures—five hundred additional entries.

This is not an indictment against the Press, neither does it reflect upon the veracity and conscientiousness of the contributors: on the contrary, both editors and writers are to be congratulated on being speech-conscious and giving expression to it.

They ought not to be held responsible for a misorientation attributable to the total mechanism of culture. They are men of affairs under an obligation to the reading public to supply up-to-the-minute news and views. To execute this duty they must keep their ears turned towards the seldom silent broadcasting apparatus: they are men of good taste who possess 'long-playing' records of the works of the master musicians and a machine for extracting the congealed sound therefrom: they are men of little leisure, hence, when 'dashing out for a quick coffee', are unable to be selective in their choice of a cafe and, in consequence are, while hastily imbibing, heavily bombarded by the jungle-howlings of the juke-box. Such conditioning of the auditory reflex renders them unable to listen to the human voice in the raw, and they assume that the slang they never hear is as dead as the donkey barrow.

People of less importance suffering from a similar sociological deafness write letters along the same lines to editors who print them: this lofty misleading occurs because 'he who lives more lives than one more deaths than one must die' and rather than run the risk of double death these arm-chair commentators upon life out-of-doors remain isolated in their own world viewing the other man's through long-distance glasses, and filling up the gaps in observation with logical deduction.

It is not easy to cross social frontiers and feel at ease in an environment other than one's own even when one is conscious of the unexplored territory to be charted: it is, however, manifestly possible to believe, even in mid-twentieth century, that one falls off the edge when past the Pillars of Hercules.

If there are fresh worlds to conquer they must be sought. The Port aspect of London, vast and important though it is, remains unostentatiously in the background of Metropolitan life. Even the multitude that passes, night and morning, over London Bridge and sees the 'breakfast boats' discharging cargo does not mentally extend the scene to cover the considerable acreage of the docks.

The watermen and the dock-workers live largely in a close world of their own: do not, when in their pubs and cafes, lay themselves open to intrusion and they are inclined, when confronted with the insensitive, objective—even aggressive—questioner, to make their answers monosyllabic.

This attitude is not, as some romantic-minded writers on London life have inferred, because of 'the natural shyness' of men who earn their living by the waters of the world, either on ocean-going ships or on the small-craft of a great tideway, but because the man of the waterfront knows how easily he may be made a cat's-paw in a smuggling plot by some plausible and apparently genuine stranger.

The Thames waterman disapproves of smuggling (which is dishonest) because it is dishonest; but he jealously guards the Englishman's right to express his political opinions, and if he is a believer in Free Trade he can fearlessly, efficiently and in a practical manner exemplify his beliefs and his ideas without the aid of strangers.

His cautiousness in casual conversation makes it more than normally difficult to tap the living spring of rhyming slang that is demonstrating, almost daily, the vital process of its creation. Names, in general rhyming slang, are often totally fictitious, and even when those of living characters are used, they seldom have direct reference to their meanings, being employed only for their phonetic value. When, however, names are used along the waterfront they are almost always those of contemporary workers, or, more importantly, those of ships. These terms are allowed to fall into desuetude when the men retire, or the ships are broken-up—or 'sold foreign'—and the names of the new men and the new ships are adopted.

Unless one is of the waterfront world there is little likelihood of this nascent slang being revealed, but fortunately Mr F. C. Wright, who has spent a lifetime linked to London's river, was, in addition to a shrewd observer during the years of his service, an industrious note-taker, and he has been generous enough to send a list of such terms all of which, appearing in the addenda, are distinguished by the description 'waterfront ephemeral'.

The present writer's frenzied efforts to obtain further specimens has, so far, met with no success, but there is surely room for that tide to rise considerably. It should perhaps be emphasized that the vulgarity or the unprintability of a term ought not to bring blushes to the cheek of anyone who knows it, but whereas it was previously suggested[1] that a postcard would make a sufficient vehicle of information, it must now be said that unprintable terms require the modest concealment of an envelope. Postmen, it seems, are easily shocked even if mitred Bishops are not.

Another specialized and industrious helper was Mr A. K. Brice, whose list covered two generations and four aspects of life. Observing that addiction to the habit of employing rhyming slang runs in families (as musical ability does) he indicated among the terms used by his father which of them were in use before 1945 (a group that includes a number handed down by his grandfather), and which had been 'picked-up' by Mr Brice senior when working between 1946 and 1952, at Ealing Studios where he was a plasterer. In addition, his own stock of terms was separated into two groups: those used by him as a boy and young man between the wars, and those by which his vocabulary was extended while serving in the Royal Air Force. These four categories are suitably indicated by the method shown in the list of abbreviations preceding the additional Glossary.

Another unselfish helper, Mr Charles Bowness, who has spent many years in the Merchant Navy, revealed a nice crop harvested in the forecastle as well as in the abode of the afterguard, and Mr Clive Graham forfeited a few gems mined upon the race-course. Non-specializing, but no less helpful, has been the material supplied by Eric Partridge *of course*—Mr A. J. Brooker, Mr Frank A. Allen, Mr Ralph A. Hadrill, and many others.

An optimist might, at this point, declare: 'there remains now no rhyming slang that is unrecorded', and lay down the pen, but clearly there must be, in addition to waterfront ephemerals, many modern Australian terms that have not yet been netted and, 'up to the time of going to press' no Irish Sportsman has tipped out the contents of his bag.

Finally, it is possible that here, on one's very door-step as it were, there lurks an unrecorded Cockney term or two, hiding behind the false front of truncation and familiarity.

[1] See page ix.

# GLOSSARY

The following abbreviations have been used:

C. = century.

*c.* = *circa* (about).

cf. = compare.

q.v. = *quod vide* (which see).

| | | |
|---|---|---|
| *American Thesaurus* | = | *The American Thesaurus of Slang*: by Lester V. Berrey and Melvin Van Den Bark. |
| Chicago May | = | *Chicago May—Her Story*: by May Churchill Sharpe. |
| Ducange Anglicus | = | *The Vulgar Tongue* . . . : by Ducange Anglicus. |
| Hotten | = | *The Slang Dictionary*: John Camden Hotten. |
| Lupino Lane | = | a private note-book, kindly lent by Mr Lupino Lane. |
| Maurer and Baker | = | *Australian Rhyming Argot in the American Underworld*: by D. W. Maurer (in collaboration with Sidney J. Baker) in *American Speech*, 1944. |

# CONTENTS

YOU CAN TAKE A BOTTLE OF SAUCE TO THE FISHERMAN'S DAUGHTER, BUT YOU CAN'T MAKE HER TUMBLE DOWN THE SINK

# ESSAY

THE *Oxford English Dictionary* informs us that 'Rhyme . . . [is] agreement in the terminal sounds of two or more words or metrical lines, such that (in English prosody) the last stressed vowel and any sound following it are the same, while the sound or sounds preceding are different. . . . The consonance may extend over more than one word. . . . Imperfect rhymes are tolerated to a large extent in English', but imperfect rhymes are nearer to true rhymes than assonances are. 'Assonance', says the O.E.D., is 'resemblance or correspondence of sound between two words or syllables'. It is characteristic of Old French, rather than of Old English verse.

Some people, even some poets, endure the labours of Hercules in writing a short, rhymed, metrical verse; others, who make no claim to literary ability, find unpremeditated rhyme flowing rhythmically into normal conversation.

At the head of the list of unconscious rhymesters are the Cockneys, some of whom have the faculty developed to a pathological pitch inasmuch as they rhyme not merely unconsciously but against their wills at most inappropriate times.

This curious ability (or linguistic disease) has not been specifically commented upon in the past by those who have written on Cockney habits, customs and peculiarities, but it has given rise to the false impression that 'Cockneys converse in rhyming slang. This erroneous idea is excusable, because in the presence of a stranger who is obviously attentive, or one who is overtly enquiring, the conversational landscape will soon become transformed in a bewildering blizzard of this arresting speech-system whereby, in place of a word, a phrase consisting of two or three words that rhyme with it, is used.' [1]

A nice discrimination must, however, be observed between rhyming slang and slang that rhymes. 'Argy-bargy', for *argument*, is one kind; another is the very general verbal euphemism, 'ruddy' for *bloody*, another is the rather weak literary expedient of writing in dialogue 'muck', 'mucker' and 'mucking'. Cockneys have, and have had for at least fifty

[1] *The Cockney*, Julian Franklyn.

years, their own little spelling joke: 'If you see Kate'. Another of the same type is: 'See you any Tuesday'.

The automatically standardized rhyming slang, evolved in the early nineteenth century, attracted educated attention reasonably soon after it had become established and popularized.

The Cultural and ideological century over-runs the Chronological century. The nineteenth century did not expire at midnight on 31 December 1900; it was bludgeoned to death on 4 August 1914; and the eighteenth century lingered in a senile state until 1837 when Queen Victoria ascended the Throne.

It should, however, in self-defence be noted that to some minds—particularly the mechanical, fact-and-figure tabulating type—the same idea could be expressed in reverse. 'Coming events cast their shadows before.' Did not the first internal-combustion engine propelled vehicle explode its concussive way along before 1901?

Nevertheless, achievement is not necessarily culture, and gentlemen of the pre-Victorian period could carouse in Seven Dials with the highwayman and the cut-purse—the prostitute being taken for granted—but in Victorian times, and particularly in the Victoria and Albert section, the chasm between the respectable and the rapscallion, the educated and the uneducated, the rich and the poor, became wide, deep and practically impassable.

Robert Peel's Police Force was a sign of the times. By 1837 it had survived its infancy. The population of Seven Dials was 'not to be mentioned to ears polite'.

There were a few outstanding characters who could and did take a full-bodied flying leap over the chasm and return with social and mental hands unsullied by the tar they had touched! Further, such men, though not missionaries, were clearly social reformers, and could not, because of their close contacts with what had come to be uncritically called 'the underworld', be denounced as renegade.

No distinction was observed between the criminal and the pauper: pauperism was regarded as a negative form of criminality, because such relief as there was for the poor was of a nature that no man of spirit could tolerate, hence, pauperism led to crime, and the undiscriminating, dignified, bewhiskered Victorian, too sincere in his hypocrisy to be lightly dismissed as a hypocrite; too sure of the sanctity of work—no matter how harrowing and poorly paid, provided it yielded him a profit—to be denounced as indifferent to the needs of the 'industrious classes', could not tolerate the existence of self-supporting poor; and he suspected every street-trader and door-to-door hawker of illicit activities. The overt occupation was condemned as merely a cover for procuring information for house-breakers.

Henry Mayhew, and to a lesser extent, Charles Dickens, ought, by their works, to have enlightened their contemporaries, but no mass mental disease is so far removed from the sphere of curability as current public opinion is, hence 'the underworld' of the mid-nineteenth century was a vastly greater territory than the character of its inhabitants justified.

Henry Mayhew, who possessed the rare ability of making an intimate sociological investigation without poisoning his system with statistics and by so doing losing sight of the fact that his material was human, discovered the street poet who, referring to the Great Exhibition of 1851, said: 'I shall be there. Me and my mates. We are going to send in a set of verses in letters of gold for a prize. *We'll* let the foreigners know what the real native melodies is, and no mistake!'

Notwithstanding, Mayhew made no specific mention of rhyming slang, with which he must have been familiar.

Francis Grose, whose (third edition) *Classical Dictionary of the Vulgar Tongue* made its appearance in 1796, gives but a vague hint at the possibility of a rhyming form of 'flash language', and even the fifth edition (1823), with extra, early nineteenth-century additions by Pierce Egan, the author of *Tom and Jerry*, does no more.

In 1839 'H. Brandon Esq.' edited *Poverty, Mendicity and Crime, or the Facts, Examinations &c. upon which the Report was founded, presented to the House of Lords by W. A. Miles Esq.* to which he 'added a Dictionary of the Flash or Cant Language, Known to every Thief and Beggar', and in that book a negligible number of rhyming slang terms were included.

It is not a very good piece of work—Brandon does not seem to have made a personal study of slang in the field but simply to have reprinted goodly extracts from *The Flash Dictionary*, a 48mo volume designed for the waistcoat pocket—its overall dimensions are $4 \times 2\frac{1}{2}$ inches—it has an engraved title-page, and was 'sold by C. Smeeton, St. Martins Churchyard' in 1821. It has fifty-five pages of Glossary, with twenty-nine lines to the page. Most of the definitions are on one line, a few extend to two or three. The rest of the pages are consumed in preliminary 'Advertisement', and appended 'The Sixty Orders of Prime Coves', and some 'Flash Songs'.

This fascinating little volume was, with a few additions and no acknowledgements, again reprinted as the appendix of *Sinks of London Laid Open* (1848), 'embellished with Humorous Illustrations by George Cruikshank, published by J. Duncombe'.

By this time, Victorianism was firmly established. The gentleman who was 'something in the City' was something quite different in the suburbs. All classes were users of slang, each according to the orbit of his activities, but the conventional, respectable attitude was one of shocked disapproval.

Charles Dickens, not in his capacity of great-hearted humanitarian and humorist but as the personification of *vox populi*, wrote a poor and priggish article denouncing the use of slang which he printed in *Household Words*, No. 183, 24 September 1853. He gave examples of slang usage in various strata of society, but he did not so much as mention rhyming slang even casually. Apart from three or four examples that had by mid-century unostentatiously crept into print, where they nestled quietly, innocent of comment, one would conclude, from the lack of evidence, that the system was not yet established. There is, however, good reason to believe that it was already a lusty youth, safely past the perils of infancy.

## II

Wise men do not tempt fate, nor set the avalanche in motion; hence, in a period when parsons preached against the use of slang,[1] and shocked parents addressed letters on the subject to the press,[2] a philologist who felt that a dictionary of slang would be a desideratum would proceed with caution and conceal his identity behind the opacity of a pseudonym.

Such a one was 'Ducange Anglicus' who was so effective in his self-effacement that a fair amount of research has so far failed to reveal the man behind the name.[3]

He produced a book of eighty pages 6 × 4 inches overall, entitled: *The Vulgar Tongue: a glossary of slang, cant, and flash words and phrases, used in London from* 1839 *to* 1859. . . . The first edition made its appearance in 1857 (the second in 1859); and both editions were published by Bernard Quaritch.

In the 'Preface to the first edition', reprinted in the second, the author says:

'This little volume has been printed with the view of assisting Literary Men, the Officers of the Law, and Philanthropists, in their intercourse with Classes of English Society who use a different Phraseology, only understood by their own fraternity.'

The intention is both laudable and sincere, each edition being limited to two hundred and fifty copies, thus prohibiting a popular market and proportionately reducing profits.

The main glossary, containing about seven hundred and thirty entries, has sixty-two specimens of rhyming slang, of which number a surprisingly large proportion are still current.

Between *The Flash Dictionary* of 1821 and *The Vulgar Tongue* of

[1] See Appendix. [2] See Appendix.

[3] The choice may have been influenced by the name of Charles du Fresne Ducange, a French historian and philologist (1610–88).

1857, rhyming slang has come to life and attracted enlightened attention.

The evolution of slang words, or phrases, or systems of usage, is as mysterious as is that of standard language. The word is evoked by some complex of circumstances at a certain level of society, and like a spilled liquid it spreads at that level, runs rapidly downward, and seeps slowly upward, the rate of dispersal being controlled by viscosity. Rhyming slang, as mobile as mercury, has thus got into print at an early age.

Among the numerous reasons for the adoption of slang expressions is the need felt by certain classes of the community for a secret language: thieves may wish to discuss, in the presence of their intended victim, the prospects of their accomplishing a successful robbery, and they may conveniently do so in the strong underworld cant, the terms of which being unrelated to, do not suggest the standard words for which they are substitute: the backslang of the coster distorts the inverted words so severely that recognition without specific knowledge is impossible, and the coster himself, in the days of backslang usage, would not, upon meeting a hitherto unknown contemporary, automatically commence a conversation in that system. He first enquired, in the language, whether its use would be acceptable.

Because the secret language theme is so well understood by philologists, all who have written on the use of rhyming slang have accepted the theory that it came into being as a secret language of the underworld. It is, however, time to revise that theory and to re-assess the value of the evidence.

That rhyming slang was discovered lurking in the underworld where it was doing duty as thieves' secret language is not evidence of its place of origin. It was annexed by the true underworld from those who inhabited the Victorian extension and that included the indigent workman.

There is a striking difference in fundamental character between the cant or flash language evolved and used by thieves and vagabonds, and the rhyming slang which they adopted. The former is grim, harsh and humourless; the latter, gay, frolicsome and amusing. The former must be learnt as a foreign tongue must be learnt, the latter is, in the main, intelligible to the uninitiated.

The reason why rhyming slang was discovered where it was discovered when it was discovered is because 'Officers of the Law' did (and they still do) make it part of their business, in the interests of public security, to learn thieves' lingo: there was (and is) no need to study that of law-abiding although humble citizens, hence, rhyming slang from its place of origin, *via* the true underworld and the police, reached respectable attention through the work of Ducange Anglicus. This took place about twenty-five or thirty years after the system was forged on the anvil of culture-clash by the hammer of friendly rivalry.

The word *navvy* made its first appearance in the language in 1832, when it could be classified as slang. In a quarter of a century it had become standard English, and soon it became a linguistic habit to prefix it with the word 'Irish'. A navvy is (or was, for the result of mechanization is the extinction of this hardy race) a semi-skilled labourer engaged on excavation, embankment, and other work demanding both strength and endurance.

The early nineteenth century was a period of titanic activity. Docks were laid down, canals were cut, railway embankments thrown up. Every pound of earth and stone displaced in these vast enterprises had to be shovelled by hand into bushel-baskets and carried on a man's back either to or from the site of the works, hence, a huge army of navvies was in employment. The ranks were filled by brawny uneducated Cockneys and massive Irishmen.

These two ethnic groups, so far asunder in many ways, yet have much in common. Each is fond of the sound of his own voice, both are lovers of words. The Cockney is renowned for his sense of humour, the Irishman for his quick temper, but the fact is, Cockneys will fight when fisticuffs are necessary, and the Irishman loves a joke. The difference in reaction is that the Cockney is tolerant and takes a great deal of annoyance, but the Irishman, considering himself a son of an oppressed nation, has developed, in common with all persecuted peoples, a tendency to make a major issue out of a minor incident. The Cockney arranges to have his fight in private, the Irishman leaps to his in public. The Cockney is amused at the Irishman's boastfulness and excitability, the Irishman amazed at the Cockney's modesty and stolid endurance.

The two people, on the whole, like each other and work well together, but while they work they talk, laugh at and chaff each other; the Irishman telling long, tall stories of which he is the hero, and the Cockney 'capping' them with brisk comment, and the assumption of Metropolitan superiority.

In this atmosphere, and under these conditions, the quick-witted Cockney created rhyming slang, as a means of mystifying 'the Micks', and having the last laugh. Verbal competition is a fine forcing house for linguistic agility. The Irishmen did not remain mystified for long: they soon mastered the system and paid back in Irish-flavoured rhyme. What could 'Rory O'More' mean to a Cockney?

This is not the only Irish name that appears in the lists of early rhyming slang, and since the Cockneys probably could not and certainly did not read Irish folk-tales, or even newspapers, these Irish references cannot be accounted for in any other way.

## III

An unemployed navvy, having nothing to support him, rapidly drifted into the ranks of the Victorian underworld, where he learned from professional beggars how to beg; and probably from professional thieves how to thieve; and they in turn learned from him the rhyming slang that had helped to laugh the day away when all was well.

Rhyming slang, having thus been adopted as a secret language by thieves, became a subject of study by the 'Officers of the Law', and grist to the mill of the lexicographer. In 1859 a far more ambitious book than *The Vulgar Tongue* of Ducange Anglicus made its appearance. This, entitled *The Slang Dictionary*, was by 'A London Antiquary', and the publisher was John Camden Hotten.

This book, a full-size dictionary, was accepted as a serious work and in the subsequent editions the 'London Antiquary' revealed his identity —none other than John Camden Hotten himself. This would have surprised no one, for he was almost a scholar and quite a gentleman: a 'bookseller' by occupation, and one who did not hesitate to compile works for his press when he felt them to be needed and could find no author to undertake their production.

The books published by John Camden Hotten have never become inhabitants of the second-hand book dealer's twopenny shelf, unless the dealer happens to be more than normally ignorant: rather have they become the catalogued stock of antiquarian booksellers. This applies very strongly to such works as *The Slang Dictionary*, and *The History of Sign Boards* (Larwood and Hotten).

*The Slang Dictionary*, which was the standard work of reference on the subject for many years, ran through five editions, the fifth appearing in 1874, fifteen years after the first, and just after John Camden Hotten's death. It had, however, clearly been edited and enlarged with its additional matter by himself.

A new impression was issued as recently as 1922 by Messrs Chatto and Windus, who took over the goodwill and assets of a number of the old-time booksellers, including the famous Moxon, who had published for Tennyson.

John Camden Hotten, who took himself and all his works very seriously, was not the man to make a mere rehash-up of older glossaries. He seems to have made contact with characters of the underworld, and to have employed them to supply him with information on the current usage of slang. He often refers to his 'informant', but he is unaware of how dangerously misleading the uneducated informant can be through no fault of his own: from no perverse desire to misinform and mislead.

In addition to his getting practical contemporary information, he studied the history of his subject and gave, as an appendix, a useful Bibliography of the literature. He was, in this, perhaps, not altogether original, for Ducange Anglicus printed a 'Bibliography of the canting and slang literature with glossaries'. The arrangement is approximately chronological and the List is a very small proportion of the entire range of that Literature; it contains only the books then being offered for sale at the publishers, hence, it may be regarded as more in the nature of an advertisement by Bernard Quaritch than as a scholarly addendum by Ducange Anglicus.

John Camden Hotten includes Ducange Anglicus in his own bibliography and comments: 'A silly and childish performance, full of blunders and contradictions.' This remark is unfortunate because John Camden Hotten's own dictionary is not innocent of errors: indeed, no glossary of slang (including that in this volume) can be totally accurate in spite of the care taken by the author, for the very nature of the subject prohibits it.

In *The Slang Dictionary*, special sections are devoted to special vocabularies, and rhyming slang enjoys a section to itself prefaced with an essay on the subject. This is the first commentary on rhyming slang and it is therefore somewhat nebulous, but its being the first makes it worthy of reproduction:

'There exists in London a singular tribe of men, known amongst the "fraternity of vagabonds" as chaunters and patterers. Both classes are great talkers. The first sing or chaunt through the public thoroughfares ballads—political and humorous—carols, dying speeches, and the various other kinds of gallows and street literature. The second deliver street orations on grease-removing compounds, plating powders, high-polishing blacking, and the thousand-and-one wonderful pennyworths that are retailed to gaping mobs from a London kerbstone.

'They are quite a distinct tribe from the costermongers; indeed, amongst tramps, they term themselves the "harristocrats of the streets", and boast that they live by their intellects. Like the costermongers, however, they have a secret tongue or cant speech known only to each other. This cant, which has nothing to do with that spoken by the costermongers, is known in Seven Dials and elsewhere as the "rhyming slang", or the substitution of words and sentences which rhyme with other words intended to be kept secret. The chaunter's cant, therefore, partakes of his calling, and he transforms and uses up into a rough speech the various odds and ends of old songs, ballads and street nick-names, which are found suitable to his purpose. Unlike nearly all other systems of cant, the rhyming slang is not founded upon allegory; unless we accept a few rude similes, thus—"I'm afloat" is the rhyming cant for "boat", "sorrowful tale" is equivalent to "three months in jail", "artful dodger" signifies a "lodger", and a "snake in the grass" stands for a "looking-glass", a meaning that would delight a fat Chinaman or a collector of Oriental proverbs. But, as in the case of the costers' speech and the old gipsy-vagabond cant, the chaunters and patterers so interlard this rhyming slang with their general remarks, while their ordinary language is so smothered and subdued, that, unless when they are professionally engaged, and talking of their wares, they might almost pass for foreigners.

'From the enquiries I have made of various patterers and "paper-workers", I learn that the rhyming slang was introduced about twelve or fifteen years ago.[1] Numbering this class of oratorical and bawling wanderers at twenty thousand, scattered over Great Britain, including London and the large provincial towns, we thus see the number of English vagabonds who converse in rhyme and talk poetry, although their habitations and mode of life constitute a very unpleasant Arcadia. These nomadic poets, like the other talkers of cant or secret languages, are stamped with the vagabond's mark, and are continually on the move. The married men mostly have lodgings in London, and come and go as occasion may require. A few never quit London streets, but the greater number tramp to all the large provincial fairs, and prefer the "monkery" (country) to town life. Some transact their business in a systematic way, sending a post-office order to the Seven Dials' printer for a fresh supply of ballads or penny books, or to the "swag shop", as the case may be, for trinkets and gewgaws, to be sent on by rail to a given town by the time they shall arrive there.

'When any dreadful murder, colliery explosion, or frightful railway accident has happened in a country district, three or four chaunters are generally on the spot in a day or two after the occurrence, vending and bawling "A True and Faithful Account", &c., which "true and faithful account" was concocted purely in the imaginations of the successors of Catnach and Tommy Pitts,[2] behind the counters of their printing-shops in Seven Dials. And but few fairs are held in any part of England without the patterer being punctually at his post, with his nostrums, or real gold rings (with the story of the wager laid by the gentleman—see FAWNEY-BOUNCING in the dictionary),[3] or savealls for candlesticks, or paste which, when applied to the strop, makes the dullest razor keen enough to hack broom-handles and sticks, and after that to have quite enough sharpness left for splitting hairs, or shaving them off the back of one of the hands of a clodhopper, looking on in amazement. And Cheap John, too, with his coarse jokes, and no end of six-bladed knives, and pocket-books, containing information for everybody, with pockets to hold money, and a pencil to write with into

[1] This was written in 1858 [J. C. H. footnote].

[2] The famous printers and publishers of sheet songs and last dying speeches thirty years ago [J. C. H. footnote]. [3] Hotten's Dictionary.

the bargain, and a van stuffed with the cheap productions of Sheffield and "Brummagem"—he, too, is a patterer of the highest order, and visits fairs, and can hold a conversation in the rhyming slang.

'Such is a rough description of the men who speak this jargon; and simple and ridiculous as the vulgar scheme of a rhyming slang may appear, it must always be regarded as a curious fact in linguistic history. In order that the reader's patience may not be too much taxed, only a selection of rhyming words has been given in the Glossary—and these for the most part, as in the case of the back-slang, are the terms of every-day life, as used by this order of tramps and hucksters.

'It must not be supposed, however, that the chaunter or patterer confines himself entirely to this slang when conveying secret intelligence. On the contrary, although he speaks not a "leash of languages", yet he is master of the beggar's cant, and is thoroughly "up" in street slang.'

Of course, in a pioneer work such as *The Slang Dictionary* is, there must be many errors, and it is unnecessary to call attention to them—at least, to the major ones—for John Camden Hotten did so himself. In the later edition he added a note, thus:

'Since the foregoing was written, matters have changed considerably, even, which I much doubt, if they ever were as is stated; for, as I have already remarked, wherever opportunity has occurred, the costermonger, the patterer, the chaunter, and the various other itinerants who "work" London and the provinces, delight in making themselves appear a most mysterious body; and this, when added to their natural disinclination to commit themselves to anything like fact so far as their natural enemies—enquirers, and well-dressed enquirers in particular—are concerned, has caused all sorts of extraordinary stories to be set afloat, which have ultimately led to an opinion becoming prevalent, that the costermonger and his friends form a race of beings differing entirely from those who mix in the ordinary humdrum routine of respectable life. Nothing could really be much further from fact. Any one who has ever been driven by stress of circumstances or curiosity to take up a permanent or temporary residence in any of the lodging-houses which abound in St Giles's, Saffron Hill, Turnmill Street, and in all parts of the eastern district of the metropolis, will bear me out when I say that a more commonplace individual, so far as his inner life is concerned, than the London itinerant cannot possibly exist. Certainly he is ignorant, and takes a very limited view of things in general, and religion and politics in particular; but these peculiarities are held in common with his betters, and so cannot be regarded as the special prerogative of any class. If you ask him a question he will attempt to mislead you, because, by your asking the question, he knows you are ignorant of his way of life; and when he does not mystify from love of mischief, as it appears he does from all published books I have seen about him, he does so as a duty he owes his natural enemies, the parish authorities and the tract distributors, the latter of whom he holds in special abhorrence.

'If the rhyming slang was ever, during its existence, regarded as a secret language, its secrecy has long since departed from it. Far easier of construction than even the back slang, it has been common, especially in several printing-offices I could name, for many years, while street-boys are great proficients in its small mysteries. The Glossary which follows here will explain a good deal of its mechanism; but it must be borne in mind that the rhymes are all matters of individual opinion, and that if one man says Allacompain means rain, another is quite justified in preferring Mary Blane, if his individual fancy lies in that direction. And now, if there is any secret about the rhyming slang, it is this—the rhyme is left out. This may at first seem extraordinary; but on reflection it will be seen that there is no other way of making the proceedings of its exponents puzzling to ordinarily sharp ears which have received the slightest clue. Thus, when the first word of a series only is used, and others in the sentence are made up from the back, the centre and various slangs, there is some hope of fogging an intruding listener to a private conversation. When a man is drunk, the rhyming slang would illustrate that fact by the words "Elephant's trunk"; but the practised hand confines himself to the statement that "Bill's Elephants". "Bullock's horn" represents to pawn, but an article is said to be "Bullocked" only; and so on through the list, providing always that the curtailed represents two syllables; if it does not, then the entire rhyme is given.

'I think that this will be sufficient to guide those readers anxious to become proficient themselves, or to understand others who are themselves proficient at this item in the world of slang; and so I have nothing more to say except to call attention to the fact that, in all the other introductions, I have made my corrections, which have been neither few nor unimportant, in the text; but that I could see no way of working on the subject of the rhyming slang fairly and explicitly other than by means of this note.'

It is interesting to observe that between his first and his last edition he had discovered the system of condensation that has mystified many more up-to-date observers, and that has enabled the end product of the process to be employed in polite society where the true meaning is unknown.

He is probably wrong in assuming that the abandonment of the rhyming element is a conscious, reasoned effort to make the not very secret language more puzzling to the eavesdropper. The explanation is more simple. Abbreviation is not only a form of verbal economy but it is a very human habit of speech. Mid-twentieth century has developed it to a point of linguistic decadence, new, short (generally very ugly) words are fused out of the initial letters of long descriptions of, or the names of, organizations and objects. (In print, the ugly little words are made of capital letters with neither full stops nor spaces between them.) Examples so readily occur to the contemporaneous reader that none will be given, chiefly in hope that the vile habit expires, and that posterity will fail to identify as a word the groups of telescoped initials.

In technical matters, and in slang usage, abbreviation is permissible, and the failure to use it by the speaker may be accepted as an insult by the hearer. Should the foreman 'iron-fighter' say: 'We'll have No. 3 Rolled Steel Joist up next,' the workman might answer: 'Wot's-a-marrer wif yeh?—Fink I've onie jes' come on na bleetn' job? Fink I don't know wot an Irish Jay is?' [1]

So it is, between friends, with rhyming slang—there is no need to insult a man by using the whole phrase as though he would not recognize the first half. Some of the phrases cannot be cut. For example, there are several that have the same first word, but widely different meanings: it is impossible to say 'Uncle' without giving his name, for Uncle Ned is not Uncle Willie.

On the other hand there are examples of severance so complete that there is danger of disassociation: even some Cockneys are not aware that *China*, a boon companion, is condensed rhyming slang, although, of course, the majority of them do know. Words like *raspberry*, an expression of disapproval, would, if associated with the rhyming element, bring blushes to many a fair cheek.

Lupino Lane, in his brilliant, entertaining and illuminating book, *How to Become a Comedian*, when commenting on the range of sounds that the professional 'comic' must learn to emit, says: 'I do not advise the use of the "Raspberry", it might give the audience an idea!'

## IV

Rhyming slang is so essentially Cockney that many people refer to it as 'Cockney slang', and, as already stated, entertain the idea that Cockneys normally converse in it. The error arises from the fact of its use being a form of Cockney ostentation: it is produced for the confusion of the obviously attentive, or the enquiring stranger, hence 'field work' in the gathering of specimens is apt to be highly inaccurate.

Cockneys are a kindly people and the average would not deliberately mislead a serious enquirer, but the dialect is a barrier to understanding and the Cockney is not conscious of having a dialect. He believes that his form of speech is plain English and that other people have a false pronunciation. Mr. George Bernard Shaw's play—*Pygmalion*—ought

[1] R.S.J.—*Rolled Steel Joist.*

to be re-entitled 'A Comedy of Errors'. This would call the attention of both readers and auditors to the fact that it should not be taken seriously and that the basic idea is a matrix error carrying gems of ignorant misrepresentation of Cockney dialect. Would a girl of Eliza Dolittle's calibre wish to change her speech form? 'Not bloody likely.' That undeservedly famous phrase is itself an error. A cockney flower-girl would have said 'No bleet'n fear!'

The Cockney, being glib-tongued and very sure of himself, rushes through his sentences at a break-neck speed and no conscious part of his mind is engaged in the selection of, or in the utterance of, the words he is using—they are, to him, simply the oral sounds that convey his meaning and if a speaker is pulled up short and asked for elucidation, he experiences a shock and is often incapable of separating word from word, much less of enunciating syllables.

If his tormentor persists in the analytical enquiry the Cockney is inclined to stammer and become confused: asked to 'write it down' and given the means of doing so, he will not merely mis-spell, but will sometimes jot down in phonetic spelling, a homophone (not necessarily a homograph). Something like this may have happened when John Camden Hotten was interrogating his 'informant' of Seven Dials who produced for him 'Daisy Recruits', which he spelt 'recroots'. The probabilities are all in favour of this having been a mere self-conscious, tongue-tied fumbling of 'Daisy-roots'.

It is noteworthy that the 'informant' of a hundred years ago could write at all, but the lack of education of the period should not be over-estimated as the cause of distortion. Today there is, practically speaking, no one who is illiterate from lack of having been taught, but many people of humble manual occupation write so infrequently that they are no better equipped than their forebears were. A modern 'informant' wrote 'Tilley Bates' for *Tiddler's Bait*, and 'Moslum Broker' for *Mozzle and brocha.*

The difficulty is not a new one. It was wittily expressed by a writer, probably Dr Maginn, in *Blackwood's Edinburgh Magazine* in the early nineteenth century and the following is an abridged version:

Of all the vulgar saws in Town,
Whose meaning I could ne'er find out,
Is that most ancient of renown,
Which tells of matters 'up the spout'.

I've asked its meaning ev'rywhere,
And searched with diligence devout,
But cannot learn, for all my care,
The origin of 'up the spout'.

One day I took a vulgar brute,
And stood him spirits, beer and stout
I asked him did he know the root
Or pedigree of 'up the spout'.

He only oped his mouth and stared;
Then grinning, like a stupid lout,
In tones oracular declared
That 'up the spout' meant 'up the spout'.

Because of these factors it is hazardous indeed for the amateur (or even for the professional) etymologist to commit himself on origins: it is equally dangerous for the philologist to speculate on reasons, because there is not an indivisible reason for the use of rhyming slang. Psychologically it gives the Cockney a superiority goal. Some of it is witty, much of it is amusing, all of it is decorative: further, it is a gentle and friendly form of expression that may carry an emotional content, hence it is often employed in addressing both children and animals. That some of the phrases have lived a hundred years and are still vital is impressive because slang, by its very nature, is ephemeral. Words, like men, 'may rise on stepping stones of their dead selves to higher things': slang-words may become colloquialisms, and then, in turn, standard English. No better example can be given than the word 'swindler'. Its parents were colloquial, its grandparents slang, its great-grandparents (mid eighteenth century) Yiddish! But slang that does not rise, generally falls into disuse with the ageing of its generation—no man under sixty years of age refers to a 'flapper' or says he is 'fed up' with the sight of one. The modern thing to be is 'browned off with the sight of teenagers'.

Rhyming slang defies the rules and appears to be immortal, and though new rhymes are applied to the old things no one can consciously and deliberately create a rhyming-slang phrase, for though any Cockney can (as previously stated) answer in rhyme, it does not follow that any other Cockney will adopt that particular rhyme for his own use. There is no satisfactory explanation of why one term should become universally employed and another, equally apt, equally witty, be ignored: there seems to be no reason why rhyming slang should have permeated the printing trade, and back-slang the butcher's.

The Oji folk of West Africa have a proverb: 'When a poor man creates a proverb it does not spread.' In what faculty is the creator of accepted rhyming slang rich? A little of it, a very small minority of the current terms, may have been coined by comedians on the music-halls, but the bulk is born spontaneously. Every universally accepted phrase was most probably uttered, for the first time, by a totally undistinguished workman. Why did that particular phrase flourish and not the ones he made use of both previously and subsequently?

A fair proportion of rhyming slang phrases are, it will be observed, merely the names of people, but if it happens that there is a relationship between the person named and the meaning, this is generally fortuitous: for example, Mae West's name might have been used even though she had possessed a 'cigarette' figure, and had acted the parts of austere matrons of homes for delinquent girls.

There is no reason to assume that any particular Duke of York had become notorious for either his use, or his misuse, of a fork; what connection had 'the intrepid Fox' with a box at the theatre? and neither Colonel Prescott nor Major Stevens had even so much as a fictitious military career—they are simply names that rhyme with their meanings: further, the names of characters from famous books are not neglected.

The mystery remains to be solved. Psychology and statistics may one day join forces and, note-books in hand, charge!—an enlightened Light Brigade: meanwhile, though a perspicacious man might make a guess, only a fool would commit it to writing!

Another mystifying quality of rhyming slang is that certain phrases have more than one meaning, and certain meanings more than one phrase to express them: John Camden Hotten in his note remarks this peculiarity, and he attributes it to mere individual preference, but this is not so now, even if it was then. A speaker often makes use of two or more rhyming phrases having the same meaning if the word for which they are the equivalents occurs more than once in his sentence. The converse usage, employment of a phrase having two or more meanings, is less worthy of note because in such cases the context makes the meaning quite clear: 'Shut that Rory O'More, will yeh!' cannot refer to the floor.

A nice discrimination is, however, shown in the usage of two different terms which, seeming to have the same meaning, actually are different. No Cockney would confuse 'crust of bread' with 'loaf of bread', neither of which are ever used in any but the abbreviated form, and both of them may be heard in conversation at social levels rather higher than 'Cockney'.

No other form of slang has travelled so far both socially and geographically as rhyming slang has. If an orator in the House of Commons should assure his auditors that the time had come for one and all to get down to brass tacks, it is almost certain that Mr Speaker would not register the disapproval of the House; and later, if twitted with having used rhyming slang, the Honourable Member for Mayfair might answer that he knew none: nevertheless, 'brass tacks' are facts, and the term is rhyming slang. Cockneys are, on the whole, so disgusted by this blatant pilfering that they are becoming more and more inclined to substitute 'tin-tacks'.

Facts and tacks, whether the latter are of brass or tin, do not rhyme and there is a very good reason for the uninitiated to place this pair in the category of assonance.

It would be most interesting if some person who knows nothing of Cockney dialect would analyse the rhyming slang glossary and place the items under three headings: 'Perfect Rhymes,' 'Imperfect Rhymes' and 'assonances', and then compare with a similar classification made by a Cockney. The totals would be very different. Facts and tacks are a perfect rhyme to the Cockney ear, for even a light Cockney accent makes 'facks' of facts: a deep Cockney is, however, needed to make 'Charing Cross' rhyme with 'horse'—the former must become 'Cherrin' Kraws' and the latter, 'awce'. In the United States of America the same rhyme—cross and horse—probably depends on the Western pronunciation, 'hoss'.

## V

Mention of U.S.A. calls for immediate clarification because the suggestion that 'Cockney Slang' is associated with 'Western' dialect is apparently absurd.

Rhyming slang is a great traveller: from its probable birth level—the gangs of navvies of early nineteenth century—it has gone down into the real underworld where it is employed by thieves, and upward into quite polite society, but this movement is abstract. Its concrete movement is a thin trickle through the printing trade by way of Periodical distribution to the provinces, and in a steady tide to Australia where it took root and produced an indigenous crop with local peculiarities. Emigration was forced upon it.

Up to 1868 'Transportation for the term of his natural life' was the first thing the 'Justices' thought of, and many a lively Cockney lad, guilty chiefly of a little high spirits, found himself en route for Botany Bay. What could not be cured had to be endured, and Cockney wit and humour must have enlivened the voyage and brightened life upon landing.

Today, in Sydney and its environs, rhyming slang has its adherents, and while the old terms survive, many new ones of peculiarly Australian flavour have been, and are still being, forged.

Sidney J. Baker, the authority on Australian English, says, in his book *The Australian Language*, 'Reviewing the subject as a whole it can be said that rhyming slang has had much smaller currency in Australia than is generally realized. Australians are inclined to resist its use if only for the fact that it is a dull, unimaginative, foolish type of slang, and that there is little of the sharp, business-like nature of other Australianisms about it.'

Mr Baker is doubtless correct in his assessment of the relative currency of rhyming slang in Australia, but few people, and none of them Cockneys, will agree that it is 'a dull, unimaginative, foolish type of slang'.

When a man holds a poor opinion of some particular thing it is clear that he will not irritate himself by going to seek it. He will, on the other hand, avoid it as much as possible. It is regrettable, therefore, that Sidney J. Baker is not an admirer of rhyming slang: had he been, he might have compiled an exhaustive glossary of the Australian rhymes, and kept it up to date. No one could do it so efficiently as he could, and there seems to be no one else qualified to make the attempt.

The effort to establish Australian usage by making enquiries through a third party who in turn writes to a fourth who is, in any case, not a trained observer, and who is himself probably in possession of but a few of the current terms, is doomed to failure: optimistically it has been tried, and in yielding 'Dad and Dave' has been of value in proving that the system is still alive in Sydney.

The next major journey undertaken by rhyming slang was from Sydney to Chicago: in the United States, where it is known as 'Australian Slang', it has again taken root and grown a goodly crop of indigenous American terms: further, some of the centenarian terms are still going strong and others have been distorted in the wine-press of trans-world travel, but can, none the less, be recognized for what they were. Who, for example, would hesitate to assert that American 'chair and cross', a horse, is distorted Cockney 'Charing Cross', a horse?

The first specimen of rhyming, or Australian, slang that has been found on record in America is a term printed in the New York *Police Gazette*, in (or soon after) 1850. This suggests that in addition to the influx from Australia entering by the West Coast ports, a certain amount was trickling across the Atlantic, either direct from its native London, or, more likely, out of Ireland to which country it had been carried by the returning Irish navvies—a matter on which more will be said later.

In New York, where there are some former Cockneys, and many former Irishmen, some rhyming slang is used but the system does not notably inform the slang speech of either the underworld or the working population, but on the West Coast the case is different.

American 'con-men' visit London when they have a gold-brick for sale, but Australian members of the brotherhood, having contempt for 'chicken-feed', take theirs to the United States where they do pretty well for themselves. In addition to these ones and twos, a small army of 'Diggers', who knew all the answers, joined in the California Gold

Rush of 1849–50; hence, Cockney rhyming slang, repacked and relabelled 'Guaranteed Pure Australian', has been assimilated in the American West Coast underworld.

'Chicago May', a 'lady crook' who operated in a fairly large and picturesque way in Chicago, New York, London and Paris, ultimately gave up crime (at least, she gave up indictable crime) and wrote a book. She did that with the confidence and competence that had marked all her other activities, and without wishing to condone or excuse criminality, one must admit that she proved herself a woman of superior mental power.

The book, entitled *Chicago May—Her Story*, was published in 1928 by Sampson Low, Marston. In Chapter 31, Chicago May says: 'I have often thought it would be interesting and instructive to get up a combination dictionary and encyclopaedia of words, names, manners, customs, [and] biographical sketches connected with the underworld. . . . I realize it will involve a lot of research, historical and otherwise.

'One of the difficulties connected with many dialects is that they are not perpetuated by their own literature. The result is that they vary, from time to time, and from place to place. This results in confusion and misunderstanding, and differences of meaning for the same word. The context is often the only clue the crook has in determining the meaning of some words.' She then proved both her pluck and her ability by breaking the back of the problem. To this chapter of her book is appended a long glossary of American thieves' terms, much of which is rhyming slang.

Chicago May did not know that during her lifetime scholars were collecting slang in the States, and in the month of May of the same year as that of the publication of her book, Ernest Booth printed in *The American Mercury* an article entitled *The Language of the Underworld*, in which he gave numerous examples including some rhyming slang.

By far the most important, and without doubt the most authoritative piece of literature on the transatlantic use of rhyming slang appeared in *American Speech* (Columbia University Press), Volume XIX, No. 3, October 1944, entitled *Australian Rhyming Argot in the American Underworld*, by D. W. Maurer (in collaboration with Sidney J. Baker).[1]

Dr Maurer observes that the predominant rhythm is either iambic or trochaic, and records that abbreviation operates in America as it does in London.

He discovered that the American crook picks up rhyming slang when

[1] David W. Maurer is a professor of English of Louisville University and is the authority on American criminals' slang with its psychological and its criminological background and implications.

in prison rather than in the course of his professional and social associations before going there. In his footnote No. 4 he says: 'Alcatraz is theoretically a "silent house". However, as one informant who has served time there comments, "There is no way to keep hooks (thieves) from talking, and even if there was, they still have their knowledge of the lingo." '

Another of Dr Maurer's informants, quoted by him in footnote No. 12, said: 'The roving British and Australian thief have played their part in bringing the lingo to the racketlands of America, but the ones who have really brought the Australian lingo into our system of speech have been the roving thief and good-time bims (chorus girls and fortune hunters) who have plied between Frisco, Shanghai and Sydney for the past fifty years. . . .'

A letter dated 14 May 1942 from Sidney J. Baker is quoted verbatim by Dr Maurer. The following is an abridged version:

'I don't know to what unkind stroke of destiny is due the reputation in the United States that the Australian crooks talk in rhyming slang. . . . Nothing could be farther from the truth . . . for the simple reason that his greatest failing is to clip and abbreviate . . . the Cockney Rhymester would use *frog and toad* for road; *plates of meat* for feet; *almond rocks* for socks . . . the Australian would [not] get past *down the frog* for down the road; *plates* for feet; *almonds* for socks.'

It is true that the Cockney rhymester seldom abbreviates 'frog and toad' but he invariably abbreviates 'plates of meat'.

It is probable that the Cockney abbreviates a far higher percentage of his rhyming slang vocabulary than does the Australian user, but until we have a complete vocabulary of Australian terms annotated with the necessary information, the matter must remain open.

Dr Maurer is not only learned, he is objective, and he applies mathematics to philology. He says, 'Now to turn to a specific analysis of the "Australian" argot as found in the United States, of the three hundred and fifty-two terms included in this Glossary [his own, of course, not the glossary in this volume], Mr Baker finds that three hundred and fourteen are *not* used in Australia, and, to the best of his knowledge, have never had any currency there. Of the remaining thirty-eight terms *only nine are definitely of Australian origin, and three have possible Australian origins.*[1] Of this group of thirty-eight, twenty-three (all of British origin) have been recorded at some time in Australia.

'Of the residue of three hundred and fourteen terms *not* used in Australia Mr Baker makes the following distribution:

75 have definitely been borrowed by the United States from England.
34 have probably been borrowed by the United States from England.

[1] Dr Maurer's italics.

34 may be either American or British in origin (definitely not Australian).

171 appear to have originated in the United States.'

To the first and the fourth items of this summary Dr Maurer appends footnotes, respectively number 22 and 23. The former states: 'Of the three hundred and fifty-two terms considered, ninety-eight come definitely from British sources (seventy-five of these being used in America, and twenty-three used both in America and Australia) while thirty-four have possible and thirty-four have probable British origins.'

Footnote 23 states: 'Only two of the total of one hundred and seventy-one terms apparently originating in America have been recorded in Australia. This is a strikingly small number in view of the known migration of criminals between the United States and Australia.'

Continuing his text after quoting Sidney J. Baker's summary, Dr Maurer says: 'In view of these figures, it would seem that rhyming argot has been badly misnamed in the United States, for it appears to be anything but Australian in origin'; on that point, Baker, quoted in a footnote (No. 24), says, 'the fault (in ascribing an Australian origin to this type of argot) is not that of American observers, but rather of Australians themselves and of people who did a hasty tour of these parts and then rushed off to write about it. . . .'

## VI

'What's in a name?' Call it Australian argot, Cockney slang, rhyming slang or what you will, its genealogy remains unchanged.

Strangely enough, one may compare its history with that of tea. This delightful herb, the infusion of which is drunk so copiously in both England and Australia, but in the United States with restraint, was indigenous to China. It was transplanted in India where it took root, flourished, and developed a local character and flavour: from India it was again transplanted to Ceylon, where the process was repeated. Ceylon tea is not Indian tea, and Indian tea is not China tea, but China tea is still the aristocrat of the tea tribe notwithstanding popular taste.[1]

Far more heat is generated by contending scholars on the subject of rhyming slang than on any other form. Eric Partridge has, however, mastered the art of keeping cool, and he sums up the situation in the introduction to his *Dictionary of the Underworld*:

'It was introduced into America, especially by way of California, by

[1] In mercy to 'tea-men', planters, brokers and merchants, it ought to be stated without delay that a kind of 'cooking-tea' was indigenous to India. That is how they got the idea that transplantation of 'drinking-tea' might be successful.

Australian crooks, mostly from Sydney, where the Cockney element is stronger than anywhere else in Australia. Rhyming slang is a Cockney invention. . . . Of . . . Australian slang only a few terms have been adopted direct from Australia . . . many have been coined in America, either by Australians or, far more often, by native Americans. The slang is "Australian" but only in that the impulse came from, the fashion was set up by, Australians. . . .'

Rhyming slang in England, more particularly in the South of England, and most particularly in London, is loved and enjoyed and, within the limits of their knowledge and ability, used by all classes of society: it is apparently not so loved and used in either Australia or America.

What is now required to complete the geographical picture is an intimate study of its history and fate in Ireland, to which country it was, in all probability, carried early by the returning Irish navvies. It is known to be employed by the 'sporting fraternity' in both Belfast and Dublin, and it is known to have acquired there a specifically Irish shape; further, it is believed to have become translated into the Gaelic, but how extensive a vocabulary the Irish sporting men have, and how far it is used outside sporting circles remains unrecorded.

At home its picturesque qualities enabled it to catch the ear of the educated classes, and to employ the pen of literary men long before slang was officially tolerated in polite society. The mature years of the nineteenth century were a brilliant, bohemian, gay and witty time when stage and music-hall flourished, when artists and writers and sportsmen prospered and were treated with respect, when certain restaurants were the rendezvous of actors, and journalists, wits and cartoonists, aristocrats and self-made millionaires, and 'characters' of every kind. Life began at eleven p.m.

In an age clean of the cinema and free of the incubus of wireless, the art of conversation was not dead and there were plenty of periodicals carrying fiction of all kinds and fun of all varieties.

Authors of the day introduced the Cockney to the non-Cockney: the character and the dialect of the coster, the hawker and the labouring man became a ready subject to write upon and around and about. Some of the matter was misleading but amusing, much of it accurate and enlightening, not a little of it was serious and even sentimental.

As king in the last category of writers stood George R. Sims; author of the *Dagonet Ballads* in which appeared *Christmas Day in the Workhouse*, but, of course, not its parody which is so well known now that few people will believe that there ever was an original.

Sims and other writers of the period were pioneers of social pity; they studied slum life intensely and became expert in their ability to portray Cockney character and to write convincing dialogue. It is perhaps because these great spirits of the nineteenth century saw the frolicsome possibilities inherent in rhyming slang that it became so widely known and appreciated. That towering pinnacle of wit, humour and caustic comment, *The Pink 'Un* (otherwise known as *The Sporting Times*),[1] specialized in terse compelling articles spiced with Cockney slang of all kinds, and the brilliant band of bohemians who were 'the staff' laughed their way through life, taking their nourishment with a dash of rhyming slang in every glassful.

John Bennion Booth, who was one of them, and who has written several most entertaining books about them, says in *Sporting Times—The Pink 'Un World*:

'[George R.] Sims knew his London well, East and West, and prided himself on his knowledge of the by-ways and underworld, being something of an authority on such abstruse sciences as the now almost-forgotten "back-slang" and "rhyming slang".

'Rhyming slang, in particular, is on its way to becoming a lost art, and is likely soon to vanish into the shades, with the coster's "pearlies" and moke, and his "donah's" fevvers.

'There was a greater expert than Sims in this curious language in A. R. Marshall, of the old *Sporting Times* staff, who for many years contributed a poem to the front page of *The Pink 'Un.*

'This remarkable character, who wrote under the pseudonym of "Doss Chiderdoss", introduced Rhyming Slang into his weekly "Pome" and occasionally wrote one wholly in that language.'

Mr Booth continues: 'At the moment back-slang and rhyming slang are not altogether dead languages in this London of ours.

'Not long ago I heard a shabby gent recounting his experiences to a pal. Moaned he: "An' s'elp me I'd 'ardly got a touch me in my sky, much less an amesjay[2] to pay for me saint and sinner!" '

Doss Chiderdoss (which meant, so the poet said, 'sleep, gently sleep') handled rhyming slang with such facility and brilliance that his work has never been equalled. Many there are who have thrown together a verse in which rhyming slang appeared, but Doss Chiderdoss wrote as though rhyming slang was the only language in the world. There is no sign of effort in his work—no obvious arrangement of a matrix of other words in which to mount the gems: they run as smoothly and as naturally into place as they do in the spoken language.[3]

Bohemianism is a thing of the past. The modern type bears the name

[1] For the benefit of the younger generation it is perhaps necessary to state that the paper's title was '*The Sporting Times*: otherwise known as *The Pink 'Un*', but as *The Pink 'Un* it was known to all and is remembered by many who have forgotten the senior section of the title.

[2] ames-J = James = £1. This system is not back-slang.

[3] C. J. Dennis, an Australian author, in his *Sentimental Bloke* and in *Ginger Mick*, displays a comparable facility with non-rhyming slang.

but lacks the nature, and no one has, in this age, written in rhyming slang for its own sake; however, it has been introduced into the dialogue of appropriate characters in Cockney and in underworld fiction, with what success may be judged from the examples appended to this volume.

The only contemporary scholar in this country who has paid any serious attention to the subject is Eric Partridge. In addition to its appearing in both *A Dictionary of Slang and Unconventional English*, and *A Dictionary of the Underworld*, he has included an article on it in *Words Words Words*, and deals with it in the appropriate places in *Slang Today and Yesterday*, as well as in 'Tract No. LV' published by The Society for Pure English.

Not to be mentioned in the same breath, none the less worthy to be mentioned, are three brave efforts by amateur lexicographers, brought out by equally amateur publishers. Two of them are clearly related. The first of them, undated, but received by the Copyright Office on 5 October 1931, consists of sixteen pages measuring approximately 7 × 5 inches but only seven of them are printed. It lacks a title page and plunges straight into a short and quite undistinguished 'Foreword'. The glossary, which is arranged in reverse order—that is the meanings in alphabetical order, as the list of meanings in this volume, but with the difference of their being followed by their equivalent terms—is printed on right-hand pages only and the last one is blank. It is in a plain grey paper wrapper on which has been written in blacklead pencil 'A Dictionary of Rhyming Slang, edited by J. [or it might be I.] Phillips'; written, also in pencil on the penultimate blank page, is the name of Mr Phillips in the capacity of 'publisher' and the name and address of the printer (which appears nowhere else).

Following the crop under each letter (not that every letter of the alphabet is represented) are examples in either prose or verse, both without reference to author, both undistinguished, and both probably the work of the editor. In some cases footnotes explain that abbreviations may be used.

One must pay tribute to Mr Phillips who, it would seem, conceived, executed and financed the publication. A noteworthy item is the final paragraph which, headed 'competition', states that a prize of a bottle of whisky will be given by the Landlord for the best verse in rhyming slang submitted before Christmas. This makes one wonder whether 'the Landlord' was none other than Mr Phillips who sold his brain-child to strangers and presented it to cronies and regulars, or whether Mr Phillips was a traveller in (say) the public-house drinking glass business who 'did' the book as a sideline. One hopes, and believes, that it was a profitable venture, for it leads to the second member of the trio.

In 1932 (Copyright Office date 4 November) the opus reappeared in the same format but with bibliological and typographical improvements. The grey paper cover is of better quality and decorated with a block title ' "Rhyming Slang" a concise dictionary' and beneath the script the likeness of two jolly fellows, veritable past-master froth-blowers pledging each other's health in foaming pints.

Within, we are greeted by a title page which, after the title, declares the opus to be 'An authentic compilation by P.P.' and a colophon—'Desti' with the address and date (Desti is no longer to be found in the London Telephone Directory). P.P. is in all probability a misprint for J.P., or it may be an attempt at difference, for there follows the same foreword, the same glossary—plus five additions (one hundred and twenty-seven in the first edition, one hundred and thirty-two in this one) and the same examples.

The invitation to win a prize for authorship of verse in rhyming slang does not, this time, commit the landlord to an 'arry of[1] I'm so[1] (Perhaps last year's proved worth no more than a small packet of do me goods[1]) but it is promoted to a full page—rouletted—and there follows a kind of index in correct lexicographical order, with one-word definitions. We are now given twenty-four pages, thirteen of them printed, but once again the printer has forgotten that it is an offence to produce a work of this kind without a printer's 'signature'.

The third member of this little band of freaks was both more ambitious and more amateurish. Entitled *A Dictionary of Rhyming Slang*, it was published by John Langdon and distributed by Simpkin Marshall (1941) Ltd., but is innocent of author's or editor's name.

It contained a *Foreword* by 'A.D.' who, without acknowledgement, quoted a four-line verse very reminiscent of Doss Chiderdoss; the Glossary was in normal lexicographical order, but the definitions consisted of one word only. It contained about as many entries as its two related works, but no detailed description can be given for, notwithstanding the apparently professional title page, it was so amateurishly produced that no copy was deposited with the Copyright Office.

These publications, making no claim to scholarship, are, nevertheless, of value to the scholar. They establish, with certainty, which rhyming slang terms were current common property at the time of their appearance.

## VII

Such ephemera are valueless in their definitions: indeed there are more ambitious works equally valueless because one word is not adequate to define a rhyming slang term.

The word might be a verb or it might be a noun, and it is not safe to

[1] Consult Glossary following.

assume that the same rhyming slang term will be used for both. In English there are too many homonyms for satisfactory one-word definitions, and further, the one word may itself be slang, or a semi-slang substitutional word: finally there are delicate shades of difference in meaning, and no good Cockney would confuse them. A particularly pertinent example is *loaf of bread*, *crust of bread*, *lump of lead*: with a one-word definition each means 'head', but consult the appended glossary under the appropriate entry and the world of difference appears.

Another bolt that must be discharged in condemnation of such inadequate definitions is the fact of one rhyming slang term sometimes possessing two or more totally unrelated meanings. Sometimes both or all of these meanings are in general use, and the context is the key: in other examples one meaning may be general and another peculiar to a certain class, group or calling, for rhyming slang has developed a number of microcosms within the macrocosm.

There are perhaps as many as one hundred and fifty terms (even two hundred) that would be recognized instantly by any rhyming slang user, but some of them, when employed by special groups, such as, for example, actors, have a different meaning than when employed by general users, and in addition, the theatrical profession has numerous terms not customarily employed outside of that world.

Even when a term is general, its meaning may be specialized. One sits comfortably by the Anna Maria, but the Fire Brigade is not called to a building on Anna Maria, hence the one word 'fire' is not sufficiently explanatory. Further, one-word definitions are misleading when applied to rhyming slang terms that are subject to abbreviation, and that phenomenon in itself could form the subject of a thesis, but whether in the department of Philology or that of Psychology it would be hard to determine. One thing only is certain: it is an aspect of rhyming slang on which scholars can disagree to their hearts' content.

When a rhyming slang term has been abbreviated so long that the non-rhyming element has become general slang, does it still qualify for inclusion among rhyming slang terms?

Why does one term become abbreviated and another not? Why is a term that is subject to abbreviation often used in full?

Michael Harrison, in a private letter (dated 4 January 1947) to Eric Partridge, says:

'It is erroneous to affirm—as so many "Philologists" do—that the slang-rhyme is always shortened to its initial element . . . "army" is always "Kate Carney" and "dinner" "Lilley and Skinner".'

The only comment required is that it is always Lilley and Skinner when it is not (say) Saint and Sinner, but it is never just 'Lilley' or just 'Saint'.

The final unanswerable (or at any rate, so far unanswered) question already posed may now be posed again. Taking into consideration the

Cockney proclivity to answer in rhyme, why does one such jingle 'catch on' and another not?

Michael Harrison, in his masterly study *Reported Safe Arrival* which, for reasons of 'National Security' at the time of its publication had to masquerade as a novel, and must therefore continue to so masquerade, thus becoming a veritable Chevalier d'Eon among books, gives two examples of what seem like extempore rhyming retorts, and one may be quite sure that they are not of Michael Harrison's own invention. Both of these have been included in the appended Glossary, but each is provided with the appropriate note of warning.

Any philologist making a study of rhyming slang is confronted with the difficulty of distinguishing between such 'local' remarks and established terms. Michael Harrison's speaker was a Cockney soldier: close enquiries (and not of an overt character) among other Cockney ex-soldiers of this character's type have failed to establish the terms, but both of them might have been in use in that particular unit, the 'disease' being caught from that character. It is because of this possibility that the terms are listed in this volume.

The present writer heard a workman turn to his boy assistant and say 'Coo! You ain't 'arf makin' a muck-up* o' that! 'Ere—gis da Jimmy Jammer!'

Subsequent very careful enquiries among workmen of the same type failed to reveal that a hammer was generally called a 'Jimmy Jammer', and guarded use of the term in the company of Cockneys who are rhyming slang users never failed to draw forth the confession that though they have understood the term they have never heard it before.

The conclusion to be reached, therefore, is that 'Jimmy Jammer' was an extemporary rhyme used by that particular workman, and that it is not one of the terms that have even a restricted or special currency. For that reason it is not included in the appended Glossary.

What is included and what is excluded from a glossary is purely a matter of knowledge, or choice on the part of the lexicographer. It would be unreasonable to assume that rhyming slang terms for vulgarisms had not been evolved at the time of Ducange Anglicus and of John Camden Hotten, but neither of them exemplified such terms in their dictionaries.[1] It would be absurd to assume that J. Phillips and 'P.P.' were ignorant of such terms, but they, too, exclude them.

The only terms purposely excluded from this Glossary are those which, like 'Jimmy Jammer', have failed to qualify—all other omissions arise from ignorance. Vulgarisms are included, because this work is not directed to girls' schools: neither is it intended to bespangle the con-

* He said 'muck'—not its rhyme.

[1] John Camden Hotten did so but quite by accident. See Glossary at MUFFIN BAKER.

versation of our modern bad-tempered bearded young men in their boogie-bars and their skiffle cellars. It is, like that of Ducange Anglicus, offered to literary men, who are warned not to attempt to put rhyming slang into the mouth of a Cockney character who might not use it, or who, using it, would do so in a different manner: to 'Philanthropists' who, translated into modern idiom as 'social workers', are often greatly in need of instruction, and frequently in need of the very treatment they are prescribing for others.[1]

'Officers of the Law', that is the Police, and particularly the 'plain-clothes policeman', of the Criminal Investigation Department of Scotland Yard, might, a century ago, have found Ducange Anglicus helpful, but the present writer does not flatter himself that such aid is, in these days, needed, for in spite of the convention of representing the police detective in fiction as a fool, the fact remains that he is highly trained and fully efficient: there is nothing in the way of slang, cant or flash lingo that is unknown to him, be it never so new.

The vulgarisms that appear herein are standard English words however 'rude' they may seem to the mealy-mouthed: the criterion is not the opinion of Mrs Simper from the suburbs, but rather that of the *Oxford English Dictionary*, hence, there seems no fitter conclusion for this essay than the closing paragraphs of Captain Francis Grose's Preface to *A Classical Dictionary of the Vulgar Tongue*:

'To prevent any charge of immorality being brought against this work, the Editor begs leave to observe, that when an indelicate or immodest word has obtruded itself for explanation, he has endeavoured to get rid of it in the most delicate manner possible; and none has been admitted but such as either could not be left out without rendering the work incomplete, or in some manner compensate by their wit for the trespass committed on decorum. Indeed, respecting this matter, he can with great truth make the same defence that Falstaff ludicrously urges in behalf of one engaged in rebellion, viz. that he did not seek them, but that, like rebellion in the case instanced, they lay in his way, and he found them.

'The Editor likewise begs leave to add, that if he has had the misfortune to run foul of the dignity of any body of men, profession or trade it is totally contrary to his intention; and he hopes that the interpretations given to any particular terms that may seem to bear hard upon them, will not be considered as his sentiments, but as the sentiments of the persons by whom such terms were first invented, or those by whom they are used.'

[1] It must be unequivocally stated that among social workers will be found men and women who have led a life of self-sacrifice, and who have wrought nothing but good. These few would agree that the criticism of the many implied above is not without strong justification.

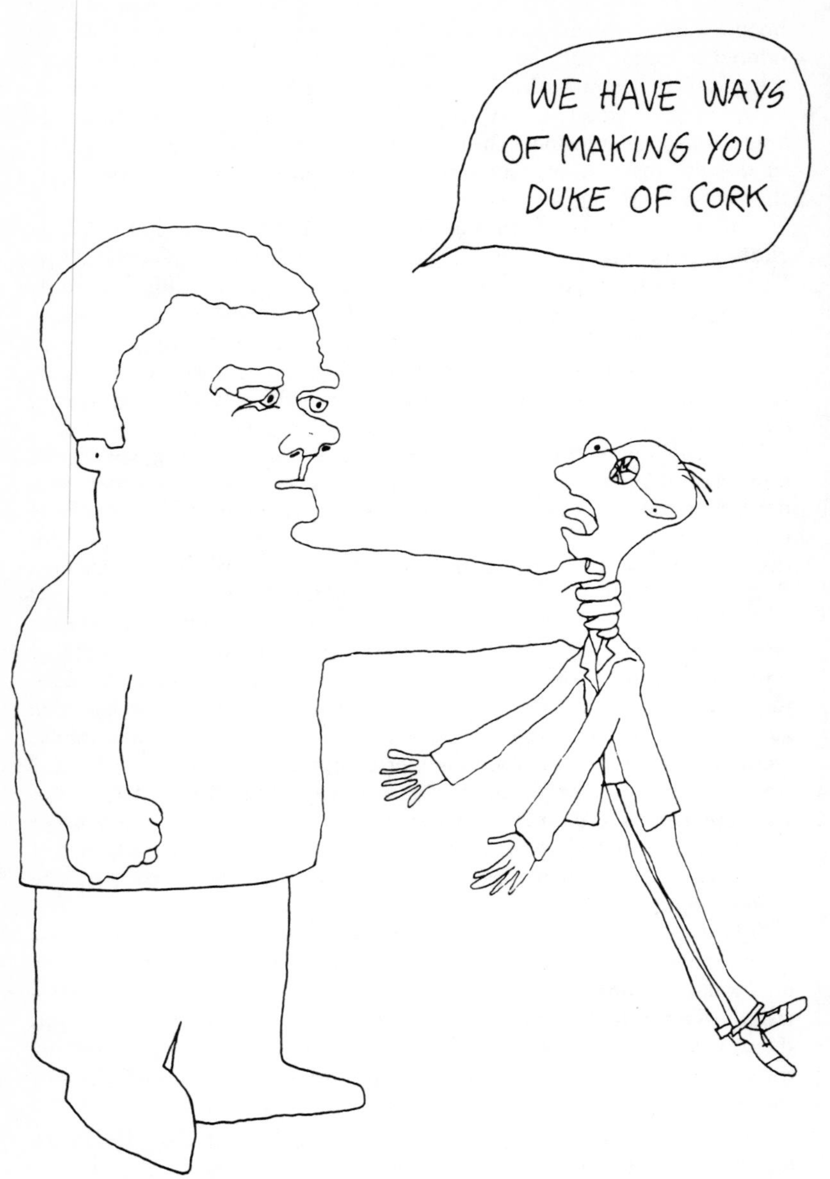
WE HAVE WAYS
OF MAKING YOU
DUKE OF CORK

# A

**Abraham's willing** *Shilling.* The term did not survive the 19 C. Hotten, 1859.

**abram** *Sham* (to feign sickness). 19 C. Recorded in *Sinks of London Laid Open*, 1848.

**Adam and Eve** *Believe.* The term, which ante-dates the 1914 war, and may have been known in the late 19 C., was always jocular, and at the present time is used chiefly to children, but also on 'leg-pulling' occasions. In the latter setting it implies disbelief—as one disbelieves the tall stories told by children.

**ain't it a treat** *Street.* 19 C. Now obsolescent. Eric Partridge, *A Dictionary of Slang . . . Addenda*, quoting Edwin Pugh, *The Spoilers*, 1906.

**airs and graces** (1) *Braces*, (2) *Epsom Races*, (3) *faces*. (1) is appropriate, since one could put on no airs and graces if that essential support failed; this meaning is, however, modern. In the first decade of this century it referred to (2) *Epsom Races*, and was not particularly suited, but earlier (last quarter 19 C.) it meant (3) *faces* and again was particularly appropriate.

**alacompain,** see ALLACOMPAIN.

**a la complain,** see ALLACOMPAIN.

**alive or dead** *Head.* A very pertinent question; one that a prospective employer might be expected to ask concerning that portion of the anatomy (early 20 C.?). Lupino Lane.

**Allacompain** *Rain.* Recorded by Hotten, 1859, and now obsolete. The word is accepted as an alternative (or mis-) spelling of *elecampane*, the wild plant 'horseheel' from which medicines and flavouring essences were made, but this is difficult to accept. It is more likely to have arisen from Hotten's mis-hearing of 'all complain', which all do when it is raining, except, we are told, the farmers; however, every Cockney knows that to travel north of Camden Town on a wet day is to hear the Chalk Farmers complain. That the theme is complaint, not herbs, is further indicated by the fact of the term taking, in America, the form A LA COMPLAIN, as recorded by Maurer and Baker.

**all afloat** *Coat.* 19 C. Recorded by Hotten, 1859, now obsolete. See I'M . . .

**alligator** *Later* (in the phrase 'see you later'); of 20 C. origin and used over a wide social range.

**almond rock** *Cock* (penis). 19 C. Generally reduced to *almond*, but seldom heard.

**almond rocks** *Socks*. Generally cut to *almonds*. Late 19 C. in origin, still current.

**Alphonse** *Ponce*. Probably suggesting that only smooth foreigners ply this trade. Recorded by Jim Phelan in *Letters from The Big House*, 1943.

**amster** *Ram* (a crook's confederate). This is the general and reduced form of *Amsterdam*. Exclusively Australian (Communicated to D. W. Maurer by Sidney J. Baker: mentioned by the former in his text, but not included in his glossary).

**Andy Cain** *Rain*. Of late 19 C. origin, and in vogue up to 1914, since when it has been decreasing in popularity, and is now seldom (if ever) used.

**Andy McGinn** *Chin*. American, Pacific Coast (Maurer and Baker, 1944).

**Andy McNish** *Fish*. Either raw or fried. Early 20 C.

**Anna Maria** *Fire*. A 19 C. term still very popular. It refers to the domestic hearth, not to disasters attended by the Fire Brigade. It should be pointed out that the pronunciation is 'Mar-eye-ah' not 'Mar-ear'. Maria is a favourite name for a girl and is generally shortened to 'Ria'. The term, when it appears in literature, is inclined to be converted to 'Ave Maria', which simply does not come within the compass of rhyming slang users. If it did, it would be correctly pronounced 'Mar-ear', and would rhyme with 'fear', not with 'fire'.

**Annie Laurie** *Three-ton lorry*. This is a specimen of imperfect rhyming slang. It was evolved during the 1914–18 war, used largely in the army (particularly in the A.S.C.), and did not long survive demobilization.

**any racket** *Penny faggot*. In use from mid-19 C. until *c.* 1910. Faggots, a form of minced liver fried with onions, were a popular proletarian supper, but the vendors of these, together with the hot-potato men, had disappeared from the streets before the 1914 war. It is recorded by Hotten, 1859. Pronounce 'ragit', and 'fagit'.

**apple and banana** *Piano*. 20 C. American in both origin and usage. Recorded by Maurer and Baker, 1944. Cf. JOANNA.

**apples and rice** *Nice*. 20 C., and generally preceding 'oh very . . .' meaning the opposite. Recorded by Michael Harrison in *Reported Safe Arrival*, 1943.

**apples and pears** *Stairs*. One of the terms recorded by Hotten, it is still very much in use: in fact, it may be described as the classic of rhyming slang, for people who know no other term know this one. They find it 'delightful', and describe it as funny which it is, but few polite users know quite how funny. To the Cockney, the phrase 'steps and stairs' describes gradation. The family, standing in a row, is 'all steps and stairs'. A war memorial on a graded plinth is standing on steps and stairs. Every good costermonger is an expert at arranging 'the front' of his stall. The selected specimens of fruit and vegetables are skilfully graded—in steps and stairs. Apples and pears are (in season) common to every barrow, and these fruits, when polished, give a particularly rewarding 'front', hence, they will be built up when time does not permit such careful arrangement of, for example, the cabbages; therefore apples and pears is most appropriate rhyming slang for stairs. Before the end of the Second World War it was unusual to condense, but in this jet-propelled age it has been reduced to 'apples'.

**apple fritter** *Bitter* (beer, not fate). It seems to be of post-1914–18 war origin, and is more often used in invitation than in ordering —'Come on ole mate—come an' 'ave an apple-fritter!'

**apple pie** *The sky*. 20 C. Evolved during the second war and is not often heard.

**applepies** *Eyes*. Americanization of British MINCE-PIES (q.v.). Recorded by Maurer and Baker, 1944.

**apple pips** *Lips*. Early 20 C. Now seldom heard, but possibly used more within the theatrical world than by the general public. Lupino Lane.

**April fools** (1) *Tools*, (2) *stools*, (3) *Pools* (football). 19 C. This term began life in the underworld, where it referred to burglar's tools, but by 1910 it had become general workman's slang. It was extended to include (2) *stools*, chiefly in public-houses, and since the Second World War has been diverted into (3), its most meaningful employment, nevertheless having such wisdom in words does not mean that it will be displayed in actions.

**April showers** *Flowers*. 20 C. Probably influenced by the verse:

> March winds, April showers,
> Bring forth May flowers.

The term may have originated in the flower-seller's trade, and has become general, although not common.

**Aristotle** *Bottle*. Very rarely spoken in full, 'Arry' being friendly, familiar and sufficient. Of late 19 C. origin, and growing less popular as the 'jug and bottle' bar trade decreases. The average cockney assumes that ''Arry Stottle' was a famous costermonger, but the 'superior' cockney knows that he wrote a little red-covered book called 'Aristotle's Work'—on obstetrics.

**army and navy** *Gravy*. Gravy was plentiful at meal-times in both services. Early 20 C.

**army rocks** *Socks*, but specifically grey woollen Army socks, which, under the umbrella of 'Government surplus', survived many years after the 1914–18 war, and with the socks, the term, which had its birth in the Army of the period. It was, of course, a specialized form of ALMOND ROCKS (q.v.).

**'Arry,** see ARISTOTLE.

**artful dodger** *Lodger.* The lodger was the butt of many late 19 C. and early 20 C. jokes; however, he was generally treated with respect, and often as one of the family. The term is recorded by Hotten, 1859, and may have some connection with Dickens' character: it is now obsolescent due to the vast change in post-war social conditions.

**artichoke ripe** *Smoke a pipe.* 19 C. Recorded by Hotten, 1859, and now extinct. See CHERRY . . . It is, of course, punning 'hearty choke'. Shag tobacco smoked in a clay pipe is inclined to have that effect.

**arty roller** *Collar.* Recorded by Sidney J. Baker in *The Australian Language*, 1945.

**Ave Maria,** see ANNA . . .

# B

**baa-cheat** *Bleat.* Sheep, hence, the trade or business (occupation or calling) of sheep-stealing. This was recorded as early as 1728 by Defoe in *Street Robberies Considered*, and is only a fortuitous rhyme. It was probably obsolete by the time rhyming slang was evolved, nearly a hundred years later. It is included here solely to prevent well-meaning people from calling attention to its omission.

**baa-lamb** *Tram* (car), of late 19 C. origin, increasing in usage as the tramways system increased, declining and dying with it.

**babbling brook** (1) *Cook*, (2) *crook*. (1) Generally shortened to *babbler*, was used in the army of 1914, and it still has a restricted currency in military circles but it never came into civilian use in England. (2) In Australia and America, it carries the meaning 'crook'—see Ernest Booth, 'Language of the Underworld', *American Mercury*, May 1928; there is, however, a special Australian usage, meaning 'unwell'.

**baby's pap** *Cap*, from *c.* 1855. Recorded by Hotten. The average cap is as shapeless a piece of headgear as a mass of bread-and-milk. The term went into decline when caps ceased to be the exclusive fashion for workmen and charwomen—*c.* 1918.

**bacon and eggs** *Legs.* American, Pacific Coast (Maurer and Baker). Not used in England, but given in *The Australian Language*, 1945, by Sidney J. Baker.

**Baden Powell** *A trowel.* Not likely to have been in use before the Relief of Mafeking, and now rarely heard.

**bag of coke** is an Australian variant of BUSHEL OF COKE (q.v.).

**bag of fruit** *Suit* (of clothes). American version of WHISTLE . . . (q.v.). Pacific Coast (Maurer and Baker, 1944).

**bag of nails** *Anything confusing.* Maurer and Baker comment thus: 'Given by an informant as rhyming argot, but the rhyme cannot be found.' This is common: 'informants', in their anxiety to oblige, will even create rhyming slang on the spot: a few questions of the right kind will always reveal the super-enthusiasm. Another kind of 'informant' is the one who, proud of his equipment, will 'spill everything'.

**baker's dozen** *Cousin.* Early 20 C. The term is rarely heard as naturally one does not discuss one's cousin or cousins very frequently. Lupino Lane.

**ball and bat** *Hat.* Popular in England before 1914, after which it was largely replaced by TIT FOR TAT (q.v.), but it still has a currency on the Pacific Coast of America (Maurer and Baker, 1944).

**ball of chalk** *Walk.* Employed mostly when to 'go for a walk' is itself slangy: as, for example, to the inefficient assistant: 'Yhus—yeu froiten eny mower customers away an' you'll go fer [or "take"] a ball o' chalk!' See also PENN'ORTH . . .

**ball of lead** *Head.* Popular in the army, 1914–18, but little used by civilians: now obsolete.

**balloon car** *Saloon bar.* 20 C. Generally reduced to 'Balloon'. It could be, but probably is not, associated with the idea that a long time spent in either results in a wobbly, sick and giddy sensation.

**band in the box** *Pox* (Syphilis). American, Pacific Coast. Recorded by Maurer and Baker, 1944.

**Band of Hope** *Soap.* 20 C. Not so popular as CAPE OF . . . (q.v.) and formed on the title of that laudable institution which, under the aegis of the Sunday School, imbues youth with ideas of Temperance. Recorded by Len Ortzen in *Down Donkey Row.*

**bang and biff** *Syph* (or siff). Short for syphilis. American, Pacific Coast (Maurer and Baker, 1944). American rhyming slang generally falls short of the British standard of appropriateness, but this specimen is well up to the mark. It suggests a careless objectivity.

**Barnaby Rudge** *Judge.* A Dickens character, but possibly influenced by *Barnaby* (recorded by Grose and defined as a quick dancing movement), itself from the name 'Barnaby', who, it seems, was an acrobatic dancer. Lupino Lane.

**Barnet Fair** *Hair.* Recorded by Hotten, 1859, and still in use, but generally condensed to *Barnet.* Changed to *barney fair*, it is used in Australia (*Detective Fiction Weekly*, 23 April 1938), and on the Pacific Coast of America (Ernest Booth, *American Mercury*, May 1928).

**Barney Dillon** *Shilling* (pronounced *shillun*). Scottish. *Daily Telegraph*, 8 November 1935.

**barney fair,** see BARNET . . .

**Barney McGuire** *Fire.* American version of ANNA . . . (q.v.). Recorded in *American Thesaurus*, 1942.

**Barney Moke** *Poke.* In Standard English, *a bag*: a *pocket*, a *purse* or *note-case*, hence an expression used largely by pickpockets (*Phenomena in Crime*, 1941, Val Davis).

**bar(s) of soap** *Dope.* American. Employed in the drug traffic. *Gang War*, 1940, J. G. Brandon. Cf. the American expression *No soap*, i.e. 'nothing doing', 'no transaction'.

**bart** *A girl.* 20 C. Recorded by Sidney J. Baker in *A Popular Dictionary of Australian Slang*, 1943. He adds, 'Now practically obsolete.' It may be rhyming on *Tart.* See JAM TART.

**basin crop** Recorded by Maurer and Baker, 1944, but it is not rhyming slang. It is Cockney slang for a crude, or bad, hair-cut, the inference being that a basin, worn hat-wise, has guided unskilled hands wielding the scissors. Generally applied to boys of school age, but also to any bad hair-cut. Maurer and Baker query whether it is 'clipped back'—abbreviated.

**basin of gravy** *Baby*. 20 C. Cockney. Suggestive of the soft foods on which babies are reared.

**bat and wicket** *Ticket*. Late 19 C. or early 20 C. Applied generally to a ticket booking seats for a music-hall.

**bath-bun** *Son*. 20 C. Cockney. A poor and pointless specimen, hence seldom used. See also CURRANT . . . PENNY. . . . Any one of the three may be employed for either 'son' or 'sun'. It is merely a matter of which appears to be the more frequent meaning that has determined selection in this work, but those who observe in Hackney may disagree with those who observe in the Borough, and Covent Garden is different again.

**battle (and) cruiser** *Boozer* (public house), post second war in origin, and in use among Cockneys.

**Battle of the Nile** *Tile*. Recorded by Hotten, 1859, it survived into the first decade of the 20 C. When 'toppers' disappeared from the City streets the slang term *tile*, a hat, fell into desuetude, and with it, the rhyming slang.

**Battle of Waterloo** *Stew*. Early 20 C. Cockney usage in both home and cook-shop.

**bazaar** *Bar* (of public house). 19 C. This is rhyming slang only when applied to a public-house bar. In general slang it means a shop counter, but in a pub it is not merely the counter, but the whole space both before and behind it that is the bar. If Mary is serving in the saloon bar she is behind the counter: Jack, drinking in the public bar, is in front of it, and when Tom leans an elbow on the bar, it is on the counter.

**Beattie and Babs** *Crabs* (crab-lice). 20 C., formed on the names of the famous entertainers. *c*. 1930.

**Beecham's Pills** (1) *Bills*, (2) *testicles*. (1) refers to the notice stating, for example, 'Ex-service man—no pension', or 'Wounded at Mons—willing to work', attached to barrel-organ or tray of matches. The famous pills not only 'get results', which it is hoped the bill will do, but the makers advertise largely on bill-posters' sites. The term evolved post-1914–18 war, when the trade depression greatly increased the number of street-beggars. See also PITCH . . . (2), invariably reduced to 'pills', demands for its rhyme the pronunciation, 'testi-kils'. It is employed extensively at several social levels, generally in the setting 'Don't talk pills', or 'That's a lot of pills', or 'That fellow talks awfully pillsie the whole time'. Respectable users are unaware that it is truncated rhyming slang, and assume that it has the simple meaning of *folly* or *foolishness*.

**beef-heart(s)** *Fart*, but is also a slang term for beans, hence there is a connection. Late 19 C.

**beery buff** *Muff*, which is itself 19 C. slang for a fool.

**bees and honey** *Money*. This holds first place among rhyming slang terms for money on account of its appropriateness: bees symbolize work, work produces money, the possession of which is sweet. First recorded by Joseph Wright in the *English Dialect Dictionary*, 1892. It is in use on the Pacific Coast of America—recorded by Chicago May, 1928, and in 'They Talk Like This', *Detective Fiction Weekly*—23 April 1938.

**beggar boy's ass** (1) *Brass*, (2) *Bass*. This is always reduced to *beggar boy's*. (1) *Brass*, money; hence the term is associative. It dates from late 19 C. (2) *Bass*, the drink (not the fish), probably later in origin than (1).

**beggar my neighbour** *On The Labour* (Exchange). To be drawing Unemployment Benefit under the National Insurance Act, is to be 'on The Labour', or 'on the Dole'. The term has an all too sound economic background. It is, of course, usually preceded by 'on the'.

**bended knees** *Cheese*. Probably late 19 C. tramps' slang implying how very hard it is to get. Lupino Lane.

**ben flake** *Steak*. First recorded in 1857 by Ducange Anglicus. It was in use in New York by 1859 (George Matsell, *Vocabulum*). It is no longer in current English slang, but may have survived in New York, where there was no war-time shortage. See JOE BLAKE.

**berkeley hunt** (see next entry). This is an accidental formation serving as an alternative for the next, but *berkeley* (without 'hunt') originally referred to the heart. In Farmer and Henley's *Slang and its Analogues* (7 vols.), 1890–4, the assumption is that *berkeley* is derived from the Romany *berk* (plural, *berkia*), the breast.

**Berkshire hunt** *C*——. This is not an objective, anatomical term, neither does it imply coitus. It connects with that extension of meaning of the unprintable, *a fool*, or a person whom one does not like. It is very often reduced to *Berk*, and in that disguise it enjoys the best of both worlds, for it is widely used by polite people in a jocular friendly way:—'Oh! you are a berk, John,' is the typical suburban girl—Clapham, Balham and Tooting—speaking. She would not, of course, utter the unprintable; what is more, confronted with it, she would declare that she did not know its meaning (and she, at least, would believe that). It is further used (but not in polite society) to mean girls and women either collectively or individually in the same context as the unprintable itself might be so employed; or the more modern word *crumpet* (developed out of 'buttered bun').

The meaning is complicated by the term's confusion (in early 20 C.) with BERKELEY (q.v.), and the spelling may be misleading.

There is, of course, no standard spelling of slang, but in this case, *berk*, the '*e*' must be retained, for *Burk* refers to Burke and Hare, the Resurrectionists, and it means to suppress, or hush-up—hence its use as military slang for the dyeing of moustaches and hair, to 'hush-up' one's age; and *birk* is a back formation of *crib*, a house to be burgled—now obsolete.

**big ben** *Ten* (£). A mid-20 C. formation brought into usage by the devaluation of money. Fifty years ago, and earlier, a rhyming slang for 10*s*. was sufficient. (In U.S.A. the same term is not rhyming slang. It refers to the whistle that spreads the alarm when there has been an attempted break from Sing Sing Prison. Godfrey Irwin, *American Tramp and Underworld Slang*, 1931, supposes that it has been suggested by some particularly efficient brand of American alarm-clock named after J. M. Dent's Westminster masterpiece of time keeping apparatus, rather than from the bell itself.)

**big bloke** *Coke*, short for Cocaine. American. In *American Thesaurus*: and also recorded by Maurer and Baker, 1944.

**big hit** *Shit*. Not excrement, but to defecate. Current Australian.

**Billy Bunter** *A shunter*. 20 C. Used exclusively by road-hauliers.

**billy button** *Mutton*. Given by Hotten, 1859, but now obsolescent. In non-rhyming slang a *billy button* is a journeyman tailor, hence, there is used on some occasions a kind of rhyming slang in reverse, when MUTTON is employed for *billy button*: as 'Come on mutton—drink up—it's time we was back at work'.

**Binnie Hale** *Tale*. 20 C. Referring to the tales told by con-men and others who hope to impose. Formed on the name of the famous actress, and now obsolescent.

**birch broom** *Room*. Given by Hotten, 1859, now seldom heard, since birch-brooms are no longer used. *Birch broom in a fit*, for disordered hair, is more common.

**bird lime** *Time*. This is old English rhyming slang—noted by Ducange Anglicus, 1857, and still widely used. By 1859 it had become Americanized and was current in New York (George Matsell, *Vocabulum*, 1859) where is seems to have sunk to the underworld, and become used for *Time* in the sense of a prison-sentence, in which form it is used (since late 19 C.) in South Africa.

**bit of blink** *Drink*. An intoxicating beverage. Recorded by J. Redding Ware in *Passing English*, 1909. The term itself seems to have passed.

**bit of tripe** *Wife*. Notwithstanding the absence of rhyme, this ranks as rhyming slang. Recorded by J. Redding Ware, *Passing English*, and now obsolete.

**black and white** *Night*, or *tonight*, late 19 C. and now obsolescent.

**blackman kissed her** *Sister*. Not very popular, since the average

Cockney, without colour prejudice, feels that kissing is going too far. The term was current in 1910, went into abeyance, and since the influx of Jamaican workers is coming back into currency.

**bladder of fat** *A hat.* Probably inspired by an old and greasy one. In use in early 20 C., but does not seem to have survived the 1914–18 war.

**bladder of lard** *A card.* The 'housie-housie' banker in the 1st Essex Regiment during the 1914–18 war, opened the proceedings by chanting 'Who says a card: a bladder o' lard, a Prussian Guard, six months' hard?' (Communicated by Mr. H. Chaplin-Smith.)

**block and tackle** *A shackle* (fetters, and probably handcuffs). Recorded in *American Thesaurus*, 1952.

**block of ice** *Shice* (to abscond). 20 C. Racecourse (and probably dog-track) slang referring to bookmakers who abscond without paying out. The term is equivalent to 'Welsh'. It is probably influenced by the low slang term, of Yiddish origin, for excrement.

**blue moon** *Spoon.* (1) Culinary implement, (2) to make love. Possibly of late 19 C. origin, the term in either sense is now seldom heard. It took a new, temporary, lease of life in the A.R.P. Services during the second war, but apparently only in (1).

**blue ruin** *Gin.* This term ante-dates rhyming slang proper, having been recorded as early as 1811 (*Lexicon Balatronicum*) and by Pierce Egan, *Life in London*, 1821. Influenced by a still older term, *Blue Riband* (or *Ribbon*), which in turn developed from *blue tape* (*c.* 1725), it may, despite the poor rhyming quality—*ruin, gin*—have helped in the transition from BRIAN O'LINN (q.v.) to MOTHER'S RUIN (q.v.).

**boat and oar** *Whore.* A rather weak rhyme—American, Pacific Coast (Maurer and Baker, 1944).

**boat race** *Face.* 20 C. Soon after the second war this term seemed to be gaining the ascendancy, but the long-established CHEVY CHASE (q.v.) has now come into its own again.

**Bob('s) my pal** *Girl*, rhyming on *gal* (Ducange Anglicus, *The Vulgar Tongue*, 1857; George Matsell, *Vocabulum*, 1859, and Maurer and Baker, 1944). The *'s* (is) seems to be an American improvement. The term may still be current in the U.S. but in England it has faded away.

**boiled rag** *Old hag.* American, Pacific Coast. Recorded by Maurer and Baker, 1944.

**bolts and nuts** *Silly*, mentally deficient, or lunatic. It is not rhyming slang since there is no rhyme, but it is on the same pattern. *Nuts*, American slang for mentally unsound (*Nut-house*, lunatic asylum), plus *bolts*, and generally cut to *bolts* only. 'He's bolts!' means he's *nuts* (*c.* 1920).

**bonnet so blue** *Irish stew.* Recorded by Hotten, 1859, now obsolete.

**Bonnie Dundee** *A flea.* This term appears to be the almost exclusive property of the theatrical profession. Lupino Lane.

**bonny fair** *Hair.* American form of BARNET . . . (q.v.). Recorded by Maurer and Baker, 1944.

**Bo-Peep** *Sleep.* Early 20 C. Equivalent to *shut-eye,* and influenced by *peepers,* eyes and *bye-byes,* sleep. The term is very popular, and is used in polite society to children.

**borrow and beg** *An egg.* Late 19 C. The term, having faded, enjoyed a fresh lease of life during the second war food-rationing period: now, again sinking into oblivion.

**Botany Bay** (1) '*Hit the hay*' (go to bed, or to sleep), (2) *run away.* Recorded by Maurer and Baker, 1944. (1) As a rhyming slang term it is indigenous to America—as *hit the hay* is. The term has numerous non-rhyming slang meanings in England. (2) *Run away* is purely Australian, recorded by Sidney J. Baker, *The Australian Language,* 1945. It is sometimes reduced to 'do a Botany'.

**bottle of Cola.** See OF KOLA.

**bottle of fizz** *Whizz* (opportunist stealing, particularly picking pockets). Of recent (post 1914–18 war) origin. It is recorded by Sharpe of the Flying Squad.

**bottle and glass** *Arse.* The buttocks (20 C.). In English usage 'on the bottle' refers to male prostitution; in America, to general prostitution. 'A bottle merchant', one engaged in prostitution.

**bottle of Kola** *Bowler* (hat). Current during the first decade of 20 C., but now as rare as the type of hat it describes. (*Kola* was a bottled drink made by R. White, and sold in London long before the Americans sublimated their world-conquering complex into the soft-drinks industry.)

**bottle of sauce** *Horse.* Of late 19 C. origin, the term referred to the horse as a draught animal and had no vogue in racing circles. It is now obsolete.

**bottle of scotch** *A watch.* Specifically a Waterbury watch, hence of 19 C. origin, but not recorded by Hotten. Now obsolescent.

**bottle of spruce** *Twopence* (rhyming on *deuce,* two). Spruce-beer was poor stuff—hence, the expression covers worthless suggestions (and objects). The term is recorded by Hotten and again by Maurer and Baker, who define it as a card-sharper's term for 'two' (Pacific Coast). *Spruce,* to deceive, may derive from it, but it is uncommon for condensed, or abbreviated, rhyming slang to retain the last (rhyming) word.

**bottle and stopper** *Copper* (policeman). There may be an inference here to *bottle,* to enclose, or to collect; and *stopper,* one who stops another from a course of action. The term is recorded in *The American Thesaurus,* 1952, by Chicago May, 1928, and by Maurer and Baker, 1944.

**bottle of water** *Daughter.* Of recent origin, and not yet fully established. *c.* 1931.

**bottles of booze** *Shoes.* Recorded in *The American Thesaurus*, 1952.

**bow and arrow(s)** *Sparrow(s).* Late 19 C. and still as popular with Cockneys as are the birds themselves.

**bowl of chalk** *Talk.* American, Pacific Coast. Recorded by Maurer and Baker, 1944. Also mistaken form of BALL OF . . . (q.v.).

**bowl the hoop** *Soup.* Recorded by Hotten, 1859. Now obsolescent. Soup-kitchens, where the 'poor' could get nourishment for a penny, were a favourite Victorian charity. The inference may be that there is nothing in it.

**box of glue** *Jew.* This usage seems peculiar to the Pacific Coast of America. Given in *The American Thesaurus*, 1952.

**box of toys.** *Noise.* Late 19 C. Rather an appropriate expression, since a box of toys, particularly a new one at Christmas-time, causes a great deal of noise to be made, even when the toys are not 'musical'.

**boy in blue** *Stew.* This is recorded by Maurer and Baker, with the one-word definition, hence, since the idea of *a stew*, meaning a 'state' of excitement, or anxiety, seems to be purely British, and since neither Maurer nor Baker is prepared to admit the term as of his own national origin (they say 'origin uncertain, but probably British'), we must conclude that it refers to Irish stew, and is of Irish origin, because it is certainly not of Cockney origin, nor is it in use by Cockneys. 'The boy in blue', meaning a policeman, is a favourite Irish expression.

**boys on ice** *Lice.* Late 19 C. and now, thanks to the Sanitary Inspector, seldom necessary.

**brace and bit(s)** *Tit(s)* (teats, breast(s)). Specifically, *nipples.* American, primarily Pacific Coast. Recorded by Chicago May, 1928, and by Maurer and Baker, 1944. The phrase is very seldom used in England. It should be noted that Chicago May prints *beasts.* It is, however, clearly a misprint for *breasts.*

**brandy snap** *A slap.* 20 C. Recorded by Maurer and Baker, 1944. Not used in England.

**brass band** *Hand.* This term, which was never very popular, had some currency in the army during the 1914–18 war, and is still used in U.S.A. Recorded in *American Thesaurus*, 1952.

**brass nail** *Tail.* (Prostitute.) More commonly heard in the North of England than in London. First appearance in print seems to be 1934, *My Selves*, Netley Lucas.

**brass tacks** *Facts.* Used in the setting 'Let's get down to brass-tacks' this rhyming slang phrase has gone so far up in the world that it has become colloquial English which, for example, a Cabinet Minister might use, if not in the House, certainly during a political talk on the broadcasting system. What is most interesting is that exalted persons who employ the term do not realize that it is slang, and when informed that it is actually Cockney rhyming slang they often indignantly deny it. Of 19 C. origin, it had become naturalized in America by 1903, and many people believe it to have been imported here from America.

**bread and butter** *The gutter.* Late 19 C. origin, still in use. It was quoted in the *Evening Standard,* 19 August 1931.

**bread and cheese** *Sneeze.* 19 C. Recorded by L. Ortzen, in *Down Donkey Row,* 1938.

**bread and jam** *Tram*(car). 20 C., and now obsolete in London, but is apparently still in use on the Pacific Coast of America. Recorded by Maurer and Baker, 1944. It appeared in the *Sydney Bulletin* 18 January 1902, and is quoted by Sidney J. Baker in *The Australian Language,* 1945.

**Brian O'Flinn,** see next entry.

**Brian O'Linn** *Gin.* Recorded in Ducange Anglicus, 1857, and generally reduced to *Brian* or even *Bri,* the term had a wide currency during the latter half of the 19 C. The very popular song 'Father O'Flinn' influenced usage in the first decade of the 20 C., and the *O'Linn* became *O'Flinn,* but this is a case where phonetics suffer total defeat by semantics. See MOTHER'S RUIN.

**bricks and mortar** *Daughter.* 20 C. Never very widely employed, and now obsolescent. It survives in the theatrical profession to stigmatize a dull heavy style of acting, but does not seem to be connected with rhyming slang because it is applied to either sex.

**Brighton pier** *Queer.* Recorded by Hotten, 1859, the term, meaning *sick* or *unwell,* had fallen into obsolescence until the 1940's when *queer* assumed the meaning of *strange,* or abnormal in sexual habits. The word *queer,* with this meaning, has become almost a colloquialism, and the rhyming slang term has emerged from oblivion. See also GINGER BEER, KING LEAR.

**Bristol City** *Titty* (breast). Early 20 C. Not very widely used. (There are several non-rhyming slang formations on Bristol, see Partridge, *Dictionary of Slang . . .*)

**broken mug** *Hug.* 20 C. American, Pacific Coast. Recorded by Maurer and Baker, 1944.

**broken oar,** see BOAT AND OAR, of which this is a variant.

**brothers and sisters** *Whiskers.* American, Pacific Coast. First recorded by Chicago May, 1928, then by Maurer and Baker, 1944. There seems to be no indication of its use in England before the second war, but it is now growing in popularity on account of the modern tendency for young men to avoid shaving.

**Brown Bess** *Yes.* Recorded by Hotten, 1859. Now obsolete.

**brown hat** *The cat.* (*Felis Domesticus,* not the whip of ninetails.) Late 19 C., it survived into the first decade of the 20 C. and is now seldom heard.

**Brown Joe** *No.* Recorded by Hotten, 1859. Now obsolete, but with the meaning *know* it is recorded by Sidney J. Baker in *The Australian Language,* 1945.

**Brussels sprout** *Boy Scout.*

The phrase was evolved *c.* 1910, when the Boy Scout's Movement was fully established, and that little masterpiece, *Scouting for Boys*, was going into its 'new and Revised edition'. (It is now in its 28th!)

**Bryant and Mays** *Stays.* Of early 20 C. origin, and now having about as much currency as there are wearers of that particular piece of 'foundation'.

**bubble and squeak** (1) *Greek,* (2) *speak.* (1) In use before 1914, and popular in the army, 1914–18. (2) American usage, recorded by Maurer and Baker, 1944. As the name applied to fried rice (or potato) and greens (with or without meat), it was first recorded by Francis Grose, 1785.

**bubbly Jock** *A turkey cock.* On this, one can not do better than quote from *A Dictionary of Slang and Unconventional English* by Eric Partridge. 'Orig. (— 1785) Scottish; but well acclimatized in England by 1840; Thackeray and Besant and Rice use it. [Captain Francis] Grose [gives it in his] 1st ed. [1785], Either it is ex the turkey's "bubbly" cry or it is an earlier rhyming synonym (see *Slang* [*Today and Yesterday*, by Eric Partridge, 3rd edn., 1950], p. 274.—2. Hence, a stupid boaster: C.19.—3. Hence, a conceited, pragmatical fellow; a prig; a cad; from *c.* 1860; ob. G. A. Sala, 1883.'

**bucket afloat** *Coat.* Recorded by Hotten, 1859, and now obsolescent.

**bucket and float** *Coat.* This form of the previous entry had a vogue in the army during the 1914–18 war, but is no longer current.

**buckle my shoe** *Jew.* Early 20 C., and used in the army 1914–18. It is still occasionally used, but it is perhaps the least popular of several rhyming slang terms having the same meaning.

**Bucks Hussar** *Cigar.* Late 19 C., implying dash and quality. Lupino Lane.

**bugs and fleas** *Knees.* Used on the Pacific Coast of America, recorded by Maurer and Baker, 1944, and probably an American product. Cockneys, who prefer *marrers*—(marrow-bones) for knees—do not use this term.

**bull and cow** *A row.* Recorded by Hotten, 1859. A nice discrimination is needed in glossing this term. The best rhyming slang users reserve it for an altercation between husband and wife only. Those who are not so particular, extend it to cover any loud quarrel or any noise, as 'the kids was kicking up such a bull and cow I come out for a ball o' chalk'. In the U.S.A., on the Pacific Coast, it is applied generally to a quarrel (Maurer and Baker, 1944).

**bullock's heart** *A fart. c.* 1890, now obsolescent.

**bullock's horn** *Pawn.* Recorded by Hotten, 1859. The term, still in popular use, is invariably reduced to *bullock.* 'I'll have to bullock my watch.' 'I have bullocked my watch.' 'My watch is in bullocks.'

**bullock's liver** *A river.* Late

19 C., and very popular in the army during the 1914–18 war, but now seldom heard.

**bull's aunts** *Pants* (trousers). 20 C. American, Pacific Coast. Recorded by Maurer and Baker, 1944, with a note that in Australia it is rendered as *bull ants*, of which it is probably a distortion.

**bundle of socks** *Think box* (head). 19 C. Recorded in *Sydney Bulletin* 18 January 1902, and quoted by Sidney J. Baker in *The Australian Language*, 1945.

**bung it in** *Gin.* A specialized, jovial form, generally addressed to a lady to whom one is standing treat—it implies that one's generosity is unbounded and money is not a matter to be thought of.

**Burchington hunt.** An uncommon mis-formation of BERKSHIRE . . . (q.v.).

**Burdett Coutts** *Boots.* 19 C. Formed on the name of Baroness Burdett Coutts whose millions built congregationless churches, buyerless market-halls, and other white-elephants with the help of Mr Charles Dickens. In the late 19 C. and early 20 C. 'the poor' were not very pleased when they received a pair of boots as an act of charity: news-vendors, for example, ran on a far more reliable foothold when bare-footed.

**Burlington hunt.** A totally erroneous formation following from the confusion of BERKSHIRE . . . (q.v.) and BERKELEY . . . (q.v.) brought about in all probability by substitution of the names of Berkeley Street and Burlington Arcade; both Piccadilly, London, W.1.

**burnt cinder** *Window* (pronounced 'winder'.) Pre-1914 formation.

**Burton on Trent** *Rent.* Late 19 C. Generally reduced to *Burton.*

**bushel and peck** *Neck.* Late 19 C. It refers more to the inside than the outside of the neck, and is generally reduced to *bushel.* 'E'yar —git that deahn yeh bushel', referring to either food or drink.

**bushel of coke** *Bloke.* Early 20 C. Usually applied to the young man with whom the daughter is 'walking out'. 'Our Ria's new bushel o' coke recons to 'ave class, he do. Works in an office.'

**Bushy Park** *A lark.* Most frequent in the slang sense, but also used to describe the bird itself. It is recorded by Hotten, 1859, but he gives no indication of which meaning was then current.

**butcher's hook** *Look.* Late 19 C. Generally reduced to *butcher's*, it is frequently heard. In Australia, where the usage is the same, it has the additional meaning, *crook* (angry).

**butter flap** *Trap* (or light cart). Hotten, 1859. Now obsolete. During the course of its career it has been used for a *cap*, but only half-heartedly, and that usage, too, is obsolete.

**by the peck** *Neck.* An American perversion of *Bushel and Peck*, recorded by Maurer and Baker, 1944, who suppose it to be of British origin, but it is not even of British usage.

# C

**cabbage hat** *Rat* (an informer). American formation with probable Australian influence. Recorded by Maurer and Baker, 1944.

**cabbage tree** *To flee.* American, Pacific Coast (Maurer and Baker, 1944). Cf. SCAPA FLOW.

**cabman's rest(s)** *Breast(s).* Late 19 C. Now obsolescent.

**Cain and Abel** *Table.* Recorded by Hotten, 1859, the term is still very popular. In America it has the additional meaning of *Chair* and table, as recorded in *American Thesaurus.*

**calico yard** *A guard* (probably a railway-train guard). 20 C. American, Pacific Coast, 1944.

**Camden Town** *A brown.* Given by Hotten in 1859 and glossed as 'a halfpenny', the phrase extended into the first decade of 20 C. with its application to pennies as well as ha'pence. The term a 'brown' for a copper is used now chiefly by buskers (who describe silver as 'white') and they also employ this rhyming slang which seems to have fallen into disuse in other circles.

**Camera Cuss** *Bus.* Early 20 C. Introduced soon after *The Vanguard* (the first motor-bus) set out on its epoch-making journey from New Kent Road to Kilburn —a miraculously preserved memory in the 'No. 1' route—now vastly extended. The new bus went by power; that is, 'works' of some kind; in the first decade of 20 C., 'works' were invariably 'clockwork', hence, the name of the famous clock-maker, happily rhyming, could not escape. The term is now obsolete—the firm Camerer Cuss & Co, established 1788, is not.

**canal boat** *Tote.* Of fairly recent origin, used by bookmakers and other racing men to describe the totalizator.

**candle-sconce** *Ponce.* Probably having reference to the smooth and greasy nature of such gentry. Recorded in *Letters from The Big House*, 1943, by Jim Phelan.

**can't keep still** *Tread-mill.* 19 C. Now obsolete. Very appropriate since persons sentenced to that particular form of 19 C. torture most certainly could not keep still for a second. It also took the form of 'never stand still'.

**Cape of Good Hope** *Soap.*

Early 20 C. Still in use. (The term as well as the commodity!)

**Captain Cook(s)** (1) England: *book(s)*, (2) American, *look(s)*. The English usage is of late 19 C. origin, coinciding with the popularization of the Public Lending Libraries, and is now used largely by racing men to describe the betting book. The American usage, recorded by Maurer and Baker, 1944, is used chiefly on the Pacific Coast. In Australia the only meaning is 'look'. Cf. TAKE A ... and, HAVE A ...

**Captain Kettle** *Settle* (to finalize or to subdue by violence). Popular during the first decade of 20 C. when this famous fictitious character was every boy's hero, but now obsolete.

**careless talk** *Stick of chalk.* Post second-war formation, the 'slogan' *careless talk costs lives* being evolved at that time. It is used in conjunction with COUPLE O' BOB (q.v.) by players of darts and was submitted to *The Evening News* 31 October 1957 by Mr R. A. Gadd.

**carpet bag** *Drag* (three-months' imprisonment). 20 C. Generally reduced to *carpet.* (The unreliability of one's 'informants' is indicated by the term 'carpet' having been explained by one of them as ''cos it's easy teh do. Cushy.') Recorded by Sharpe of the Flying Squad.

**carving-knife** *Wife.* Current in the army 1914–18, now obsolete.

**castle rag** *Flag.* A 'flag' was slang for a fourpenny piece (groat). Given by Hotten, 1859, but now as obsolete as the coin. Is one justified in assuming, from this, that the Cockney of mid-19 C. knew that the armorial banner flies from the flag-staff when the head of the family is in residence?

**cat and kitties** *Titties* (breasts). American, Pacific Coast (Maurer and Baker, 1944). Not used in England.

**cat and mouse** *House.* Hotten, 1859, and still in use. The phrase is suggestive of the domestic environment. What is home without a cat? The place where the mouse may live in peace.

**cat cuff** *A bluff.* 20 C. American, Pacific Coast. Recorded by Maurer and Baker, 1944. In Australia it is a boxer's term for a feint.

**Catherine Hayes** *Long days.* American, Pacific Coast. Recorded by Maurer and Baker, 1944.

**cellar flap** (1) *tap* (to borrow), (2) *tap* (dance). Early 20 C., the term still has a restricted usage in sense (1). (2) is now obsolete, but tap or 'clog' dancing was once so popular that no music-hall performance was complete without at least one such 'turn'—with speciality attitudes and rhythms it could even carry two—and Cockney street-boys spent much time in developing the art.

**centre lead** *Forehead.* 20 C. American, Pacific Coast. Recorded by Chicago May, 1928. The term may be derived from a sport—possibly baseball.

**chair and cross** *Horse.* An American debasement of CHARING

. . . (q.v.) probably rhyming on Western pronunciation 'hoss'. Recorded by Maurer and Baker, 1944, who recognize it as a version of Charing Cross, but who do not commit themselves further. One would like to rationalize the semantics, *chair*, on which one sits (as a horse) and *cross*, moral responsibility, or burden.

**chalk boulders** is an alternative form recorded by Chicago May, 1928, of ROCKS AND . . . (q.v.).

**Chalk Farm** (1) *arm*, (2) *harm*. (1) is given by Ducange Anglicus, 1857, and it has travelled all the way to the Pacific Coast of America, appearing in Chicago May, 1928, by which time it had become obsolescent in England. (2) does not seem to have developed before about 1928, and is used, chiefly, in the statement that 'something' will not do 'somebody' any *Chalk Farm*. It is doubtful whether the American users are aware that it is the name of a quite unimportant part of London—it is also doubtful whether the inhabitants of Chalk Farm would accept the American usage as a compliment.

**channel fleet** *Street*. 20 C. Irish usage. (Rhyming slang is heard mainly in Belfast and Dublin.)

**Charing Cross** *Horse*. The rhyme is not apparent unless the Cockney dialect is used. *Kraws*, 'cross', and *awce*, 'horse'. Recorded by Ducange Anglicus, 1857. The term was used mainly by costermongers and applied to their own draught animals. It seems never to have been used for a racehorse, and is now obsolescent.

**Charles James Fox** *Box* (in the theatre or music-hall). Usually reduced to a Charles James. Mentioned by Edward Shanks in *John o' London's Weekly*, 8 December 1934, but belonging to late 19 C.

**Charlie Beck** *Cheque*. American (spelt *check*). It refers to a forged, or other worthless cheque. Used mostly on the Pacific Coast, recorded by Maurer and Baker, 1944.

**Charlie Brady** *Cady* (a hat), of 19 C. origin, now falling into disuse with the word *cady* itself.

**Charlie Chalk** *Talk*. American, Maurer and Baker, 1944. Cf. CARELESS . . . .

**Charlie Dilke** *Milk*. Seldom heard since the milk trade became centralized, and impersonal. Late 19 C. and early 20 C. the milkman had individuality. Recorded by Lupino Lane.

**Charlie Freer** *Beer*. *c*. 1909. Now obsolete.

**Charlie Horner** *Corner*. American variant of JOHNNIE . . . (q.v.). Recorded by Maurer and Baker, 1944. In its English form it refers always to a street corner, or corner of a room—not to the abstract 'in a corner' (difficult position).

**Charlie Howard** *A coward*. 20 C. Recorded by James Curtiss, *The Gilt Kid*, 1936.

**Charlie Lancaster** *Handkerchief* which, in mid-19 C., was pronounced ''an'ke'cher' and is recorded by Hotten, 1859. The term is now obsolete, and the word is pronounced ''ain-kin-choof'.

**Charlie Mason** *Basin.* Early 20 C. Still in use with a changed meaning. It no longer refers to an article of kitchen-ware, but 'I'll have a Charlie Mason' means 'I'll have a basin *full*'; that is, a try, or a share, or a ticket in a sweepstake.

**Charlie Pope** *Soap.* Army, 1914–18. Fraser and Gibbons, *Soldiers' and Sailors' Words and Phrases*, 1925.

**Charlie Prescot** *Waistcoat.* Recorded by Hotten, 1859. The term is still in use, although it is going out with the garment for which a 'pull-over' is substituted. Pronounced 'Preskit' and 'weskit'. It is also used in America, and is recorded by Maurer and Baker, 1944.

**Charlie Rocks** *Socks.* American variant of ALMOND . . . (q.v.). Maurer and Baker, 1944.

**Charlie Roller** (1) *Dollar*, (2) *collar.* Usage (1) given by Chicago May, 1928: usage (2) in *Detective Fiction Weekly*, 21 April 1934 (also Maurer and Baker, 1944). Sometimes spelt *Rollar*.

**Charlie Ronce** *Ponce.* An alternative form of JOE . . . (q.v.), but the latter is never, and the former is always, reduced. 'He's a Charlie' is so frequently used that its rhyming slang association is being lost sight of. See also OATS AND BARLEY.

**Charlie's Coat** *A Carley float.* 20 C. Recorded by Sidney J. Baker in *A Popular Dictionary of Australian Slang*, 1943, as Royal Australian Navy slang.

**Charlie Wheeler** *Sheila* (a girl). Recorded by Sidney J. Baker in *The Australian Language*, 1945.

**Charlie Wiggins** *Diggings* (lodgings), current chiefly in the theatrical profession. 19 C. Lupino Lane.

**charming mottle** *Bottle.* 19 C. Recorded in *Sydney Bulletin* 18 January 1902 and quoted by Sidney J. Baker in *The Australian Language*, 1945.

**charming wife** *Knife.* Army, 1914–18. Fraser and Gibbons, *Soldiers' and Sailors' Words and Phrases*, 1925. Cf. CARVING . . . , DRUM AND . . .

**Chatham and Dover** *Give over.* Early 20 C. A curious combination, Chatham and Dover being South of England, and 'give over' a North of England equivalent of Cockney *nark it*, stop it.

**cheese and kisses** *Missus.* Has more currency in Australia (where it is generally reduced to *cheese*) than in England. Also used on the Pacific Coast of America. Ernest Booth, in *American Mercury*, 1928. Maurer and Baker, 1944.

**cheese and spices** (Starting) *prices.* Bookmakers and other racing men, Pacific Coast of America. Maurer and Baker, 1944.

**Cheltenham bold** *Cold.* 20 C., and not of frequent use. It is sometimes rendered *Cheltenham cold*—as though 'Cheltenham' was a profane adjective.

**cherry ace(s)** *Face(s)*. 20 C. Evolved during the second war, now obsolete.

**cherry hog** *Dog*. 20 C. Used chiefly by dog-racing enthusiasts (cherry hog is a cherry stone). To go to 'the cherries' is to go to the dog-track.

**cherry ripe** (1) *Pipe* (tobacco), (2) *tripe* (nonsense). (1) is recorded by Hotten, 1859, and probably has reference to the cherry-wood pipe which, up to 1914, cost only one penny. It is still in use, and may be applied to even the most expensive pipe. (2) Seems to be a late 19 C. development which has grown with the word 'tripe' applied to inferior authorship and other nonsense.

**Chesapeake shad** *Not bad*. American, chiefly Pacific Coast. Maurer and Baker, 1944.

**chevy chase** *Face*. Recorded by Ducange Anglicus, 1857, and Hotten, 1859. The term has become widely applied in its reduced form *chevy* (pronounced 'chivvy') and is a favourite with many people who do not connect it with rhyming slang. (To *chivvy* is also to 'chase'.) Maurer and Baker record its American use and, probably unaware of the very prevalent *chivvy*, 'face', assume that is is obsolete in England.

**chews and molasses** *Glasses* (spectacles). American—Maurer and Baker, 1944.

**china plate** *Mate*. This is an old-established expression and is invariably reduced to *China*. It is almost universal among Cockneys, who are themselves often unaware that the word 'plate' ought to be attached. It has a somewhat emotional content, and is applied seriously to one's best and most intimate friends, not to mere work-mates. It is often used jocularly by referring to someone's enemy as his *china*. It is also in constant use in Australia. (See *The Cockney*, Julian Franklyn.)

**chip and chase** *Face*. An Americanization of CHEVY . . . (q.v.). Recorded first by Chicago May, 1928, and by Maurer and Baker, 1944.

**chirrup and titter** An alternative form of GIGGLE AND . . . (q.v.).

**Chopper** *Copper* (policeman). 20 C. American, Pacific Coast. Recorded by Maurer and Baker, 1944. (It is more in the nature of slang that rhymes, than of rhyming slang.)

**chop sticks** *Six*. 20 C. In the game of House (Housie-Housie), played a great deal in the army, 1914–18. Sometimes rendered CHOPPING STICKS.

**Christmas card** *Guard*. Current in the theatrical world, 20 C. Lupino Lane. Since actors spend Sundays on railway siding, the term probably refers to a railway guard, but it might mean a fire-guard, or a Grenadier Guard.

**Christmas Eve** *Believe*. 20 C. formation, but not so popular as ADAM . . . (q.v.).

**chump of wood** A debased form of CHUNK . . . (q.v.).

**chunk of beef** *The chief* (employer, manager or foreman). 20 C. Australian. Generally reduced to *Chunka*. Cf. HAM AND BEEF.

**chunk of wood** *No good*. Recorded by Hotten, 1859, now rarely heard.

**cinder shifter** *A drifter* (tramp). 20 C. American, Pacific Coast. Recorded by Maurer and Baker, 1944.

**clever mike** *Bike*. 20 C., and probably influenced by the outrageous antics that adolescent youth is inclined to perform on a bicycle, particularly when showing off for the benefit of the opposite sex.

**clickety click** *Sixty-six*. Score used in the game House, known as *Housie-Housie*, and very popular in the army during the 1914–18 war.

**clink and blank** *Bank*. American, Maurer and Baker, 1944.

**clothes peg** *Leg*. 20 C. An alternative form of SCOTCH PEG (q.v.) and erroneously written for 'egg'.

**club(s) and stick(s)** *Dick(s)* (detective(s)). *Detective Fiction Weekly*, 21 April 1934, also Maurer and Baker, 1944, and *American Thesaurus*.

**coachman on the box** *Pox* (syphilis). The phrase was current in the first decade of the 20 C., but suggests an earlier origin. It is applied to all forms of venereal disease, not to syphilis alone.

**coal heaver** *Stiver* (a penny), late 19 C. Reduced to *coal*, and misspelt *cole*, it is widely used for a penny and its origin is not suspected, since the word *stiver* is obsolescent. Also short: *heaver*.

**coals and coke** *Broke* (penniless), late 19 C. Apt, since both coal and coke used to be supplied in large nodules that had to be broken before use. It is less popular than HEARTS . . . (q.v.).

**coast about** *Roustabout*. 20 C. American, Pacific Coast. Recorded by Maurer and Baker, 1944.

**coat and badge** *Cadge*. 19 C., and sometimes given in full as DOGGETT'S. . . . It may have some reference to the fact that holders of the Doggett Coat and Badge could charge higher fares than those without, and watermen plied for hire until well past mid-19 C. The term is still in use, and is generally prefixed with 'on the'—'He's on the C. and B. again!'

**Cobar shower** *A flower*. American, Pacific Coast, given by Maurer and Baker, 1944, but clearly of Australian origin—from Cobar, a town in New South Wales, where it has a different, non-rhyming meaning.

**cobbler's awls** *Balls* (testicles), of 19 C. origin, the term, reduced to *cobblers*, is very popular, and is used in circles where it is accepted as a euphemism and not recognized as reduced rhyming slang.

**cobbler's stalls** *Balls* (testicles), a variant of COBBLER'S AWLS (q.v.).

**cockie's clip** *Dip*. Probably sheep dip. Recorded by Sidney J. Baker in *The Australian Language*, 1945; but on the Pacific Coast of America it refers to a pickpocket (Maurer and Baker). A 'Cockie' in Australian slang is a small farmer, and country-folk visiting town are favourite victims of thieves.

**cock(le) and hen** (1) *ten* (shillings), (2) *pen.* Late 19 C., it served for both ten shillings and ten pounds when the latter was rarely mentioned; it is now restricted to *shillings*: for *pounds*, see BIG . . . The *Cockle* pronunciation has no reference to the bivalve mollusc of the genus *cardium* (a favourite Cockney foodstuff), but is merely a slovenly pronunciation of *cockerel.* The second meaning is as old as, if not older than, the first, but is rarely heard. 'A Cockle' is also a 'ten-stretch' of prison.

**cocked hat** *Rat* (an informer). 20 C. American, Pacific Coast. Recorded by Maurer and Baker, 1944. Cf. CABBAGE . . .

**cock linnet** *Minute.* Often prefixed with 'half' meaning, 'pause to consider'. (Early 20 C.) Lupino Lane.

**cockroach** *Coach* (motor). 20 C. This term has been evolved since the second war, and has grown in popularity as long-distance road journeys have been considered more entertaining than railway travel.

**cock sparrow** *Barrow.* 19 C. Still in frequent use among costermongers.

**coffee and cocoa** *Say so.* This term, unlike most others that are used in a reduced form, retains the last, not the first word. 'Why didn't you cocoa?' In its extended form it is sometimes altered to TEA AND COCOA. Often used in emphasis: 'Is thay pleny o' dough there? I should cocoa!'

**cold potato** *Waiter.* 20 C. Current in the theatrical world. See also HOT . . . Lupino Lane.

**collar and cuff** *Puff* (an effeminate person). Suggested either by the neatness of attire, or by 'powder puff'. Recorded by Philip Allingham in *Cheapjack*, 1934, but see also IRON . . .

**collar and tie** *A lie.* 20 C. but never popular, since Cockneys do not require a substitute for a robust word. Occasionally used to admonish children, so long as the untruth is not of a serious nature. (Polite people use the euphemism 'a whopper'.)

**Colleen Bawn** *Horn* (erection). The Colleen Bawn is the heroine of 'The Lily of Killarney; an opera in three acts, the music by J. Benedict, the words by J. Oxenford and Dion Boucicault: first produced at the Royal English Opera, Covent Garden, Monday, February 10, 1862', hence the term must have originated after that date. It is still in currency.

**Colney Hatch(es)** *Match(es).* Current in the theatrical world. 20 C. Lupino Lane.

**Colonel Prescot** *Waistcoat.* 20 C. Variant of CHARLIE P. (q.v.).

**Colonial Puck** *F——.* American. Recorded by Maurer and Baker—defined as 'fornication' —1944.

**Conan Doyle** *Boil.* Arthur Conan Doyle achieved fame in 1892 with his first series of *Sherlock Holmes* stories, hence the origin of the term is after that date.

It has currency in the theatrical world, but is seldom heard elsewhere. It is used in reference both to water at 100° Centigrade, and a septic focus on an adolescent neck.

**constant screamer** *Concertina.* 19 C. The mechanized music of modern times has resulted in the abandonment by the Cockneys of both the concertina and the mouth-organ, which is to be regretted, and the term is now obsolete.

**cop a flower pot** *Cop it hot* (get into serious trouble), possibly suggested by the effect of a flower pot dropped from an upper window on to some person below. 20 C.

**corns and bunions** *Onions*, late 19 C. and still in use, chiefly in the vegetable trade, but also implying sophistication, as in, 'She knows her corns and bunions all right!'

**corroboree** *Drunken spree.* This native Australian word means a ritualistic gathering of male adults. It is admissible as rhyming slang when used to describe a convivial gathering of white men. It was brought to London during the 1914–18 war by the Anzacs; it fell into desuetude, and was revived during the second war. It is still a favourite word among topers, to whom it is a euphemism.

**cough and sneeze** *Cheese.* Current in the theatrical world. 20 C. Lupino Lane.

**council houses** *Trousers.* A modern form of ROUND . . . (q.v.).

**country cousin(s)** *Dozen(s).* Early 20 C., used largely on the racecourse.

**couple of bob** *A damp swab.* Post second war. Used by dart-players—'couple o' bob and some careless talk', *a damp swab and a piece of chalk.* See CARELESS . . .

**Covent Garden** *Farthing* (pronounced *fard'n*). Recorded by Hotten, 1859. Current up to early 20 C., but now obsolete since the smallest sum a child will accept is sixpence, which buys no more than a pre-1914-war farthing did.

**cow and calf** (1) *laugh*, (2) *half.* 19 C. (1) is recorded by Hotten, 1859, and is in use, with the same meaning, on the Pacific Coast, America, as recorded by Maurer and Baker, 1944. In Britain (1) is obsolescent, but (2) is current among racing-men.

**cows and kisses** *Missus.* Recorded by Hotten, 1859, it became obsolete in England, but had (or has) currency in U.S.A. (Maurer and Baker, 1944).

**cowhide** *Wide* (aware of). Irish usage—one is 'cowhide' to a certain fact. 20 C.

**crack-a-boo** *Bill and coo* (to make love). American, Pacific Coast (Maurer and Baker, 1944).

**cracks-a-cry** *Die.* American. Recorded by Maurer and Baker, 1944.

**crackers on toast** *Winning post.* American, possibly used in racing circles (Maurer and Baker, 1944).

**crown sheet** *Seat* (of trousers). Recorded in *The American Thesaurus*, 1952.

**crust of bread** *Head.* Early

20 C. This term, which is invariably reduced to 'crust', refers to the physical head, not to mental activity. 'When Jack fell off his bike he got a bad crack on the crust.' See also LOAF . . .

**cuddle and kiss** *Miss* (a girl). 20 C. Recorded by L. Ortzen, in *Down Donkey Row*, 1938.

**cup of tea** *See*. This term, which is recorded by Maurer and Baker, 1944, as of American usage is of questionable origin. Americans drink so little tea that one assumes it to be of Australian origin, but Baker disowns it. Maurer says it is probably of either American or British origin. It is most certainly not used or known in this sense in London, is unlikely to be American, but could very well be Irish, for much tea is imbibed in the Emerald Isle.

**currant bun** *The sun*. 20 C., probably suggested by the prevalent idea entertained by country folk that in London the sun always appears as a reddish-brown disc with well-defined contours, but see BATH BUN, PENNY BUN. Any one of the trio can be used for either *sun* or *son*.

**currant cakie** *Shakey*. 20 C. Generally applied in a tone of jocular admonition with reference to the condition of one's hands on 'the morning after the night before'.

**currants and plums** *Thrums* (threepence). Recorded by Hotten, 1859, but *thrums*, from *thrups*, from *threp*, as a slang (or dialect) word for threepence has long been forgotten in London, hence the rhyming slang term is now obsolete.

**cut and carried** *Married*. 20 C. This is applied only to the female, who is cut from the parental stem and carried (provided for) by the husband.

**cut and slicer** *Dicer*. American for *hat*. The term *dicer* is very rarely heard in England (Maurer and Baker, 1944).

**cuts and scratches** *Matches*. 19 C. Probably suggested by poor quality (imported) safety matches (sold at a penny a dozen boxes—best quality, British made, were only three-halfpence), which frequently proved dear in the long run as a large percentage cut and scratched the sensitized side of the box without igniting.

DIEU ET
MON
DROIT

# D

**Dad and Dave** *Shave.* Australian: from a radio serial which commenced *c.* 1930, featuring the two characters.

**daffadown dilly** *Silly.* Current in the theatrical world. Lupino Lane. Cf. the slang 'daffy' (probably from 'daft', silly).

**Daily Mail** (1) *Ale,* (2) *tail,* (3) *tale.* All these are 20 C. (1) and (2) are obsolescent—(2) refers to an animal's tail, not to a prostitute. (3) is the major usage, and refers to the glib patter of a con-man. See also BINNIE . . .

**daily tell the tale** *Daily Mail.* 20 C. Jocular, and used chiefly in the inevitable discussion following the stock query: 'Which one do you take?'

**daisy beat** *To cheat.* 19 C. Originally British, having reference to a burglary, the term journeyed to U.S.A. where it assumed the meaning of *a swindle.*

**daisy beaters** *Feet.* 19 C. Of sound semantics, but poor phonetics, the term is rarely employed.

**Daisy Dormer** *Warmer.* This term has currency in the theatrical world. Daisy Dormer was a famous music hall artiste. Lupino Lane. The word 'warm' has numerous slang meanings; sexy, wealthy, nearing the solution to a problem: no indication is given, it may therefore refer merely to a change in the weather.

**daisy recruits,** see DAISY ROOTS.

**daisy roots** *Boots.* The term is an old one, recorded by Hotten, 1859 and is still in popular use. As a rule it is reduced to *daisies,* and seems to have evolved about mid-19 C., when it was confused with DAISY RECRUITS, which is now totally obsolete, if it ever actually existed. It has currency in Australia, in South Africa, and in the U.S.A., both in New York and on the Pacific Coast, Eric Partridge, *Dictionary of Slang* and *Dictionary of the Underworld*; Chicago May, 1928; Maurer and Baker, 1944.

**damager** *Manager.* 19 C. It is theatrical slang, highly charged with sarcasm (damageress for the manageress of a London tea-shop had a short vogue in early 20 C., but it fell before the impact of the far more witty *Miss Manageress*—mis-manageress).

**Danny Rucker** *Butter.* American, Pacific Coast. Maurer and Baker, 1944. Cf. DAN TUCKER, and LAY ME . . .

**Dan O'Leary** *Weary*. American tramps' term for walking, generally reduced to *O'Leary*. Quoted by John Chapman, in *The* (New York) *Sunday News*, and recorded (but not as rhyming slang) by Eric Partridge in *Dictionary of the Underworld*.

**Dan Tucker** *Butter*. Recorded by Hotten, 1859, now obsolete in England but survives in America where it is interchangeable with Danny Rucker. Both terms recorded by Maurer and Baker, 1944.

**Darby and Joan** *Alone*. 20 C. A rare substitution for JACK, or PAT, generally reduced to DARBY.

**Darby Kelly,** see DERBY KELLY.

**day and night** *Light* (ale). 20 C. This seems to be a post-second war formation, and has a restricted currency. It will be interesting to observe 'whether it flame or fade' in the next decade.

**day's a-dawning** *Morning*. Late 19 C. The term is confined in its usage to night workers, and those who commence their labours in the small-hours—milkmen, Covent Garden Market men, and others.

**dead spotted ling (of)** *Dead ring* (*of*), that is, *likeness*. 20 C. Australian. Sidney J. Baker quoted by Eric Partridge, *Dictionary of Slang . . . Addenda*.

**Derby Kelly** *Belly*. Late 19 C. or early 20 C. The term was brought into great prominence by Harry Champion's song, 'Boiled beef and carrots' which contains the couplet: 'That's the stuff for your derby kel, makes you fat and keeps you well.' The term is always reduced as in the song, and is also in use on the Pacific Coast of America. Chicago May gives it, 1928, so do Maurer and Baker, 1944.

**Derry and Toms** *Bombs*. 20 C., during and after second war. The reference here is not only to the famous London store, but to 'derry', to 'have a derry on' means a dislike of—from *down on*, prejudiced against, from DERRY DOWN (Ireland): the dialect word *deray* also may be formative, from old French, *desroi* or *derroi*; confusion, destruction.

**derry-down-derry** *Sherry*. Theatrical usage. 20 C. Lupino Lane.

**deuce and ace** *Face*. Given by Fraser and Gibbons in *Soldiers' and Sailors' words and phrases*, 1925. It seems to have enjoyed some popularity in the army, 1914–18. It is now rarely heard, but was recorded by Michael Harrison in *Reported Safe Arrival*, 1943.

**dickory dock** *Clock*. 19 C. from the nursery rhyme, and generally used by mothers to children at bedtime. 'Look at that dickory dock! Up them apples and pears, into Uncle Ned!'

**Dick Turpin** *Thirteen* (score at darts). *Evening News*, 2 July 1937.

**Dicky bird** *Word*. The term does not refer to a word as a unit of language, but as an oath, 'I give you my dicky bird for that', or as a serious admonition, 'Oi—'ere—

come 'ere—I want to 'ave a dicky bird with you. What do you mean by . . .' The term was in use in the late 19 C., and in the early 20 C. had extended its meaning to include an 'informer'—a 'stool pigeon', the 'little bird' who whispers in the ear of the police.

**Dicky diddle** *Piddle* (urination). 20 C. A juvenile form of *Jimmie Riddle*, and generally reduced to *diddle*, however, the first element is not discarded because it is all-sufficient as a rhyming slang reduction: Dick(y)—*prick* (the penis). It remains juvenile in its usage.

**Dicky dirt** *Shirt.* Invariably reduced to *Dickey*, and totally fused with an older term first recorded in 1781 by George Parker in *A View of Society* who defines it as 'cant for a worn-out shirt'. By 1811 it had improved its status by rising to the level of slang, and by the end of the 19 C. it was standard English for a detachable shirt-front. Dickeys are now used only by waiters, but they served their turn in the late 19 C. to early 20 C. by enabling people to 'keep up appearances'.

**didn't ought** *Port* (wine). Late 19 C. to early 20 C. Based on the simpering of ladies who, when asked to 'have another', replied that they 'didn't ought'.

**Dieu et mon droit** (pronounced *dright*) *F—— you Jack, I'm all right.* Army, 1914–18. The term was critical and condemnatory of all who acted in a selfish manner, and was not an expression of one's own attitude. The comradeship and good-nature of the soldiers, irrespective of civilian social status, was the good that came out of the evil, and it paved the way to the Social Reforms we now enjoy. One half of the world discovered how the other half lived.

**dig and dirt** *Shirt.* American formation, see DICKY . . . and DINKY. Recorded in this form by Chicago May, 1928.

**dig in the grave** *A shave.* 19 C. Much used during the 1914–18 war in the army, where, no doubt, it was influenced by the 'issue' open razor, it is still current. Recorded in *Sydney Bulletin*, 18 January 1902, and quoted by Sidney J. Baker in *The Australian Language*, 1945.

**dilly** *Silly.* This term is recorded by Sidney J. Baker in *A Popular Dictionary of Australian Slang*, 1943. He points out that it may be extended to *dilpot*, *dillypot* and *dollypot*: however, the term may be the reduced form of DILLYPOT (q.v.) and have rhyming significance in only a secondary way.

**dillydonce** *Ponce.* American, recent formation; *Letters from The Big House*, Jim Phelan.

**dillypot** *Twat* (a fool). 20 C. Australian. (*Twat* has, of course, another meaning, which itself is used for 'fool'.)

**dime a pop** *Cop* (policeman). 20 C. American, Pacific Coast. Recorded by Maurer and Baker, 1944: probably an expression of ridicule and contempt comparable with the British 'three shies a penny'.

**ding dong** *Song*. So defined by Hotten in 1859 when it may have been adequate, but in mid-20 C. the term carries much more. It is one of the rare examples of both words in a rhyming slang phrase matching up with their partners, for a DING DONG is a *sing song*, that is, an impromptu party at which the entertainment takes the form of singing popular songs, lustily and in unison, sometimes into the small hours, with or without musical accompaniment. A ding dong may just happen, when one or two hilarious neighbours get together and attract more, or it may be mildly organized to celebrate a birthday, or on any other excuse. The Cockney ding dong is the direct ancestor of the modern, very respectable, and often clergyman-led 'Community Singing'. The basic necessity of a ding dong is community of voices. A gathering whereat the entertainment is provided by a local soloist is not a ding dong, and the singer does not give a ding dong. He or she 'obliges'. Such a solemn occasion can warm up into a ding dong when the soloist, having 'obliged', and having responded to the polite request for an encore, leads into a chorus song. The term is as curiously and as exclusively Cockney as the cultural expression it represents. There is no American equivalent; in the States Ding Dong means merely a song and is so defined by Maurer and Baker, 1944. See DINKY . . .

**ding the tot** *Steal the lot*, as, for example, removing the safe instead of breaking it open and stealing the contents. To *ding*, 'steal', is an 18 C. word defined by Captain Alexander Smith in *A Thieve's Grammar*, 1719. The rhyming element is probably a 19 C. addition. Eric Partridge, *Dictionary of the Underworld* and *Dictionary of Slang* . . .

**dinkey dong** See DINKY.

**dinkie do,** an alternative spelling of *Dinky-doo* (q.v.).

**dinky dirt** *Shirt*. An American debasement of the English *dickey* . . . (q.v.) Pacific Coast, recorded by Maurer and Baker, 1944.

**dinky dong** *A song*. Thus defined by Maurer and Baker, 1944. The term is more likely to be an American formation than a debasement of Cockney DING DONG (q.v.). The spirit is expressed rather in *dinky*, neat, small, dainty, from Scottish *dink*, neat, than in its rhyming element.

**dinky doo** *Twenty-two*. Score in the game of House (Housie-Housie) extensively played in the army, 1914–18.

**dip south** *Mouth*. An American form of NORTH . . . (q.v.). Recorded by Maurer and Baker, 1944.

**dirty old Jew** *Two*. Score in the game of House (Housie-Housie) extensively played in the army, 1914–18.

**dirty 'ore** *Thirty-four*, score in the game of House (Housie-Housie) extensively played in the army, 1914–18. *'ore* is 'whore'. This is double rhyming slang, both words being engaged.

**do and dare** *Underwear*

(? feminine). 20 C. American, Pacific Coast, recorded by Chicago May, 1928.

**Doctor cotton,** see JOHNNIE...

**Doggett coat and badge,** see COAT . . .

**dog's dinner** *Deaner* (shilling). Recorded by Sidney J. Baker in *The Australian Language*, 1945. See also RIVERINA.

**Dolly Cotton,** see JOHNNIE . . .

**dollypot,** alternative spelling of DILLYPOT (q.v.).

**Dolly Varden** *Garden.* 20 C. The term is not used by gardeners, who are grim men, worried by worms and slugs; but by parents, who put children to play in the Dolly Varden. It is, however, not one of the popular expressions.

**do me good(s)** *Wood(s)*, short for Woodbines, the famous small cigarette that, together with Bruce Bairnsfather, the humorist, did much to win the 1914–18 war. The term was evolved at that period, and fell into abeyance, but the mid-20-C. anti-tobacconist 'cancer-of-the-lungs' scare revived it as an expression of Cockney defiance.

**don't make a fuss** *Bus.* 20 C. Chiefly theatrical.

**dook(s),** see DUKE OF YORK.

**door to door** *Four* (or any number ending in four, as 24, 34, 44, . . .). 20 C.

**Dora Gray** *tray* (three, hence a threepenny piece). 20 C. Recorded by Sidney J. Baker in *A Popular Dictionary of Australian Slang*, 1943. It is sometimes reduced to a *Dora.*

**dot and dash** *Moustache.* 20 C. American, Pacific Coast. Recorded by Chicago May, 1928.

**down the drains** *Brains*, meaning 'mental ability', not foodstuff. 20 C., not popular.

**drags** *Rags.* The reference is to feminine attire worn by male homosexuals in the practice of transvestitism. It seems to be a condensation of 'dress' and 'rag' and also has reference to the clogging effect of skirts on a masculine stride. American in origin, its usage is largely confined to the States, although it is not unknown here.

**drum and fife** (1) *Wife*, (2) *knife.* Both meanings are almost exclusive to the army. (1) is the more popular, and may have an oblique reference to noise both shrill and heavy.

**drummond and roce** (No rhyme) *Knife and fork.* Recorded by Michael Harrison in *Reported Safe Arrival*, 1943, who elucidates in a footnote specifically stating 'Cockney rhyming slang', but records no rhyme. The explanation was given in a private letter 7 October 1958. *Drum and fife—knife*; reduce to *drum and*, pronounce *Drummond. Roast pork—fork*; reduce to *roast*, pronounce *roce.* Connect the two with an intrusive 'and'. This is a magnificent specimen of Cockney verbal agility and subtle humour. Messrs. Drummond & Roce sound like an old-established very dignified firm of Sheffield manufacturers producing table cutlery. It is a classic example of the possibilities in rhyming slang—even without rhyme.

**dry land** *Understand.* Recorded by Hotten, 1859, now obsolete.

**Duchess of Teck,** an alternative form of DUKE OF . . . (q.v.).

**duck and dive** *Hide.* 20 C. Good semantics, but poor phonetics. A duck dives and is hidden beneath the surface of the pond. To *duck* is to avoid a blow by a quick dropping movement executed by bending the knees.

**Duke of Cork** *Talk.* An American formation, Irish influence, from DUKE OF YORK (2) (q.v.). Ernest Booth in *American Mercury*, 1928; Maurer and Baker, 1944.

**Duke of Fife** *Knife.* Late 19 C., used largely in the army.

**Duke of Kent** *Rent.* 20 C., but less frequently used than BURTON . . . (q.v.).

**Duke of Teck** *A cheque.* Theatrical. Lupino Lane.

**Duke(s) of York(s)** (1) *Walk*, (2) *talk*, (3) *cork*, (4) *chalk*, (5) *fork.* (1) is given by Hotten, 1859, and is now obsolete: (2) developed *c.* 1873: (3) is modern, but uncommon: (4) in use about 1890: (5) perhaps the earliest sense, and may possibly go back to 18 C. An interesting metamorphosis has taken place: *forks* is an early 19 C. (possibly late 18 C.) slang term for 'fingers'; *fingers* represent 'the hand'; the *hands* can be bunched into 'fists'. Duke(s) of York(s) is reduced to Duke(s) and pronounced in Cockney dialect *dooks.* Dooks, as a slang term for hands, and particularly for fists, has climbed the social scale, and is used widely by people who do not know that it is merely the Cockney form of Dukes. 'That boy is very handy with his dooks', meaning he is a good boxer, is used in quite polite circles, so is 'keep your dooks off', do not 'borrow'.

**dumb waiter** *Elevator.* Used by workmen only. Evolved *c.* 1920. *John O' London's Weekly*, 9 July 1934.

**Dunlop tyre** *Liar.* 20 C. Less popular than HOLY . . . (q.v.).

**Dutch pegs** *Legs.* A 20 C. development of SCOTCH . . . (q.v.).

**Dutch Street** *To eat.* 20 C. Generally in the form of 'to eat in Dutch street', meaning each member of a party at a restaurant will pay his own bill.

**Dutch Treat,** a variant of DUTCH STREET (q.v.).

YOU FILTHY LITTLE DUNLOP TYRE

# E

**early door** *Whore.* 19 C., and based on the custom of paying a few pence extra to be admitted to the Music Hall before the bulk of the crowd. (The admirable self-imposed civic discipline of forming a queue was unknown in 19 C.)

**early doors** *Drawers.* 19 C. The term is obsolescent, because ladies' intimate undergarments, so blatantly displayed in advertising photographs, are no longer a subject of robust masculine jesting, and are no longer called drawers, but scanties, panties, knic-knics and the like.

**early hours** *Flowers.* 19 C. and still in use among the vendors who have to keep very early hours to purchase their wares in the great glass flower hall of Covent Garden Market.

**east and south** *Mouth.* Early 19 C. Recorded by Ducange Anglicus, 1857, and by Hotten, 1859. It is now rarely heard, having been converted into NORTH AND SOUTH. The change has been influenced by semantics. N. being vertically opposed to S., it suggests the opening of the mouth, whereas E. and S. suggest nothing but a crooked smile. The term is applied to the act of talking rather than to the physical mouth. 'You know what the trouble is—'e's bin shootin' e's Norf un Sarf!' or, 'Oi! 'ere! Shut your bleetn' Norf un Sarf!' It is one of the few rhyming slang expressions to be used in anger.

**east and west** (1) *Vest*, (2) *breast*. Both meanings are in use on the Pacific Coast of America. Recorded by Maurer and Baker, 1944, and in *The American Thesaurus*, 1952.

**eat a fig** *Crack a crib.* Given by Hotten, 1859, but now quite obsolete as today one does not crack a crib; one heists a joint.

**Edna May** *Way* (on your, on my). Edna May was a famous music hall artiste, and the term survives only in the world of the theatre. (Modern youth knows nothing of the Music Hall, or the genius it fostered.) Lupino Lane.

**Egyptian Hall** *A ball* (dance). Recorded by Hotten, 1859, when the Egyptian Hall, Piccadilly, was a fashionable place at which society functions, art exhibitions and the like were held. The term was demolished with the building.

**eighteen pence** *Sense.* Of 19 C. origin, this term is still frequently heard chiefly in a challenging voice from a workman to his juvenile assistant: 'Ain't you got no eighteen pence? Don't you know no better yet?' In the U.S. it seems to have a wider application. James Curtis in *The Gilt Kid*, 1936, says, 'He did not know Masie had all that eighteen-pence.' (*Note:* 'penny' is used in the States for a cent, as 'a dollar' is in Britain for 5/-.

**Elephant and Castle** (1) *The anus* (arse - hole, pronounce 'arsole'), (2) *hell.* (1) is the more commonly used; (2) is weak, depending on a special stressing of Castle—*cars-ell*—for its effect. The Elephant and Castle, originally a public-house at the commencement of the Old Brighton Road, has given its name to an area, a style of Cockney swagger, and a special toughness of character. The story that the House received its name through a sign-writer's error when instructed to paint *Infanta of Castille*, is only a story.

**elephant trunk** is an American clipping of:

**elephant's trunk** *Drunk.* This is among the oldest of rhyming slang terms and is recorded by Hotten, 1859. It is still constantly in use, and is generally reduced to 'Elephants'. To 'cop an elephant' is to get drunk. Its formation is probably influenced by the idea that pink elephants lunge lustily through alcoholic hallucinations. In the U.S.A. it refers to the affected person: 'Jack-rolling elephant's trunks' is the act of picking the pockets of drunken men—a favourite form of juvenile delinquency.

**Ellen Terry** *Jerry.* 'Jerry' is a shortened form of *Jeremiah*, a slang term for a chamber-pot. It has currency in the world of the theatre (Lupino Lane). According to Eric Partridge, *Dictionary of Slang* . . . it is *Jeroboam*, hence, *Jeremiah* is probably a specifically Cockney form.

**engineers and stokers** *Brokers.* 19 C. Not 'City gentlemen', but the down-at-heel people employed to 'take possession' in a case of non-payment.

**Epsom races** (1) *Braces*, (2) *faces.* Recorded by Ducange Anglicus, 1857, both meanings are now obsolete.

**Ernie Marsh** *Grass.* This term is very rarely used; it refers to grass in the parks, and the Cockney habit of sleeping a summer Sunday on the grass. Probably formed on the name of some once notorious sleeper-out.

**Everton toffee** *Coffee.* Recorded by Ducange Anglicus, 1857, and by Hotten, 1859. Now obsolescent, but indicative that this particular sweetmeat was enjoyed by our ancestors.

**eye me float** is an American perversion of I'M AFLOAT (q.v.).

# F

**fal** *Gal* (girl). Given by J. Redding Ware in *Passing English*, 1909. Now quite obsolete, and probably never well established, as Cockneys seldom call a girl a 'girl'—and in any case, *gal* is not, and never was, the Cockney pronunciation of 'girl'. *Gal* is stage-cockney, or literary-cockney, the real dyed-in-the-wool dialect makes of it 'gaow'.

**fall down the sink,** see TUMBLE . . .

**false alarm(s)** *Arm(s)* (limbs), current in the army, 1914–18, but seldom used in England now. It is, however, current in the U.S.A. *American Thesaurus.*

**fancy sash** *Smash* (physical blow. '. . . gave him a fancy sash on his I suppose.' Recorded in *Sydney Bulletin*, January 1902, and quoted by Sidney J. Baker in *The Australian Language*, 1945.

**Fanny Blair** *Hair*. Current in England 19 C. but now seldom heard. In New York it was in use as early as 1859 (Matsell's *Vocabulum*) and is current on the Pacific Coast. Maurer and Baker, 1944.

**far and near** *Beer*. 19 C. Of secondary importance in England (see PIGS . . .), but in U.S.A. it has greater popularity. Recorded in *American Thesaurus*.

**feather and flip** *Kip*, that is, 'sleep', and by extension of meaning, the bed itself. The rhyming slang is more frequently applied to the latter. 20 C.

**fiddle and flute** *Suit* (of clothes), an American form of WHISTLE . . . (q.v.). Maurer and Baker, 1944, and *American Thesaurus.*

**fiddley did** *Quid* (£1). 20 C. Generally reduced to *fiddley*. Recorded by Sidney J. Baker in *The Australian Language*, 1945.

**field of wheat** *Street*. Recorded by Hotten, 1859. A strong motif of Cockney humour is inversion of meaning. Nothing could be further removed from a field of wheat than a London street. The term is also current in Australia.

**fife and drum** *Bum* (the buttocks). Early 20 C., and when applied to children very appropriate, since the drum, too, is beaten.

**fifteen and seven** *Heaven* (good, or enjoyable). American in origin and use. Maurer and Baker, 1944.

**fifteen and two** *Jew*. Current on the Pacific Coast of America, Maurer and Baker, 1944, and heard occasionally in England since the second war, but here it is condensed to FIFTEEN-TWO.

**fig and post** *Toast* (toasted bread). Current in the army during the second war, now obsolescent. See also PIG AND . . .

**fillet of veal** (1) *Tread mill*, (2) a *wheel*, (3) *prison*. (1) is recorded by Hotten and is now as obsolete as that particular instrument of torture. (2) is in current use on the Pacific Coast of America, recorded by Maurer and Baker, 1944. (3), rhyming on *steel*, refers to the proverbial 'bars' behind which a convict is confined. Ducange Anglicus, 1857, defining rhyme (3), gives 'a house of correction'.

**fine and dandy** *Brandy*. 19 C. Cockney term, now obsolete in England, but current on the Pacific Coast of America. Maurer and Baker, 1944.

**finger and thumb** (1) *Rum*, (2) *drum* (road). (1) Recorded by Hotten, by Henry Mayhew, and by Ducange Anglicus, it is of respectable antiquity and still has a restricted currency in England; however, the term 'mur' (back-slang) became so general during the 1914–18 war, that all other slang terms for rum faded. It is in use on the Pacific Coast of America (Maurer and Baker, 1944). A second, and somewhat specialized meaning, is *Road* rhyming on 'drum', Romany for a highway.

**Finsbury Park** *Arc* (lamp). In use by cinematic technicians since *c*. 1945. It is a studio (filming) not a laboratory (cutting and editing) term, generally shortened to *Finsbury*, as in 'Cut the Finsburies!', switch off the arc-lamps.

**first of May** *Say* (acrimonious speech), to speak up for one's self. 'So she went round there, and didn't 'arf 'ave 'er first o' May!' 'I'll 'ave my first o' May when I get in front o' the beak.' Ducange Anglicus gives the term, but defines it as 'tongue'. It might have some connection with May-Day Saturnalia.

**fish and shrimp** *Pimp*. An American term, recorded by Maurer and Baker, 1944, and *American Thesaurus*. This term, with others, is disowned by Maurer and Baker, who suppose it to be of British origin. It is not: and is unknown in London.

**fisherman's daughter** *Water*. It is very seldom applied to water in bulk—river, lake or sea—generally only to a drink of water, but as much as a bucket or a basinful seems to be permissible. It is nearly always reduced to *fisherman's*, and is very widely used. Since every fisherman's business or 'sport' demands the presence of water, it is closely associated with its meaning.

**five-acre farm** *The arm*. 19 C. Quoted by Augustus Mayhew in *Paved with Gold*, 1857, but now obsolete. There may be a pun in *acre* and *acher*.

**five to two** *A Jew*. This

refers to racing odds, not to the time, hence it is the favourite rhyming slang for Jew among bookmakers, their associates, and habitual punters. Reduced to *five*.

**flag unfurled** *Man of the world*. Recorded by Hotten, 1859, but now obsolete.

**flash of light** *A sight*. A 'sight' is a term applied to a gaudily, or unbecomingly, dressed woman. 'Coo! Look at 'er! Reg'lar flash o' light—ain't she!' Early 20 C. Recorded by J. Redding Ware in *Passing English*, 1909. Eric Partridge, *Dictionary of Slang* . . . , suggests that the usage is confined to South London, localization of rhyming slang is not an uncommon occurrence hence the suggestion is acceptable. No closer enquiry can be made, as the expression is now obsolete, but the word *flash*, which has the same meaning: 'Coo! ain't she flash!', and which may be an example of reduced rhyming slang, is still extant, and is widely used. 'Flash' has numerous other meanings, all of which are to be found in Eric Partridge, *op. cit.* A 'sight', in the sense of an ugly, or otherwise striking sight, may itself be a reduction of 'a sight for sore eyes'.

**flea and louse** *House*. Hotten records this, but is content with a one-word definition; however, it is probable that a *bad* house (a brothel) was indicated, which is the current meaning on the Pacific Coast of America (Maurer and Baker, 1944). The term is now obsolete in England.

**fleas and ants** *Pants* (trousers). Has a currency in America only, since trousers are not called pants in England. It is recorded by Maurer and Baker, 1944, and in *American Thesaurus*, 1952: cf. the American expression 'ants in her pants' said of a restless, energetic person.

**flounder and dab** *Cab*. This is recorded by Hotten, 1859, and is now obsolescent in England; it survives, however, on the Pacific Coast of America where it has become mechanized—meaning taxi-(cab) (Maurer and Baker, 1944).

**flowers and frolics** *Ballocks*. 20 C. Irish usage; an alternative form of FUN AND FROLICS.

**flowery dell** *Cell* (prison). Late 19 C. or early 20 C., and from the total inversion, clearly of Cockney origin. Often abbreviated to 'flowery'.

**fly flat** *Gat* (gun). American, Pacific Coast. Recorded by Maurer and Baker, 1944, who suggest that in England it refers to a 'would-be sport; a wise-guy', but it does not. To be 'fly' is to be sharp, wide; and a 'flat' is a fool, mug; so the two words, in English usage, never meet: 'flat' is seldom used at all.

**fly my kite** *A light* (ignition). Recorded by Ducange Anglicus, 1857: now obsolete.

**fork and knife** *Life*. Quoted by Alan Hyder in *Black Girl, White Lady*, 1934.

**found a nail** *Round the tail*. Australian; a sheep-shearing term. Sidney J. Baker, quoted by

Eric Partridge, *A Dictionary of Slang*, *Addenda*.

**four by two** *A Jew*. This is of 1914–18 wartime origin. A 'four by two' was the piece of rag, measuring four by two inches, that was issued to the troops for the purpose of cleaning the bore of the short Lee-Enfield rifle (it was applied by means of a cord with an eye-splice, called a 'pull-through'. The same four by two was used for pistol cleaning, and was applied by a ram-rod.) Old soldiers still employ the term, but the 'time' references are more general. See HALF . . . ; QUARTER . . . ; TEN . . . Also (in error?) FIVE BY . . . but see FIVE TO . . .

**fourth of July** *A tie*. This does not ante-date the 1914–18 war, and must then have been brought over by the Americans because the Fourth of July means nothing at all to any Englishman, and Cockneys in particular hold the opinion that it exists as a red-letter day simply because Yanks do not know that Guy Fawkes' Day is the fifth of November.

**forty-four** (1) *Door to door* (salesman), (2) *whore*. (1) is of 20 C. origin, following the popularization of Hire-Purchase. Cf. MOZZLE AND . . . (2) is American, recorded in *American Thesaurus*.

**fowl roost** *Boost*. A 'boost' is an assistant to a pickpocket. His (or her) part is the creation of a diverting situation. It is a Pacific Coast of America term recorded by Maurer and Baker, 1944.

**France and Spain** *Rain*. Of 19 C. origin, but revitalized during the 1914–18 war probably because of the prodigious quantities of rain-water that flooded the trenches in France, most particularly in 1917.

**Frank and Hank** *Bank* (savings). The employment of these two Christian names suggests the intimate familiarity that is so outstanding a feature of the American way of life (Maurer and Baker, 1944).

**Friar Tuck** *F*——. (1) *Coitus*, (2) *expletive*. (1) is jocular, and is generally used in the form of a Spoonerism. 'Blimey! You don't 'arf look 'appy [meaning miserable]. Why don't you Friar Tuck?' The conventional reply is, 'I'd sooner fry a sausage', which does not seem to have a double meaning but might have. (2) is never violent, as the unprintable word itself often is: generally, 'I don't give a Friar Tuck!' equivalent to 'I don't give a damn', or in modern parlance, 'I couldn't care less.' Also, 'What the Friar Tuck in Hell . . .'

**fried eggs** *Legs*. 20 C. Australian. A. A. Martin in a letter (1937) to Eric Partridge. See *Dictionary of Slang . . . Addenda*.

**frilled gizzard** *A lounge lizard*. 20 C. American, Pacific Coast. Recorded by Maurer and Baker, 1944.

**frog a log** *Dog*. American, recorded by Maurer and Baker, 1944.

**frog and feather** *Leather* (a pocket wallet: bill-fold). Recorded by Maurer and Baker, 1944.

**frog and toad** *Road.* Recorded by Hotten, 1859, and still very popular. It may have been influenced by the fact that Cockneys who went out into the country to sell their wares—in mid-19 C. the country started just beyond Streatham—would encounter frogs on the road and nowhere else, since they, the Cockneys, never left the road. See Henry Mayhew, who tells of a coster who explained how his boy had refused to take the donkey into a field for a feed of grass—and, incidentally, how the donkey himself brightened up, trotted faster, and seemed to take a less jaundiced view of life when he came within smelling distance of Vauxhall Gate. See also *The Cockney* (*Appendix*), by Julian Franklyn, giving details of Lady (then Mrs) B. L. Q. Henriques' experience of Cockney children who became ill (from shock) on their first visit to the country. The foregoing may, however, be too fanciful. Ducange Anglicus (1857) gives *Frog and Toe*—not rhyming slang. 'Frog' may therefore refer not to the amphibious quadruped of the genus *Rana*, but to the springy sole of a horse's hoof; in which case the following word will be *toed*—past tense of *to toe*, and not toad, the amphibious quadruped of the genus *Bufo*.

According to Ducange Anglicus, the phrase 'We will take it on the frog and toe' means we will take the proceeds of the robbery back to London and there share out. This seems to involve a long tramp by road because thieves of mid-19 C. would not go by rail.

**frog-in-the-throat** *Boat.* In use during the 1914–18 war: now dropped.

**front wheel skid** *Yid.* Of post-1914–18 war origin, and not very often heard. It is based on the fact of a driver rarely coming out of a front wheel skid with a smile on his face.

**full as an egg** *A slug in the head.* This is recorded as of American origin and usage by Maurer and Baker, who query whether it is bona fide rhyming slang. Its inclusion certainly seems to call for a generous expansiveness.

**fun and frolics** *Ballocks.* 20 C., Irish usage, the phonetics well supported by semantics.

# G

**Gar and Starter** *Star and Garter* (Inn, Richmond, Surrey), but it is more in the nature of a jocular Spoonerism than of rhyming slang.

**garden** *Pardon* (form of, 'I beg your pardon—what did you say?'). Recorded by Michael Harrison in *Reported Safe Arrival* but, apparently, very local. See ONE AND ELEVEN . . .

**garden gate** *Magistrate*. Recorded by Hotten, and still enjoying a moderate currency in England. It is also in use on the Pacific Coast of America (Maurer and Baker, 1944).

**garden gates** *Rates*. There is but little use of this term because most Cockneys pay an 'inclusive rental'. It is inclined to come out of hibernation every three years in order to take part in the Municipal Elections.

**garden hop** *Shop* (to inform, betray or turn Queen's Evidence). Of post-1914–18 war formation, it appears in *The Missing Million*, by Edgar Wallace.

**garlic and glue** *Stew*. American, Pacific Coast (Maurer and Baker, 1944).

**gates of Rome** *Home*. A 20 C. development of POPE . . . (q.v.).

**gay and frisky** *Whisky*. A lively, apt and descriptive term it has wide currency, both in Britain and in the United States. It is recorded by Chicago May, 1928, and by Maurer and Baker, 1944. See I'M SO . . .

**gear** *Queer* (of abnormal sexual habits). This term has not yet established itself, and one dare not prophesy of its future: its fate depends entirely on that of 'queer' which, in mid-20 C., seems to be becoming a polite euphemism, but which might at any moment be submerged beneath some new term.

**George Robey** *Toby* (Road, from *tobar*, a form of Gipsy language). Recorded by Matt. Marshall in *Tramp Royal on the Toby* (cf. FROG . . .). George Robey, a famous comedian, *c.* 1930.

**gerbera** *Yarborough* (in the game of 'Bridge'). Recorded by Sidney J. Baker in *The Australian Language*, 1945. See also LUBRA.

**German band** *Hand*. The closing decades of 19 C. and the first decade of 20 C. were rendered hideous by this particular form of street-noise. 1914 put an end to it, and the term died a natural death.

**German flutes** *Boots.* This term, which is recorded by Ducange Anglicus, 1857, and by Hotten, 1859, was defeated in Britain by the far better semantics of DAISY ROOTS (q.v.); however, in America—the hot-house where discarded English slang words luxuriate—it is popular on the Pacific Coast (Maurer and Baker, 1944, also in the *American Thesaurus*, 1952).

**Gertie Gitana** *Banana.* In the first decade of 20 C., this term, on account of the music-hall fame of Gertie Gitana, became a catch-word through the popular song: *Let's all go down the Strand*, the refrain of which was frequently changed from 'Have a banana!' to 'Gertie Gitana'. It is now fading away with the generation that lived its youth in those glittering days.

**Gertie Lee** *Thirty-three* in the game of House (Housie-Housie, played excessively in the army, 1914–18).

**giddy goat** *Tote* (totalizator). 20 C. Recorded by Sidney J. Baker in *The Australian Language*, 1945.

**giggle and titter** *Bitter* (beer, not fate). This very apt and witty term has its greatest currency in the theatrical profession. Lupino Lane.

**giggle stick** *Prick* (penis). 20 C. American, Pacific Coast. Recorded by Maurer and Baker, 1944. (It may be spelt as one word.) This is probably of Australian origin where it is not rhyming slang, but is descriptive of a stick used for mixing drinks.

**gimp** *Limp* (defective gait). The term appears to be exclusively American, and has been traced only to the *American Thesaurus.* It probably refers to an assumed limp as an adjunct to begging, but might, of course, include a natural physical defect.

**ginger ale** *jail.* American, Pacific Coast. Recorded by Maurer and Baker, 1944, who assume it to be of British origin, but it is unknown in London.

**ginger beer** (1) *Engineer* (ships), (2) *tear* (lachrymal), (3) *queer* (homosexual). (1) is British usage and uncommon outside of the Merchant Navy and the docks. (2) is American usage recorded by Maurer and Baker, 1944. (3) is post-second war in origin, of Cockney usage, and of growing popularity. It is frequently reduced to 'a ginger' and sometimes enhanced to 'a dead Eighteen-carat Ginger' (ex Michael Harrison in a private letter, 7 October 1958). In Australia The Ginger Beers are the (Military) Corps of Engineers.

**ginger pop** *Slop.* Late 19 C., *slop* is a backslang formation for police(man): *ice* (eci) becomes '*s*': This may seem a roundabout way to seek a meaning when *pop* rhymes so obviously with *cop*, but the Americanization of English 'copper' to *cop* (catch) has been imported into England during the 20 C. and not even in its first decade. The term *Ginger pop* is old enough to overlap with the heyday of backslang.

**gipsy's warning** *Morning.* This term is not so popular as DAY'S . . . (q.v.) and may have in its formation an inversion, since the gipsy's warning would surely be more appropriate at dusk than at dawn.

**girl abductor** *Tram conductor.* Recorded in the *Sydney Bulletin*, January 1902, and quoted by Sidney J. Baker in *The Australian Language*, 1945.

**girl and boy** *Saveloy.* This term, which is recorded by Hotten, 1859, is obsolete here, but in use in the States (Maurer and Baker, 1944).

**give a cook** *Look* (from the Yiddish *guck*). Post-second war. Also TAKE A . . . and HAVE A . . .

**give and take** *Cake.* 20 C. A very appropriate phrase since no cake can be eaten that has not been given (if only by a shopkeeper) and taken. 'Cake' also means money—'a cake of notes': that, too, needs to be given and taken.

**Glasgow boat** *Coat.* 20 C. Irish usage.

**glass case** *Face.* Recorded by Augustus Mayhew in *Paved with Gold*, 1857; now obsolete.

**glimmie glide** *Side.* 20 C. Specifically 'other', or 'far', side (of the street, boxing-booth, dog-track, etc.). Irish usage.

**glorious sinner** *Dinner.* Recorded by Hotten, 1859, and now obsolete in England. It is probably formed out of the endeavour made by pioneer social-workers to point out to 'the industrious classes' that their mode of life was extravagant, and that with better organization the week's pay would buy more. (See the Alderman and the tripe in *The Chimes*, by Charles Dickens.) The people did not take the good advice in the right spirit. They simply formed the opinion that 'the gentry' begrudged them not only their few luxuries, but even the necessaries of life. The Cockney still nurtures an undercurrent of resentment against social-workers and they, in turn, have learned not to tread on dangerous ground. The term is still in use on the Pacific Coast of America (Maurer and Baker, 1944).

**goanna** *Piano.* Recorded by Sidney J. Baker in *The Australian Language*, 1945. See also JOANNA.

**Goddess Diana** *Tanner* (sixpence). Recorded by Hotten, 1859, now obsolete.

**God forbid(s)** (1) *Kids* (child or children), (2) *Yids* (Jews), (3) *lid* (hat). (1) The average Cockney is fond of children, inclined to spoil them, and may even be seen crawling about on all fours, playing moke and driver. He is, however, very self-conscious and shy, hence when under observation he reacts gruffly. *God forbid(s)* implies that he does not wish for any (or any more) children. In America the term carries the same superficial meaning, though the spirit must be rather different. It is recorded (without comment) by Maurer and Baker, 1944. The use of the word 'kids' has, in U.S.A., a wider currency and the same meaning as it has in England, but the value is different. (2) This is not intended to express disparagement. The Cockney, xenophobic though he may be, is not an anti-Semite: in fact, since both Jews and Cockneys have the faculty of pointing jokes against themselves they enjoy poking fun at each other without giving or taking offence. The term is formed on the street-trading Jew's pious ability to include the Deity in a business transaction. 'God forbid that I should sell you a damaged pair of stockings, dear!' 'God forbid that I sell a coat that does not fit you, dear!' 'God forbid the quality of this compact should not be first-class, dear!' In conversation with the next stall-holder: 'God forbid it should rain!' Hence, GOD FORBIDS is self-created rhyming slang for *Yids*. In this usage the term has no footing in U.S.A., perhaps because of the different social conditions there. (3) is often employed but is far less popular than TIT FOR . . . (q.v.).

**goose and duck** *F——* (coitus). This term is recorded by Maurer and Baker, 1944, and is therefore current on the Pacific Coast of America, but it is assumed by them to be of English origin. It is not now used in London, and there is no trace of its ever having been. Baker is emphatic on its not being known in Australia, and Maurer's assumption that it is English implies his certainty that it is not American: therefore it must be Irish.

**gooseberry pudding** *Old woman.* Even when pronounced *pudd'n* the phonetics are poor, and as the semantics are not superior it is a wonder that the term, recorded by both Ducange Anglicus, 1857, and Hotten, 1859, survives, even in the reduced form of *Gooseberry*. Probably the suggestion of sourness is a saving grace. It is noteworthy that some Cockneys who use the word 'gooseberry' do not know 'gooseberry pudding' and they deny that it is a reduced form of rhyming slang. From a Cockney the words: 'Well—*I* ain't never 'eard it', is condemnation indeed.

**gooseberry tart** *Heart*, but merely a variant of RASPBERRY . . . (q.v.).

**Gordon and Gotch** *A watch.* It is hard to understand how the name of this old-established firm of book and periodical exporters has gone beyond the confines of the export trade. That GOTCH rhymes with 'watch', and that exporters must impose strict time-limits on the delivery of supplies, is the point of association, but why should the term be used by people who do not know, even, that books or periodicals are exported, much less that Gordon & Gotch are the firm who do it?

**grape vine** *Clothes line.* Recorded in *John o' London's Weekly*, 9 June 1934. [In the present writer's opinion it is of doubtful authenticity—wide enquiries 'in the field' have not produced a single person who owns to knowing it, and Cockneys are apt to claim more knowledge (not less) than is justified.]

**grasshopper** *Copper*. This term is applied to not only the Policeman proper, but to the informer (cf. GARDEN HOP). To 'grass' is to inform. Of late 19 C. origin, the term is still in use.

**greengage** *The stage*. It is exclusive to the theatrical profession. Lupino Lane.

**greengages** *Wages*. 20 C., and nearly always reduced to GREENS.

**grey mare** *Fare* (tramcar or omnibus), late 19 C. The inference is that one cannot ride without a grey mare!

**grocery store** *Door*. American. Recorded in *American Thesaurus*, 1952.

**grumble and grunt** *C——*. Generally *coitus*, sometimes a collective disrespectful term for 'girl', 'girls', or 'woman', used in the same way as *crumpet*; never used as an expletive. 20 C.

**Gungah Din** *Chin*. Rudyard Kipling's hero's fame has spread when Gungah Din can be used in the Pacific Coast Underworld (Maurer and Baker, 1944).

# H

**Hackney Marsh** *Glass* (of liquor). Late 19 C. and now obsolete.

**hail and rain** *A train.* 20 C. Recorded by J. Manchon, *Le Slang*, 1923.

**hair and brain** *A chain.* American, Pacific Coast (Maurer and Baker, 1944).

**hairy float** *Coat.* American, Pacific Coast (Maurer and Baker, 1944).

**hairy goat** *Throat.* American, Pacific Coast (Maurer and Baker, 1944).

**half-a-dollar** *Collar.* Late 19 C. Recorded by Brophy and Partridge in *Songs and Slang of the British Soldier 1914–18*, 3rd edn., 1931.

**half-a-lick** *Sick.* 20 C., as recorded by Maurer and Baker, 1944, in American usage, but a one-word definition does not make the term clear. Does it refer to a fit of vomiting, to a feeling of depression, or to general illness?

**half-an-hour** *Flour.* 20 C. Australian. Recorded by Sidney J. Baker, 1943.

**half an Oxford scholar** *Half-a-dollar*, that is, half-a-crown (2s. 6d.). It is nearly always reduced to 'half-an-Oxford'. Late 19 C.

**half a peck** *Neck.* Of late 19 C. origin, and now fading away in favour of BUSHEL AND . . . (q.v.). It is in use on the Pacific Coast of America, and is recorded by Maurer and Baker, 1944.

**half inch** *Pinch* (steal). This is an old term that was certainly very well established before the 1914–18 war, and is probably of 19 C. origin. As a euphemism for 'stealing', it stands shoulder to shoulder with such terms as 'swipe', and is widely used by polite people who do not regard the 'lifting' of a pencil, or some other minor thing, as an act of stealing by their friends. In the underworld it refers also to an arrest.

**half ounce** *Bounce* (cheat). 19 C. and still in use. 'When I come to count my change proper I found they 'adn't 'arf 'arf-ounced me!'

**half-past two** *A Jew.* Early 20 C. One of several terms rhyming on Jew, and as likely to be used as any other.

**ham and beef** *Chief* (warder). Recorded by Jim Phelan in *Murder by Numbers*, 1941.

**ham and eggs** *Legs* (always

girls' legs). Current in South Africa, recorded by Eric Partridge (from a private letter) in *A Dictionary of Slang . . .* , but in use in England with the same meaning before 1914.

**hammer and tack** (1) *Back*, (2) *track*. (1) is American, and refers to the dorsal surface of the body. (2) is Australian and may be applied to any track, including a metalled road. Maurer and Baker, 1944.

**Hampstead Heath** *Teeth*. First printed in *The Referee*, 7 November 1887, it displaced the older HOUNSLOW . . . (q.v.) and is still in use, generally reduced to *Hampsteads*.

**Hampton Wick** *Prick* (the penis). The term is of 19 C. origin, and by the first decade of the 20 C. in the reduced forms of both *Hampton* and *Wick*, it had become a polite euphemism. They are still very widely employed by people who do not know that they are using reduced rhyming slang. Whereas *Hampton* has given rise to the story of the young lady who said her luxury flat was furnished by Waring & Gillows although it had been furnished by Hamptons, *Wick* occurs especially in 'He gets on my wick'; that is, 'he irritates me'. Hampton Wick is a suburb of London and it is impossible to understand why it should have been chosen for this piece of rhyming slang when Hackney Wick—much nearer to Charing Cross, and far more Cockney—would have served the purpose just as well. No reliance can be placed on the suggestion that it is influenced by 'hamper'—a basket.

**hang-bluff** *Snuff*. Recorded by Ducange Anglicus, 1857, now obsolete. See HARRY . . .

**happy hours** *Flowers*. Early 20 C. theatrical currency (Lupino Lane), but also used on the Pacific Coast of America and recorded by Maurer and Baker, 1944.

**harbour light** *All right*. 19 C. Still in use but nearly always reduced to 'all harbour'. It is an expression of satisfaction and well-being, as: 'I fixed up wiv da guv'nor to gimme Sahtdee awf, an' it's all 'arbour!' 'All right' itself can be a threat: for example, the boy who, having broken a window, runs off, knows, if he is followed by a cry of 'all right!' uttered in a certain tone, that he will not ultimately go unpunished.

**hard and flat** *Hat* (derby). 20 C. American, Pacific Coast. Recorded by Maurer and Baker, 1944.

**Harry Bluff** *Snuff*. Recorded by Hotten, 1859, and still used occasionally by the few remaining snuff-takers.

**Harry Lauder** *Border* (stage hangings). Early 19 C. and current only in the theatrical world. Quoted in *The Evening Standard* 19 August 1931.

**Harry Randall** (1) *A candle*, (2) a *handle*. Harry Randall was a famous comedian at his zenith, *c.* 1900, hence the term does not ante-date 20 C. (2) was the earlier usage; (1) was added by the troops during the 1914–18 war, when candles for illuminating dug-outs were commodities of high value. (1) has survived, but is rarely heard since candles are now rarely used.

**Harry Tagg** *Bag.* Current in the theatrical world where when 'on tour' numerous bags have to be packed and unpacked, hauled to the railway station, and 'looked after' on trains, hence bags play a larger part in the life of an actor than in that of the ordinary man. Lupino Lane.

**Harry Tate** (1) *Late,* (2) *plate,* (3) *R.E. 8,* (4) *state.* Harry Tate was a comedian famous in the first two decades of 20 C. for his burlesque on motoring, hence the term was young when war broke out in 1914. (1) was its pre-war meaning; (2) displaced (1) by about mid-1915; at that period (3) displaced (2). An R.E. 8 was an observer's aeroplane. Since 1918 (4) has come (it seems) to stay. It refers to a state of nervous excitement or irritability.

**Harry, Tom and Dick** Alternative form of TOM . . . (q.v.).

**Harry Wragg** *A fag* (cigarette). 20 C. Cockney usage, probably not prior to 1930: formed on the name of the jockey. Now obsolescent, OILY RAG (q.v.) being in the ascendant.

**Harvey Nichol** *Pickle.* 20 C. This is reduced from HARVEY NICHOLS (q.v.) but does not refer to pickle as a condiment. It means a predicament, or unenviable situation.

**Harvey Nichols** *Pickles.* Early 20 C. The famous London fashion house is not a general store, and therefore has no grocery department. Their conscription into this is one of the penalties of their being famous.

**hash - me - gandy** *Handy.* American, Pacific Coast (Maurer and Baker, 1944).

**hat and cap** *Clap* (gonorrhoea). American, Pacific Coast. Recorded by Maurer and Baker, 1944.

**have a cook,** see GIVE A . . .

**Hawkesbury Rivers** *The shivers.* 20 C. Australian. Recorded by Sidney J. Baker, also by Maurer and Baker, 1944.

**head and tail** *Jail.* 20 C. American, Pacific Coast. Recorded by Maurer and Baker, 1944.

**heap of coke** *Bloke.* This is an occasional variant of BUSHEL . . . (q.v.) but in the world of the theatre it is generally applied to the Manager. 20 C.

**heart and dart** *Fart. c.* mid-19 C., and now obsolete.

**heart and lung** *Tongue.* American. Recorded by Chicago May, 1928. Probably using 'tongue' in the sense of talk (as 'lip' and 'jaw' in English usage), but it might refer to the tongue as an organ.

**hearts of oak** *Broke* (penniless). 19 C. There may be an inverted reference to the Building Society which inculcates thrift: on the other hand it may imply that when in that condition one must be stout of heart. It is generally reduced to ***hearts.***

**heavenly bliss** *Kiss.* American, Pacific Coast. Maurer and

Baker suggest British origin, but it is untraceable in England.

**heavenly plan** *A man.* 19 C. Recorded in the *Sydney Bulletin* 18 January 1902, and quoted by Sidney J. Baker in *The Australian Language*, 1945.

**Heaven and Hell** *A shell.* Army, 1914–18, then appropriate, but now obsolete.

**hedge and ditch** *Pitch.* In use in early 20 C. and probably of 19 C. origin. It may have originally referred only to a stall-holder's pitch, which meaning it retains, but by 1914 it was extended to Cockney schoolboys for a football or a cricket pitch.

**here and there** *A chair.* American, Pacific Coast. Recorded by Maurer and Baker, 1944, and in *The American Thesaurus*, 1952.

**Herman Finck** *Ink.* 20 C., and current in the theatrical world. Lupino Lane.

**hey-diddle-diddle** *Fiddle.* 20 C. The term is used mostly on hilarious occasions, such as during a DING DONG (q.v.). It seems to be exclusively Cockney, and is of course derived from the nursery rhyme. It is inclined to be pronounced 'oi-diaw-diaw'.

**hickory dock** *Clock.* Recorded in *The American Thesaurus.* It is interesting to compare this with the British form, DICKERY ... The nursery rhyme is variously printed, sometimes 'h', sometimes 'd', but the 'h' form has taken root in the States, probably because of the indigenous North American tree of that name—hickory—(genus *carya*). American troops, during the 1914–18 war, brought a rhyme over with them:

'Mother, may I go out to swim?'
'Yes, my darling daughter.
Hang your clothes on a hickory tree,
And don't go near the water.'

**Highland frisky** *Whisky.* 19 C. Recorded by C. Bent in *Criminal Life*, 1891. See GAY AND . . . I'M SO . . .

**high seas** *Knees.* American. Recorded by Chicago May, 1928.

**high-stepper** *Pepper.* 20 C. American, Pacific Coast. Recorded by Maurer and Baker, 1944.

**hit (and) or miss** (1) *Piss* (urine), (2) *kiss.* (1) is recorded as American usage by Maurer and Baker, 1944, and is of Australian antecedence; (2) is given by George Orwell in *Down and Out in Paris and London*, 1933.

**hit the deep** *Sleep.* 20 C. This seems to be exclusively Australian.

**hobbledehoy** *Boy* (adolescent). This is not strictly rhyming slang; not only can it be traced back to 1540, but it is a colloquialism verging on Standard English. *Yob*, backslang for 'boy', seems to be a fellow traveller.

**Hobson's choice** *Voice.* 19 C. Generally reduced to *Hobson's*, it is exclusive to the theatrical world.

**hod of mortar** *Porter.* Recorded by Hotten, 1859, and now as out of date as the drink itself.

**holloa boys, holloa** *Collar.* 19 C. (Generally pronounced 'oller), and still in use.

**holy friar** *Liar.* 19 C. This is still in use, and is the favourite among the various terms for 'liar', but it is not used in a serious vein. No euphemisms are needed to tell a man when he is a dangerous liar: adjectives suffice. Rhyming slang refers to a playful or harmless liar.

**Holy Ghost** (1) *Post,* (2) *toast.* (1) This, one assumes, refers in English usage to the Post Office. Defined simply as 'post' it was recorded in Lupino Lane's notebook, and is probably theatrical slang. In America, however, it is race-course slang, and defined by Maurer and Baker as *winning post.* (2) In the army, during the second war, the term became conscripted to 'toasted bread'. See also FIG AND . . .

**hook of mutton** *A button.* American, Pacific Coast. Maurer and Baker, 1944. (Can it be a perversion of *hock* . . . ?) An alternative spelling, HOOK A . . . does not help the semantics. Baker's note: 'In New Zealand . . . *hook one's mutton* . . . "go away".' In London,*s ling one's hook, hook it,* or *hook off,* is 'go away', but neither the one nor the other sheds light on this term.

**hoot and holler** *Dollar.* Not English 5s. (see OXFORD . . .) but American $ (Maurer and Baker, 1944).

**hop toad** *Road.* 20 C. American, Pacific Coast. Recorded by Maurer and Baker, 1944. Cf. FROG AND . . .

**horse and cart** *Heart.* Late 19 C. Recorded by J. Redding Ware in *Passing English,* 1909. At that time J. R. W. did not realize that the animals and the vehicles were passing too.

**horse and trap** (1) *Clap* (gonorrhoea); (2) *crap* (to defecate). Both are 20 C. Cf. both COACHMAN . . . and PONY . . .

**horses and carts** *Darts.* 20 C. This does not seem to be used outside the world of the theatre. Lupino Lane.

**horse's hoof,** often shortened to *horses,* is an alternative form of IRON . . . (q.v.).

**hot-cross bun** *On the run* (in hiding from the police). 20 C., post-second war.

**hot hay** *The bay.* 20 C. This may be geographical; on the other hand it may be rhyming slang for rhyming slang for non-rhyming slang: HOT HAY—*the bay,* short for BOTANY BAY (q.v.)—*hit the hay*—to go to bed. American, Pacific Coast, recorded by Maurer and Baker, 1944.

**hot potato** *Waiter.* 19 C. This must be pronounced per-tay-ter to get the right effect. The temperature is sometimes changed to 'cold' but it does not affect the pronunciation or the meaning. HOT P . . . ought to refer to an efficient waiter; and COLD P . . . to a slow one, but no such nice distinction is made.

**hot-scone** *John.* Australian general slang for a policeman, hence, a detective. Quoted in footnote No. 14 by Maurer and Baker. It is arresting to note that Australians pronounce it *scon* (they certainly do not pronounce the name *Joan*). Cockneys say *skoan.*

**Hounslow Heath** *Teeth.* Recorded by Ducange Anglicus in 1857 but, by 1890, largely displaced by HAMPSTEAD . . . (q.v.).

**house to let** *A bet.* 20 C., never very strongly established, and now obsolescent, if not obsolete.

**how-d'ye-do** (1) *Shoe,* (2) *stew.* 20 C. (1) is now obsolescent. (2) refers not to food but to a condition of alarm, excitement or irritability. 'Blimey! 'ere's a noice ah'd-ye-do! Gawn an' spent this week's Burton on pig's ear 'e 'as!'

**hundred and worst** *Hundred and first* (101st Regiment). This is military nicknaming of Regiments, and is rhyming only as a secondary quality. It is recorded by J. Brett Young in *Jim Redlake,* 1930. It classifies as rhyming slang by courtesy only.

**hurricane deck** *Neck.* 20 C. This is not naval, but theatrical. Lupino Lane.

**husband and wife** *Knife.* American, Pacific Coast (Maurer and Baker, 1944).

**hutch** *Crutch* (a sheep's). 20 C. Recorded by Sidney J. Baker in *A Popular Dictionary of Australian Slang,* 1943. It is, perhaps, merely slang that rhymes, not true rhyming slang.

# I

**ice-cream freezer** *A geezer*, that is any adult of either sex, and often preceded by 'old'. 20 C., and popularized since ice-cream has been so heavily ballyhooed by the big manufacturers. In the days of the 'Ice-cream Jack' (the itinerant Italian vendors), the term was unknown.

**I declare** *A chair*. American, Pacific Coast (Maurer and Baker, 1944). (Cf. I DON'T CARE.)

**I desire** *A fire*. Recorded by Hotten, 1859, and now obsolete in Britain, but in use on the Pacific Coast of America. (Maurer and Baker, 1944). (See ANNA . . .)

**I don't care** *Chair*. Recorded by Maurer and Baker, 1944, annotated as probably British in origin, but it certainly is not—it is most likely American in origin as well as usage, and the reference is probably to the Electric (execution) chair—the 'hot-squat'—and is an expression of defiance.

**if and and** *Band*. American, Pacific Coast. Maurer and Baker, 1944, but as unsatisfactory as a one-word definition can be. What kind of band—jazz, or elastic? The term is unknown in London.

**I'm afloat** (1) *Coat*, especially an overcoat, (2) *boat*. (1) is recorded by Hotten, 1859, and is still in use both here and in America, where it is listed by Maurer and Baker, 1944. (2) seems to be as old as, if not older than (1), but usage restricted to waterfront and dock workers.

**I'm so frisky** *Whisky*. 19 C. An alternative form of GAY AND . . . (q.v.). Often reduced to 'I'm so.'

**in and out** (1) *Snout*, (2) *stout*, (3) *gout*. 20 C. (1) has both phonetics and semantics to aid it—the snout is the nose through which healthy people breathe, both in and out. (2) Stout, the alcoholic drink, is also in a strong position for it goes in (at the mouth) and out—down the drain. (3) is totally unconvincing. That particular chalky disorder of the foot does not lower itself to the level of panel patients. (See also SALMON . . .) Perhaps the reference is to 'toffs' who limp!

**inky smudge** *Judge*. Recorded by James Curtis in *The Gilt Kid*, 1936.

**insects and ants** *Pants*. 20 C. This, being British and not American, refers to men's nether undergarments. See also FLEAS . . .

**in the book** *Hook* (a thief)—

one who hooks. American, Pacific Coast (Maurer and Baker, 1944). (It might have a reference to the book in which Police records are kept.) Cf. JOE HOOK.

**in the sleet** *In the street.* American, Pacific Coast (Maurer and Baker, 1944). It probably refers to homelessness due to pennilessness.

**Irish Kerby,** see:

**Irish Kirby** *A derby* hat. (Also spelt Kerby.) American, Pacific Coast (Maurer and Baker, 1944).

**Irish lasses** *Glasses* (spectacles). 20 C. American, Pacific Coast. Recorded by Chicago May, 1928, and by Maurer and Baker, 1944.

**iron duke** *A fluke.* Late 19 C. The term, which was employed by billiard players, is dying with the game.

**iron hoof** *Pouf* (effeminate male). Recorded by Eric Partridge, 1938, and by Val Davis in *Phenomena in Crime*, 1941. The term seems to be influenced by the Cockney habit of inversion of meaning. Frequently reduced to *Iron.*

**iron horse** (1) *Toss* (a coin), (2) *course.* (1) Pronounced with Cockney dialect, *tawce*—hence the challenge—'I'll iron you for it!' (2) The race-course, either horse-racing or dog-track.

**iron-tank** *Bank.* 20 C., often, but not necessarily, a Savings Bank. See also TIN . . .

**Isabella** *Umbrella.* Recorded by Hotten, 1859, now obsolete (*gamp* is the slang word used for an umbrella by all classes, and it has not attracted a rhyming slang equivalent. *Brolly* seems to be gaining in popularity).

**isle of fling** *Coat.* Recorded by Eric Partridge, *Dictionary of Slang and Unconventional English*, who localizes it to the East End of London; dates it *c.* 1875–1910; and suggests the rhyme falls on *lining.*

**Isle of France** *A dance.* Recorded by Hotten, 1859, and perhaps influenced by the alleged gaiety of Paris. Now obsolete.

**Isle of Wight** *Right.* 20 C. Expressing approval, but also sometimes allied to the right hand side or direction.

**I suppose** *Nose.* Recorded by Ducange Anglicus, 1857, and by Hotten, 1859, but now obsolescent in Britain, where *snitch*, *conk* and *beezer* have overlaid it. It is, however, still current in U.S.A., and is recorded in the *American Thesaurus*, 1952.

**itch and scratch** *A match* (ignition), used largely in the army, 1914–18, now obsolescent.

**it's a breeze** *It is easy.* Recorded by Sidney J. Baker in *The Australian Language*, 1945.

**ivory band** *Hand.* Recorded in *Detective Fiction Weekly*, 21 April 1934. (American.)

**ivory float** *Coat.* American, Pacific Coast. Recorded by Chicago May, 1928, and in the *American Thesaurus*, 1952.

**ivory-pearl** *A girl.* Recorded in *John o' London's Weekly*, 9 June 1934, but the term does not seem to have been widely used and is now obsolescent.

# J

**Jack-a-dandy** *Brandy.* 19 C. Recorded by Ducange Anglicus who omits the connective 'a'. Hotten gives it with the 'a'. Jack-a- (or Jack-o-) Dandy is another folk-name for Will-o-the-wisp, namely, methane, or marsh, gas which, igniting spontaneously, is sometimes seen as a blue light, close to the ground, and is an object of superstition: thus the meaning is probably implied by the blue flame of ignited brandy.

**Jack and Jill** (1) *Till,* (2) *hill,* (3) *bill.* (1) is probably its earliest meaning and was well established in the first decade of 20 C. (2) seems to have been evolved after 1918, and is sometimes applied to the stairs since they are frequently called the *wooden-hill.* (3) is applied chiefly to public expenditure, particularly when it is unpopular; for example, a rise in wages for M.P.s means that 'we' pay the Jack and Jill. (1) also has a currency in U.S.A. where its use is recorded by Maurer and Baker, 1944.

**Jack Dandy** American form of JACK-A-DANDY (q.v.). The omission of the connective 'a', which is the spelling favoured by Ducange Anglicus (1857), is noteworthy. Recorded by Maurer and Baker, 1944.

**jackdaw** *Jaw* (physical). Recorded by Augustus Mayhew in *Paved with Gold,* 1857.

**jackdaw and rook** *Book.* 20 C. Theatrical usage; the 'book' being the words of a (musical) play. Lupino Lane.

**jacket and vest** *West-*(end of London). Recorded by Charles Prior in *So I Wrote It,* 1937. (Among numerous slang terms applied to the West End two others come near rhyming slang, one; *the worse end* and the other; *the best end,* but as the assonance (or the rhyme) is internal, they do not seem fully to qualify for rhyming slang.)

**Jack Horner** see JOHNNY . . .

**Jackie Lancashire** *Handkerchief* (pronounced hankacher). Australian. Recorded by Sidney J. Baker in *The Australian Language,* 1943. See also CHARLIE LANCASTER.

**Jack-in-the-box** (1) *Pox* (syphilis); (2) *socks.* (1) is an alternative for COACHMAN . . . (q.v.). (2) is used on the Pacific Coast of America. Recorded by Maurer and Baker, 1944.

**Jack Jones** *Alone.* The term

may have originated in late 19 C., was certainly in use before 1914, but came very much to the fore during the first war. It is expressive more of isolation than loneliness, and often carries a tincture of admiration. A man who is described as 'all on his Jack' is one at the apex of his calling: or a youth having received instruction is informed, on being permitted to function alone, that 'from now on you're all on your Jack'. It is a form of encouragement. See also PAT . . . , and TOD . . .

**Jack Malone** *Alone.* 20 C. A formation on JACK JONES (q.v.) and PAT MALONE (q.v.).

**Jack O'Brien** *Train* (railway). 20 C. The term seems to be the exclusive property of American tramps (who do a lot of illicit railway riding). Recorded in the *American Thesaurus*, but see also JOHNNIE O'BRIEN.

**Jack Randle** *Candle.* 19 C. Recorded by Hotten, 1859, who explains 'the noted pugilist', but he spelt the name *Randall.* The term took a new lease of life when candles for dug-out illumination assumed an importance. See also HARRY . . .

**Jack's alive** *Five* (pounds sterling), or the number five in the game of House (Housie-Housie), hence, pre-1914 in origin.

**Jack Scratch** *Match* (illuminant). American, Pacific Coast. Recorded by Maurer and Baker, 1944.

**Jack Shay** (1) *Tea,* (2) *slay* (to kill). Australian, where the old English, and present Irish, pronunciation 'tay' lingers. It is extended, by the Australian tramp, to include the can in which tea is brewed. (2) is American Pacific Coast usage. Recorded by Maurer and Baker, 1944.

**Jack Sprat** (1) *Fat* (of meat, not the figure), (2) *brat.* (1) is used chiefly to children when they show a tendency to eat only the lean part of their meat; (2) is current on the Pacific Coast of America. Recorded by Maurer and Baker, 1944.

**Jack Surpass** *Glass* (of liquor). First recorded by Henry Mayhew, *London Labour and the London Poor*, 1851, now obsolete.

**Jack Tar** *Bar.* 20 C. Current in the theatrical world, and very apt since the 'bar' is where one would expect to encounter Jack ashore. Lupino Lane.

**Jack the ripper** *Kipper.* 19 C., influenced by the famous 'Ripper' murders, and by the fact that a kipper is open.

**jam-jar** (1) *Tramcar,* (2) *motor-car.* (1) was the original late 19 C. meaning which, during the first decade of 20 C. became displaced onto (2). In the R.A.F. during the second war, an armoured car was meant. See also JAR OF . . .

**jam-tart** (1) *Sweetheart,* (2) *mart.* The term arises in mid-19 C., and from its restricted use to describe one's own particular 'best girl', it was extended to include all girls and young women. It is one of the few rhyming slang terms to be reduced to its second element instead of its

FLOUNDER AND DAB MA'AM ?
I HAVE MY OWN PRIVATE JAM JAR

first. Its second meaning *mart* was originally applied to (or on) the Stock Exchange, and the fusion of the two had the effect of implying immorality to a girl or woman described as a 'tart'. This word is used by all ages, both sexes, and in every social class, hence it is almost a colloquialism. Among boys and young men the word generally means simply 'girl' with no reflection on her morality. When immoral women make use of the word they are often doing so in order to be 'tough' and express contempt for their respectable sisters. Used by respectable, middle-aged, and particularly married women, the word always carries an inference of immorality, and is strongly tinctured with spite.

**Jane Shaw** An alternative (and more usual spelling) of:

**Jane Shore** *Whore.* 20 C., and probably of naval origin, since the term has also a non-rhyming association to tinned meat as supplied to Her Majesty's Ships; also, the mis-spelling of 'Shaw' seems to suggest the sailor's unconscious mind.

**jar of jam** *tram*(car). 20 C. Recorded by L. Ortzen in *Down Donkey Row,* 1938, perhaps influenced by crowded vehicles during the rush-hours; it cannot be dismissed as an alternative form of JAM-JAR (q.v.) because in that the rhyme is on 'car', not on 'tram'.

**Jem Mace** *Face.* Late 19 C., and formed from the name of the pugilist (1831–1910). The term is now obsolete, but in U.S.A. it has currency other than rhyming slang.

**Jenny Hills** *Pills.* Late 19 C., and now obsolescent. Jenny Hills was a music-hall artiste at the zenith of her fame *c.* 1870. There is no record of the term's application in the past, hence it is unknown whether it referred to pills in the medicinal sense. In so far as it is still in use, it means testicles, 'pills' being a substitution for 'balls'.

**Jenny Lea** (1) *Tea,* (2) *flea,* (3) *key.* (1) late 19 C. in origin, is the most frequent usage: probably influenced by RIVER LEA (q.v.). (2) is seldom used in the singular, but JENNY LEES cannot be regarded as a separate term. (3) this, though not very common, is used in both singular and plural. The spelling, *Lee,* is an alternative, although the champions of the idea of gipsy influence regard it as the correct form, the Romany family of Lee being exemplified as the origin. (Lea—meadow: gipsies live in meadows, hence the name.)

**Jenny Linder** *Window.* 19 C. Recorded by Ducange Anglicus, 1857, and by Hotten, 1859. The Cockney pronunciation of *winder* is required to fit the rhyme, hence, it is rather surprising to find that it has currency on the Pacific Coast of America. The origin is influenced by the name of Jenny Lind, 'the Swedish Nightingale'.

**Jeremiah** *Fire.* Late 19 C., or early 20 C., but not exactly an alternative for ANNA MARIA (q.v.) since it is used by road-workmen to describe the fire in a brazier that cheers the night-watchman. OBEDIAH is sometimes substituted.

**Jerry-cum-mumble** (1) *Tumble.* (2) *rumble.* Eric Partridge, in *A Dictionary of Slang and Unconventional English*, gives: 'to shake, tousle, tumble: C. 18 early 19 . . .' It has survived in rhyming slang but not in relation to a physical fall—to 'tumble' is to understand suddenly—to tumble to it. See also UNDER-CUM-STUMBLE. (Fortuitous rhyme.)

**Jerry Diddle** *Fiddle.* Of late 19 C. origin, this term originally applied to dishonest (or not quite honest) transactions. It journeyed to the United States where, on the Pacific Coast, it is in use for a fiddle (violin) but, it seems, not for a dishonest transaction. Recorded by Maurer and Baker, 1944.

**Jerry Linda** *Window.* 20 C., American, used by thieves, and meaning entry by a window. Cf. JENNY LINDER. Quoted by J. F. Fishman in *Startling Detective*, 1947.

**Jerry McGinn** *The chin.* Pacific Coast of America (Maurer and Baker, 1944).

**Jerry O'Gorman** *A Mormon.* 20 C. Rarely used, probably American in origin. It is applied to one who is seen in the company of numerous different women.

**Jerry Riddle** *Piddle* (urination). Late 19 C., an alternative form of the much more popular JIMMIE . . . (q.v.), but this may be influenced by 'Jerry', a chamber-pot.

**Jersey City** *Titty* (breast). American, Pacific Coast (Maurer and Baker, 1944). (Also in the plural.)

**Jew chum** *Bum* (a tramp). 20 C. The meaning of the word 'bum' differs widely between England and America, hence this term has no currency this side of the Atlantic. It is recorded by Maurer and Baker, 1944, but its American and its Australian usage differs. In the latter country a newly arrived immigrant is a 'new chum': when, *c.* 1936, Central European refugees began to arrive 'Jew-chum' was inevitable. The American usage is more difficult to understand because it is very doubtful if there is such a thing as a Jewish 'bum'. American citizens planning a visit to Europe (which in the American language means 'England', and is not intended to be a term of disparagement), ought to take the precaution of getting 'wised-up' on 'bum', 'crap', 'fanny', 'trash' and 'tramp'.

**jig and prance** *Dance.* American, Pacific Coast, recorded by Maurer and Baker, 1944, but it is a far too accurate description of the activity to really be regarded as slang.

**Jim Crow** *Saltimbanco.* 19 C. A street-clown or busker, now obsolescent.

**Jimmy Britts** *The shits* (diarrhoea). Australian, generally reduced to *The Jimmys*, hence excluded from the glossary by Dr. Maurer but mentioned in his article.

**Jimmy Hope** *Soap.* 20 C. American. Recorded in the *American Thesaurus,* 1952. This term has no currency in England where CAPE OF . . . (q.v.) is popular.

**Jimmy Low** *Go slow.* 20 C. American, Pacific Coast. Recorded by Maurer and Baker, 1944.

**Jimmy O'Goblin** *Sovereign.* Late 19 C., of theatrical origin, it soon won adherents and was widely used during the first decade of the 20 C. With the disappearance of gold coinage the term fell into abeyance and is rarely applied to a one-pound note. Reduced to 'a Jim' it is used in Australia.

**Jimmy Riddle** *Piddle* (to urinate). 19 C., the term is used over a wide social cross-section.

**Jimmy Skinner** *Dinner.* 19 C. The term is quoted by L. Ortzen in *Down Donkey Row,* 1938. It has currency in America (*American Thesaurus*). It is sometimes rendered as Jim . . . , Joe . . . , and Johnnie . . .

**Joanna** *Piano* (pronounced *Joanner* and *pianner*). Early 20 C., when the hire-purchase trade of this particular musical instrument was at its height; now rarely heard because wireless receiving apparatus has killed all forms of self-entertainment. Sometimes spelt JOHANNA.

**Joan of Arcs** *Sharks.* Recorded by Sidney J. Baker in *The Australian Language,* 1945. See also JOE MARKS.

**jockey's whip** *kip* (bed or sleep). 20 C. Evolved during the second war and now obsolescent.

**Joe Blake** (1) *Cake,* (2) *snake,* (3) *steak.* (1) is English usage, but not very popular, (2) is Australian. (3) is American Pacific Coast as recorded by Maurer and Baker, 1944. All three must be regarded as of comparatively recent origin; but (1) might go back to late 19 C.

**Joe Brown** *A town.* 19 C., and probably evolved by circus men. Recorded by P. H. Emerson —*Signor Lippo,* 1893.

**Joe Erk** *A jerk.* 'Erk' is British, and 'jerk' is American for a fool. 20 C.

**Joe Goss** *The boss.* The term is applied to any person whose signature is valid on a cheque, and it seems to be employed by forgers. (Recorded by Maurer and Baker, 1941.) American in origin, is not unknown in Australia, but has no currency in England.

**Joe Gurr** *Stir* (prison). 20 C. Recorded by F. D. Sharpe in *Sharpe of the Flying Squad,* 1938.

**Joe Hook** (1) *Crook,* (2) *book.* As rhyming slang it seems to be of 20 C. origin, but to 'hook', to thieve, and 'a hook', a thief, is far older. (2) refers not, as might be expected, to the bookmaker's book, but to reading matter—any publication that is folded and wire-stitched is a 'book'. See also JOE ROOK.

**Joe Hunt** *C——.* 20 C. A fool —nothing else. Often reduced to (a Joey): for example, 'Don't be such a Joey'.

**Joe Marks** *Sharks.* Recorded by Sidney J. Baker in *The Australian Language,* 1945. See also JOAN OF ARCS.

**Joe Morgan** *Organ* (street). 20 C. Recorded by Sidney J. Baker in *The Australian Language*, 1945. It is an Australian form of MOLLY . . . (q.v.).

**Joe Rocks** *Socks.* 20 C. A development of ALMOND . . . (q.v.).

**Joe Roke** *Smoke* (tobacco). In the sense of 'to have a smoke'. Recorded by Chicago May, 1928.

**Joe Ronce** *Ponce.* Hence, one so engaged may be described as 'on the Joe Roncing Stakes'. Recorded by James Curtis in *The Gilt Kid*, 1936. See RONSON.

**Joe Rook** *Crook* (a thief). Recorded by F. D. Sharpe in *Sharpe of the Flying Squad*, 1938. An alternative spelling, and perhaps the more correct, is *Rourke.* See also JOE HOOK. JOE ROOK is sometimes, but very rarely, applied to a book.

**Joe Rourke,** see JOE ROOK.

**Joe Savage** *Cabbage.* 19 C. Recorded by Hotten, 1859, and now obsolete.

**Joe Skinner,** see JIMMY . . .

**John Hop** *Cop* (Policeman). 20 C. Used in Australia and New Zealand, where the American word 'cop' is more frequently heard than English 'copper'. It is sometimes condensed to *Jonnop*, and even further to *hop.*

**Johnnie Cotton** *Rotten.* 20 C. This is merely a form of DOLLY . . . (q.v.) or of DOCTOR . . . (q.v.), and is as likely to be used as either of them.

**Johnnie Horner** *Corner.* Specialized to mean the street corner and, as so many streets have pubs at the corner, it may imply a visit to a pub. It is generally reduced to *Johnnie.* 'Jus' goin' roun' the Johnnie.' It is one of the rhyming slang terms that is used over a wide social field.

**Johnnie O'Brien** *Iron.* American tramps' slang for the railway, hence this term is interchangeable with JACK . . . (q.v.). Recorded in the *American Thesaurus*, 1952.

**Johnnie Raw** (1) *Saw*, (2) *jaw.* 20 C. American, Pacific Coast, in both senses. Recorded by Maurer and Baker, 1944.

**Johnnie Ronce** *A ponce.* 20 C., an alternative for JOE . . . (q.v.).

**Johnnie Rousers** *Trousers.* 20 C. Recorded by Chicago May, 1928. Also to be found in the *American Thesaurus*, 1952, where it is recorded as JOLLY ROUSERS, hence, the latter is probably an alternative.

**Johnnie Rump** *A pump.* American, Pacific Coast. Recorded by Maurer and Baker, 1944, but what kind of pump? Petrol, bicycle, village or stomach? It could also mean an effort to extract information by subtle questioning.

**Johnnie Russell** *Hustle.* To hurry. American, Pacific Coast. Recorded by Maurer and Baker, 1944. The term is of Australian origin, where it rhymes with *bustle*, which has the same meaning, 'to hurry'.

**Johnnie Rutter** *Butter*, but is seldom applied to anything other than bread and butter. It is of 19 C. origin, and in its youth it may have been applied simply to butter, but by the 20 C. it had specialized to bread and butter in which meaning it is still in use.

**Johnnie Skinner,** see JIMMY SKINNER.

**Jollopp** *Stop.* 20 C. American, Pacific Coast. Recorded by Maurer and Baker, 1944. A better definition is required. Does it mean to terminate, to pull the car into the lay-by, a rubber buffer to prevent a door swinging wide, or 'to kill'?

**jolly rousers,** see JOHNNIE ROUSERS.

**Jonnop,** see JOHN HOP.

**joy of my life** *Wife.* 19 C. Either jocular or derisive. Still in use.

**Joynson Hicks** *Six.* 20 C. Theatrical slang. Mr. Joynson Hicks, during his period of office as Home Secretary, assumed so schoolmasterlike an attitude towards the general public, and was so very unpopular, that his name was used in some most uncomplimentary settings.

**just as I feared** *Beard.* Current in the theatrical profession. Lupino Lane.

# K

**kangaroo** *A Jew.* 20 C. Recorded by Michael Harrison in *Reported Safe Arrival*, 1943.

**Kate Karney** *Army.* Popular during the 1914–18 war, now obsolescent. Kate Karney was a famous music-hall artiste.

**Keith and Proctor** *A doctor.* American, Pacific Coast. Recorded by Maurer and Baker, 1944.

**Kelly Ned** *Head.* American, Pacific Coast (Maurer and Baker, 1944), but clearly of Australian origin. Ned Kelly was a famous Bush-Ranger. (See also NED KELLY.)

**Kennedy Rot** *Sot* (a drunkard). American, Pacific Coast (Maurer and Baker, 1944), but of Australian origin. Kennedy Rot is a disease similar to scurvy that was a problem in Australia, not in U.S.A.

**Kentucky horn** *Corn* (whisky). Recorded in the *American Thesaurus*, 1952. Probably 'hard' whisky produced in the illicit stills of the Kentucky mountains.

**Khyber Pass** *Arse*, not the buttocks but the anus. Usually 'He can (you can) (they can) stick it up his (your) (their) Khyber!' It is an expression of disapproval. Late 19 C.

**kick and prance** *Dance.* An alternative form of JIG AND . . . (q.v.).

**kidney pie(s)** *Eye(s).* An American form of MINCE . . . (q.v.). Recorded by Maurer and Baker, 1944, but not unknown here in 1920. It seems that in the States only the singular is used.

**kidney punch** *Lunch.* 20 C. Theatrical. Lupino Lane.

**kidstake(s)** *A fake*, or 'telling the tale'—'on the Kidstakes'. 20 C. American, Pacific Coast. Recorded by Maurer and Baker, 1944.

**kiko,** alternative spelling (an attempt at Cockney phonetics) of *Cocoa* (q.v.).

**Kilkenny** *Penny.* Late 19 C., now obsolete.

**Kilkenny cats** *Scats* (scatty—silly) and *bats* (same meaning, form 'bats in the belfry'). 20 C., and generally applied to silliness that partakes more of daring, or foolhardiness, than of folly.

**King death** *Breath.* Of doubtful authenticity. If the term ever had a currency it must have been very restricted.

**King Lear** (1) *Ear*, (2) *queer*

(homosexual). (1) is chiefly of theatrical currency, where the term 'ear biting' means borrowing. Cockneys occasionally use the term, but prefer non-rhyming slang, either 'burr-hole', or 'lug' (which latter is not really slang at all). (2) is also more popular in the world of the theatre than among Cockneys.

**kitchen range** *Change.* 20 C. Current in the theatrical world, but a better definition is required. Does it mean change of scene, of costume, or change of a pound? The last has better semantics, being suggestive of weight.

**kiss the cross** *The boss.* 20 C. American, Pacific Coast. Recorded by Maurer and Baker, 1944, who query whether it is of American or British origin. It is certainly not the latter for apart from its being unknown here it is not in English idiom.

**knock me silly** *A billy*(can). 20 C., generally reduced to *Knock me.* Recorded by Sidney J. Baker in *The Australian Language*, 1945.

# L

**la-di-dah** *A car* (motor). 20 C. Generally disparaging (and envious) of a new or smart vehicle.

**Lady Godiva** *A fiver* (£5). 20 C. Obsolescent, but likely to experience a revival as the new five pound notes become established.

**Lady of the Manor** *Tanner* (sixpence). Late 19 C. Rare variant of LORD . . . (q.v.).

**Lakes of Killarney** *Balmy* (feeble-minded). 20 C. Recorded by Phillip Allingham in *Cheapjack*, 1934. It is more often than not reduced to 'Lakes' or 'Lakie'.

**lamb(s) fry** *Tie* (necktie). 20 C. American origin and usage. Recorded by Maurer and Baker, 1944, and in the *American Thesaurus*, 1952. Cf. PECKHAM . . .

**lame duck** *F——*. Coitus. 20 C. American, Pacific Coast. Recorded by Maurer and Baker, 1944.

**lard and pail** *Jail.* American, Pacific Coast (Maurer and Baker, 1944).

**Larry Happy** *Sappy* (feeble-minded). American, Pacific Coast. (The happiest people are those who have been wise enough to get themselves into a lunatic asylum.) Recorded by Maurer and Baker, 1944.

**Larry Simon** *Diamond.* American, Pacific Coast (Maurer and Baker, 1944). The term cannot, however, have a wide currency since the word 'ice' is the mcst popular term in the U.S.A.

**last card in the pack** (1) *A snack*, (2) *back*. (1) current in the theatrical world. 20 C. (2) is now obsolete: recorded by Augustus Mayhew in *Paved with Gold*, 1857.

**lath and plaster** *Master.* 19 C. First recorded by Ducange Anglicus, 1857, given by Hotten, 1859, and now obsolescent. It probably arose in the building trade.

**laugh and joke** *A smoke.* 20 C. Recorded in *John o' London's Weekly*, 9 June 1934.

**lay me in the gutter** *Butter.* Recorded by J. Manchon in *Le Slang*, 1923. It is a variant of DANNY RUCKER and DAN TUCKER.

**lean and fat** *A hat.* 19 C. Both Ducange Anglicus, 1857, and Hotten, 1859, record the term. It is seldom heard in England, but had currency in America.

**lean and lake** *A steak.* 20 C.

American usage, given by Maurer and Baker, 1944. Cf. JOE BLAKE.

**lean and linger** *Finger.* American. Recorded in *The American Thesaurus*, 1952, but a one-word definition is unsatisfactory. Does it refer to the digit—the physical finger, or to 'touch'—'don't finger the goods if you're not buying!'? Has it a sexual significance of either the one kind or the other? Employed by Damon Runyon, 1930–40.

**lean and lurch** *A church.* 19 C. Recorded by both Ducange Anglicus, 1857, and Hotten, 1859, the term is obsolescent in England, but current on the Pacific Coast of America. Recorded by Maurer and Baker, 1944.

**leaning fat** is Chicago May's spelling of LEAN AND FAT (q.v.).

**left in the lurch** *A church.* Late 19 C., now obsolescent. Based on a popular comic song:

There was I
A'waiting at the church,
Waiting at the church,
But he'd left me in the lurch.

**leg-rope** *Hope.* American, Pacific Coast. Recorded by Maurer and Baker, 1944.

**Levy and Frank** *Wank* (masturbation). 20 C., and formed on the name of a well-known firm of public-house and restaurant proprietors, Levy and Franks.

**Lewis & Witties** *Titties* (breasts). Lewis & Witty were a trading house in Melbourne, now extinct, but thus commemorated in rhyming slang. Recorded by Sidney J. Baker in *The Australian Language*, 1945.

**light and dark** *Park.* 20 C., probably having oblique reference to the London County Council's notice to the effect that a bell will be sounded, and the gates locked, at dusk. ('Accidentally' getting locked in the park is a time-worn excuse of the adolescent boy and girl.)

**Lilian Gish** *Fish.* 20 C. Current in the theatrical world, and probably referring to fried fish. Formed on the name of the actress. Lupino Lane.

**Lilley & Skinner** *Dinner.* 19 C. This famous firm of shoemakers was established in 1835, and the term was probably in use fairly early in 19 C.

**linen draper** *Paper.* 19 C. Recorded by Ducange Anglicus and still current. It refers not to paper, in general, but specifically the newspaper, which is described as a (or the) 'linen'.

**lion's lair** *Chair.* 20 C., probably having reference to the danger of disturbing father when he is taking his afternoon nap in an easy chair 'of a Sunday'.

**live eels** *Fields.* 19 C. Recorded by Hotten, 1859: of poor phonetics and even poorer semantics, the term is now obsolete.

**load of hay** *Day.* 19 C. Recorded by Hotten, 1859, and now obsolete. Probably influenced by the sentimental print published mid-19 C. of a loaded hay-wain on which some children are riding home at sunset.

**loaf of bread** *The head.* Late 19 C. This term is invariably reduced to *loaf*, and although it may indicate the physical head, it refers far more often to the mental head. 'Use your loaf' means, not merely *think*, but 'be extremely careful'. It generally has a bearing on some minor infringement of rules and regulations: 'If you want to pop out and have one before they close, use your loaf and look sharp.' It is the method by which 'authority' intimates that its eyes are, within reason, closed. It also serves as a warning that the circumstances demand caution tinctured by cunning: 'If you want the afternoon off next Friday, you want to use your loaf.' As a synonym for common sense, particularly in social relationships, the term is employed over a wide cross-section of the public. LUMP OF BREAD is a very rare substitute, and LUMP OF LEAD was evolved during the 1914–18 war. The term is current on the Pacific Coast of America, recorded by Maurer and Baker, 1944, but with no indication of the extensions of meaning there (if any).

**lollipop** (1) *Drop* (a tip—money), (2) *slop* ('police' in back-slang), (3) *shop* (to inform). (1) is by far the widest usage, particularly in its extension of meaning: to 'drop' is to give a tip, a tip is easy, hence sweet, money, therefore all money is referred to as LOLLI OR LOLLY. Lollipop as a term for sweets is of 18 C. origin. A sweet-shop is a lolli(y) shop, (3) to 'shop' is to inform and by inversion, (since it is not sweet) to *lolly*, or to *lollipop* is to 'shop', that is, *inform*. The police receive the information, and *slop* is back-slang—ice—eci—s—for 'police'. See Eric Partridge, *A Dictionary of the Underworld* and *A Dictionary of Slang and Unconventional English.*

**London blizzard** *Leighton Buzzard.* This term is current among railway-workers, but nowhere else. It was recorded in *The Daily Herald*, 5 August 1936.

**London fog** *A dog.* 20 C., recorded by Eric Partridge in *A Dictionary of Slang and Unconventional English.*

**Long Acre** *A baker.* 19 C. Recorded by Ducange Anglicus, 1857, and by Hotten, 1859, now obsolescent.

**long(ers) and linger(s)** *Fingers.* This term in both its forms is an alternative for LEAN AND . . . (q.v.). LONG AND L. is recorded by Chicago May, 1928.

**loop the loop** (1) *Hoop* (a finger ring), (2) *soup*. (1) is American, recorded by Chicago May, 1928. (2) is Australian—current.

**Lord John Russell** *A bustle.* Recorded by Hotten, 1859, the term expired at the end of the 19 C. with that not unbecoming item of feminine attire. In its day it may also have meant *bustle*, to hurry.

**Lord Lovel** *A shovel.* 19 C. First recorded by Ducange Anglicus, 1857, included in Hotten's list, 1859, now obsolescent in England but still current on the American Pacific Coast. Maurer and Baker, 1944.

**Lord Mayor** *Swear.* 20 C. The term is not often heard, and refers to profane, not to judicial, swearing.

**Lord of the Manor** *Tanner* (sixpence). This term was recorded by H. Brandon in *Poverty, Mendicity and Crime*, 1839; it is therefore among the first rhyming slang terms to be noted, and shows that the system has been evolved during the first third of 19 C. Reduced to *Lord* it is still in use.

**lost and found** *A pound* (£). 19 C. Recorded by J. Redding Ware in *Passing English* as £10, in which sense it has indeed passed, but is enjoying a new lease of life at ten per cent. of its former value.

**Lousy Brown** *Rose and Crown.* A common inn sign, particularly frequent in the London area. 20 C. in origin—probably post-second war. It may have originated at the Rose and Crown pub kept by a landlord named Brown, and it may have reference to brown ale.

**lubra** *Yarborough* (in the game of 'Bridge'). Recorded by Sidney J. Baker in *The Australian Language*, 1945. See also GERBERA.

**lump of bread** *The head*, an alternative form of LOAF . . . (q.v.) but never used in substitution and seldom used at all. See also LUMP OF LEAD, CRUST . . .

**lump of coke** *Bloke.* 19 C. Recorded by Hotten, 1859, but now seldom heard. See BUSHEL . . .

**lump of ice** *Advice.* 20 C., to receive which, after having angled for financial aid, is very cold comfort indeed.

**lump of lead** *The head.* An alternative for LOAF (q.v.). This term was evolved during the 1914–18 war, and is now seldom heard in England, but it is current in America, where its use is recorded by Chicago May, 1928, Maurer and Baker, 1944, and the *American Thesaurus*, 1952. In so far as it has currency in England, it is specialized to refer to the head on the morning after the night before—'I woke up wiv a marf like a carsey an' I couldn't lift me lump-o'-lead orf da ti-willer to git at the fisherman's.'

# M

**macaroni** *Pony* (£25). 19 C. and still current, employed mainly by bookmakers and their associates. (In Australia it seems to refer to pony, a horse, and is often reduced to *macker*.) See Sidney J. Baker, *The Australian Language*, 1945.

**maccarony** mis-spelling of MACARONI (q.v.).

**Mac Gimp** *Pimp*. Current in the Western States of America; recorded by Jackson and Hellier in *Vocabulary of Criminal Slang*, 1914. It is sometimes given a final 'er', and also spelt as one word.

**MacIntire and Heath** *Teeth*. American, Pacific Coast (Maurer and Baker, 1944). These two gentlemen may have been noted dentists. See also Addenda.

**Madam De Luce** *Spruce* (deception). Late 19 C. Still used very widely in its reduced form: 'Don't give me any of your *madam*': 'It's no use you coming the *madam* with me.'

**mad Mick** (1) *Prick* (the penis), (2) *pick*. Both senses are current in Australia. (2) is generally in combination: 'Mad Mick and a banjo', a pick and shovel. Sense (2) is also current in America, where it stands alone. Recorded in this last by Maurer and Baker, 1944.

**mad mile** *Smile*. 20 C. In use on the Pacific Coast of America (Maurer and Baker, 1944).

**Mae West** *Breast* (female). Popular when this celebrated film-star was making news, now obsolete.

**Maggie Mahone** *Telephone*. American, Pacific Coast, recorded by Maurer and Baker, 1944. The favourite term in England for the 'phone is 'the blower' from the old-fashioned 'speaking tube' through which one had to blow in order to sound a whistle and attract attention.

**Maggie Moores** *Drawers* (women's). 20 C. Australian. Generally reduced to *Maggies*. Recorded by Sidney J. Baker in *The Australian Language*, 1945.

**Magimp(er),** alternative spelling of MAC GIMP (q.v.).

**maids adorning** *Morning*. Recorded by Hotten, 1859, and now seldom heard in England. It has currency on the Pacific Coast of America, where its use is recorded by Maurer and Baker, 1944.

**Maidstone jailer** *A tailor*.

Recorded by Hotten, 1859, now obsolete.

**Major Loder** *Soda.* 20 C. Chiefly as *whisky and soda.* Cf. ROSY . . .

**Major Stevens** *Evens.* 20 C. The reference is to betting odds, and the term is current in the world of bookmakers, their satellites and their victims.

**Malcolm Scott** *Hot.* 20 C. Theatrical usage, but does it refer to the weather, the shaving water, or is it an expression of appreciation, as 'John put on a very hot performance last night'? It might, too, have a sexual significance.

**mallee-root** *Prostitute.* American, Pacific Coast, recorded by Maurer and Baker, 1944, but clearly of Australian origin. Mallee bush, scrubby *Eucalyptus dumose,* grows in South Australia.

**man and wife** *Knife,* specifically a pocket knife. Current in the army during the 1914–18 war and now obsolescent. (The custom of carrying a pocket knife is dead. Modern youth does not know what they are (or were) for. The final blow has been dealt by the popularization of the 'ball-point pen': in place of the blacklead pencil. The average young person cannot sharpen a pencil with a knife, but depends on the twist-round pocket pencil sharpener.)

**Maria Monk** *Spunk* (in all its senses). Late 19 C. From the title of the pornographic novel, which is still obtainable in 'chemist' shops.

**Mark Foy** *Boy.* 20 C. Recorded by Sidney J. Baker in *A Popular Dictionary of Australian Slang,* 1943. Cf. ROB . . . SAN . . . The term is clearly of Cockney origin, being based on the name of a firm of cartage contractors who functioned in the London area in late 19 C. to early 20 C.

**Marquess of Lorne** *Horn* (erection). Very rare, see COLLEEN . . .

**Martin-Le-Grand** *Hand.* Of 19 C. origin, the term is now obsolescent. Formed on the name of the street (St. Martin le Grand) made famous by the General Post Office of London being situated there.

**Mary and Johnnie** *Marijuana.* American, Pacific Coast, recorded by Maurer and Baker, 1944, with the note that the rhyme is probably accidental in translation from Mexican Spanish, but a rhyming slang rhyme cannot be *accidental*: it may be suggested by, or strongly influenced by, but not accidental. It may be fortuitous.

**Mary Ann** *Hand,* particularly fist. In Cockney dialect 'Ann' and 'hand' come very close together, for the aspirate is dropped and the final 'd' is swallowed: however, the term is seldom used.

**Mary Blane** (1) *Train,* (2) *rain.* (1) To meet a train, and impose upon inexperienced persons which was, in the 19 C., a fairly common practice. It led to the formation of *The Travellers' Aid Society.* The term can be traced back to 1891, and it survived into the first decade of the 20 C. See Eric Partridge, *A Dictionary of the Underworld.* (2) Given by Hotten, 1859, now obsolete.

**me and you** *Menu.* Early 20 C., perhaps even late 19 C., but barely admissible as rhyming slang.

**megimp,** see MAC GIMP.

**Melbourne pier** *Ear.* Recorded in *Sydney Mirror,* October 1942, and quoted by Sidney J. Baker in *The Australian Language,* 1945.

**me mother's away** Dialect distortion of MY . . . (q.v.).

**Mickey Mouse** *House.* 20 C. Current in the theatrical world. The 'House' is the theatre—the auditorium—the audience: also —particularly in the music-hall— the time of a performance. 'Two Houses Nightly.' 'First House.' 'Second House.' Lupino Lane. Based on Walt Disney's cartoon masterpiece.

**miller's daughter** *Water.* 20 C. This is a variant of FISHERMAN'S . . . (q.v.).

**mince pie(s)** *Eye(s).* 19 C. Recorded by Ducange Anglicus, 1857, and Hotten, 1859, and by Augustus Mayhew. It is still the favourite term in England. In America, where it is recorded by Maurer and Baker, 1944, by Chicago May, 1928, by the *American Thesaurus,* 1952, and several more, it shares the honours with other terms. See MUTTON . . . , STEAK . . .

**misbehave** *Shave.* 20 C. Current in the United States of America, and recorded in the *American Thesaurus,* 1952.

**moan and wail** *Jail.* 20 C. In use on the Pacific Coast of America. Recorded by Maurer and Baker, 1944.

**mocking bird** *Word.* 20 C. Current in the theatrical world. Lupino Lane.

**Molly O'Morgan** *Organ* (barrel). Early 20 C., formed on a popular song: 'Molly o' Morgan, with her little organ . . .' which, of course, had a double meaning, just as the term may have.

**mortar and trowel** *Towel.* Late 19 C., or early 20 C., now obsolescent.

**moslum broker** is a misspelling of MOZZLE AND . . . (q.v.).

**mother and daughter** *Water.* This is recorded by Hotten, 1859, and is now obsolete in England: it has currency in the United States of America and is recorded by Maurer and Baker, 1944, and in *The American Thesaurus,* 1952.

**Mother Hubbard** *Cupboard.* Late 19 C., still in use: formed on the nursery rhyme:

Old Mother Hubbard,
She went to the cupboard,
To get her poor doggie a bone.

**mother of pearl** *Girl,* but not a young, unmarried girl: 'my old girl', *wife,* invariably reduced to *mother,* and very popular, hence strangers hearing a middle-aged Cockney say: 'No mate, I won't have another drink: my mother will tear me up for waste-paper', open their eyes in amazement.

**mother's ruin** *Gin.* Early 20 C. The phonetics are poor—*gin*, ru*in*; but the semantics are sound. This is now the most popular slang term for gin and has currency in social circles where rhyming slang is not normally employed. It comes from BRIAN O'LINN (q.v.) through BLUE RUIN (q.v.).

**mountain passes** *Glasses* (spectacles). Early 20 C., now obsolescent.

**mozzle and brocha** *On the knocker.* 20 C. Generally 'on the m. and b.', referring to the occupation of a door-to-door canvasser. The words are Yiddish, and may have a background in Hebrew: m. is good luck; b. is good health. These are two only of the six 'goods' required by a door-to-door salesman. The other four being good looks; good temper; good voice and good manners. The term is not very common, and may have originated in a Cockney member of the profession having overheard Jewish members exchanging greetings and compliments.

**Mrs Chant** *Aunt.* 20 C. This term is used in reference to the sister of either of one's parents, but more frequently in the setting, 'I'm going to see Mrs Chant', rhyming with 'I'm going to see my aunt', which is euphemistic for going to the W.C. (generally for the minor function). It is more frequently employed by women than by men.

**Mrs Duckett** (1) *Bucket*, (2) *f—— it!* (1) has its greatest usage in the fishmonger's trade, where buckets full of fish, full of ice, full of water, are in frequent use. (2) is a comment rather than an expletive: the workman who hits his thumb with a hammer uses no euphemism; the workman asked his reaction to doing overtime on Tuesday (or some other evening) may answer: 'I think Mrs Duckett', which means: No!

**mud in the eye** *Tie* (necktie). 20 C. Recorded in *The New Statesman*, 29 November 1941, and quoted by Eric Partridge in *A Dictionary of Slang . . . Addenda.* This term is suspect: no amount of diligent enquiry 'in the field' has produced confirmation.

**muffin baker** *A quaker.* 19 C., and still in use. It is applied to excrement, particularly when costive, or when retained uncomfortably long, in which case it may have some reference to the fear of a mishap. (To quake, to tremble.) The rhyme may be influenced by 'hard bake', another expression having the same meaning. Hotten records the term, and (in the first edition) gives a one-word definition using a capital 'Q'. From this it would seem that he missed the inference and assumed that a member of the Society of Friends was indicated, and that meaning seems to have been accepted by most philologists, though why Cockneys (and particularly at that period) should have a slang term for Quakers does not seem to have presented itself to them. It is recorded by Maurer and Baker as of Pacific Coast of

America usage, and over there it may refer only to the Friends who take a more noticeable share in social work (and are therefore more likely to be discussed at a low social level), than they do here; but it must be emphasized that English Quakers are probably the most active, and least ostentatious true charity workers in the world. Elizabeth Fry, the Friend, carried the Bible into Newgate Jail—and was not derided by the inmates.

Later Hotten discovered his error. It was in—he could not take it out, so leaving the standing type alone, retaining the initial capital letter, he filled the line by adding: '(a slang term for excrement)'—in brackets.

**mumbley pegs** *Legs.* 20 C. American, Pacific Coast. Recorded by Maurer and Baker, 1944.

**Mutt and Jeff** *Deaf.* 20 C. Current in the theatrical world, and formed on the names of the two famous strip-cartoon characters.

**mutter and stutter** *Butter.* Early 20 C., and particularly bread and butter.

**mutton pies** *Eyes.* 19 C. An alternative form of MINCE . . . (q.v.) but not popular.

**my God** (pronounce Gawd) *Sword.* 19 C. Sometimes prefixed by 'Oh', but seldom used in either form.

**my mother's away** *The other day.* 20 C. Recorded in *Sydney Bulletin*, 18 January 1902, quoted by Sidney J. Baker in *The Australian Language*, 1945.

**my word** *Turd.* Early 20 C., generally used jocularly in reference to dogs fouling the footway: 'My word, I trod on a my word.'

# N

**Nancy Lee** (1) *Tea*, (2) *flea*. (1) is a rare variant of ROSY . . . (q.v.). (2) the more usual meaning, but neither is in frequent use.

**Nancy Prance** *A dance*. 20 C. American, Pacific Coast. Recorded by Maurer and Baker, 1944.

**nanny goat** *Boat*. 20 C. Evolved during the second war: meaning transferred to *Tote*.

**nap** *Slap*. A term used in the world of the theatre in the form of 'take the nap'. It refers to one who receives a blow, usually on the face, as part of a performance. Such blows are often, but not always, a skilful illusion, the 'victim' creating the sound by clapping his hands. The term is old—even very old. It may go back to the days of the mountebanks, and perhaps, after all, it is not really slang, but something in the nature of a technical term. Be that as it may, the psychological mechanism that operates rhyming slang has been formative.

**nap and double** *Trouble*. Recorded by Margery Allingham in *Mystery Mile*, 1930. Probably it has reference to the card-game 'nap'.

**narky** *Sarky* (sarcastic, or otherwise offensive). Recorded by Michael Harrison in *Reported Safe Arrival*, 1943, Eric Partridge, *Dictionary of Slang . . . Addenda*, says, '. . . perhaps, in part at least, rhyming s . . .' Narky, in addition to the foregoing meaning, describes a person who is in an irritable state. *Nark* is from Romany *nak*, the nose, hence nark, a police spy, extended to a dangerous person. Sarcastic people and irritable people are dangerous, therefore, *narky*.

**National debt** *Bet*. 20 C. Theatrical usage. In both cases the banker gets the best of it; and perhaps also influenced by the Grand National Horse Race. Lupino Lane.

**Navigator Scott** *Baked potato hot*. Recorded by Hotten, 1859, and now obsolete. The perambulating hot-potato can did not survive 1914, but is reviving.

**navigator's** *Potatoes* (pronounce *taters*). Recorded by Hotten, 1859, now obsolete.

**near and far** (1) *Bar* (public house), (2) *car*. (1) involves the idea of 'so near and yet so far'—in a busy pub at the peak hours the counter is fenced off from the casual customer by the immobile throng of topers. (2) A motor-car in which both near and far destinations may be reached. The term is current in both senses in America, and is recorded by Maurer and Baker, 1944, who date (1) as *c.* 1910, but it was well established by then, and may be of late 19 C. origin. (See FAR AND NEAR and THERE YOU ARE.)

**near and there** *A chair*. 20 C. American, Pacific Coast. Recorded by Maurer and Baker, 1944. It is probably a slovenly form of HERE AND . . .

**near enough** An alternative form of NIGH ENOUGH (q.v.).

**Ned Kelly** *Belly*. Late 19 C. Australian. N.K. is a national hero down-under. See KELLY NED.

**Ned Skinner** *Dinner*. Recorded by J. Redding Ware in *Passing English*, 1909, but this term is still passing.

**needle and pin** *Gin*. 20 C. This term is rare, and the tendency is for it to be used by habitual gin-drinkers who prefer it to MOTHER'S RUIN (q.v.).

**needle and thread** *Bread*. Recorded by Hotten, 1859, now obsolete.

**Nellie Blighs** *Flies*. 20 C. This term is frequently employed by children but not by adults, who are more inclined to be irritated by flies than children are, and who therefore think of the creatures in rather more robust terms.

**Nelly Bly's,** see NELLIE BLIGHS.

**Neptune's daughter** *Water*. American development of FISHERMAN'S . . . (q.v.), recorded by Maurer and Baker, 1944, and by the *American Thesaurus*, 1952.

**never fear** *Beer*. Recorded by Hotten, 1859, and now very rarely used. Cf. PIGS . . .

**never stand still,** see CAN'T KEEP . . .

**Newgate Jail** *A tale*. Late 19 C. The specific kind of tale is the 'hard luck', or other sympathy inducing story.

**Newington Butts** *Guts*. Late 19 C. It may refer to either the physical guts (abdomen) as: (. . . so I give (gave) 'im a poke (punch) in da Newingtons . . .'; or the moral fibre, as '. . . she twists 'im rahnd 'er finger an' 'e ain't got da Newingtons teh slosh 'er one . . .' In either sense, and in any setting, it is used in the reduced form. Newington Butts is a thoroughfare in South London.

**new south** *Mouth*. 20 C. American, Pacific Coast. A form of EAST AND . . . , or of NORTH AND . . . (q.v.), but clearly influenced by Australian slang where the term is an abbreviation of New South Wales. Recorded by Maurer and Baker, 1944.

**New York Nipper(s)** *Kipper(s)*. 20 C., but very rarely used.

**Niagara Falls** (1) *Balls* (testicles), (2) *stalls* (theatre). (1) is less popular than ORCHESTRAS (q.v.). (2) is employed chiefly within the theatrical profession. Also in use in America and recorded by Maurer and Baker, 1944, who give as a meaning also 'meatballs'.

**nickel and dime** *Time*.

Purely American, since the coins named are not used elsewhere. Recorded by Maurer and Baker, 1944, but the one-word definition is inadequate—is 'time' the passing of the hours, is it a prison sentence, or both?

**nigh enough** *Puff* (pouf). A homosexual prostitute. Recorded by James Curtis in *The Gilt Kid*, 1936.

**night and day** *A play*. Recorded by Hotten, 1859, and now obsolete in England. In use on the American Pacific Coast, and recorded by Maurer and Baker, 1944.

**nits and lice**(s) *Starting price*(*s*). In use among bookmakers and others in the horse racing world since the first decade of 20 C. Recorded as in use on the American Pacific Coast by Maurer and Baker, 1944.

**Noah's ark** (1) *Nark* (an informer), (2) *park*. (1) has been in use in England since the first decade of the 20 C. It is also used in the form of a Spoonerism *'oah's Nark*, the first word having the inference '*whore's*', and when thus inverted it is the supreme expression of contempt. (2) is American Pacific Coast usage, recorded by Maurer and Baker, 1944.

**non-skid** *Yid*. 20 C. Recorded by Richard Llewellyn in *None but the Lonely Heart*, 1943. Cf. FRONT WHEEL . . .

**no Robin Hood** *No bloody good*, used extensively in the army 1914–18, now obsolescent.

**north and south** *Mouth*. Developed from EAST AND SOUTH (q.v.) and recorded by Augustus Mayhew in *Paved with Gold*, and by Chicago May, 1928. Maurer and Baker define the term and date it 1880.

**north pole** *Hole* (the anus). 19 C. Now seldom heard. Cf. KHYBER . . .

**nose and chin** *A win*, in which sense it has been in use by bookmakers since the first decade of 20 C., and exported to the United States of America it is recorded by Maurer and Baker, 1944. It is, however, given by Hotten, who glosses it, not as a *win*, but as a *winn*, which was an early- to mid-19 C. slang name for a penny. (Also spelt whinn.)

**noser my knacker** *Tobacco* (pronounce bacca, or backer). This term, recorded by both Ducange Anglicus, 1857, and Hotten, 1859, is now obsolete, but it may not have been quite so silly as it looks. A hundred years ago the public attitude towards smoke, smokers, and smoking was one of disapproval. There were few smoking compartments on local trains, and magistrates delighted in imposing the full 40s. fine on persons 'indulging the vile habit' in prohibited places. Non-smokers, within and without rights, frowned, protested, and offensively fanned with newspapers at smokers. The phrase 'noser my knacker' may customarily have been 'innocently' incorporated in a persecuted Cockney workman's reply because of the double meaning of *knacker(s)* (testicles). The final 'r' on *nose* may be due to a mishearing. Cockneys are inclined to put intrusive syllables into single words, and very apt to do so in order to slur two words into one. The 'r' sound lends itself to the blending process. Words ending in 'e' and in 'a' are rendered 'er'. Henry Mayhew, *London Labour and the London Poor*, gives it as 'nosey my . . .', which strengthens the foregoing theory.

**not much frocks** *Socks*, but children's socks only, meaning when one was young. Eric Partridge, in *Dictionary of Slang . . . Addenda*, quotes Edwin Pugh, *The Spoilers*, 1906: 'Never doin' no honest work . . . from the time when they was in not much frocks . . .' The term is now obsolete.

# O

**oak** *Joke.* 20 C. Recorded by J. Redding Ware in *Passing English,* 1909, but it has survived with an altered meaning. It now refers to rough jocular play, or 'larking about', as, ''Arry were oakin' abaht in da boat, on da Turps an' in 'e flops.'

**oak and ash** *Cash.* 20 C. Current in the theatrical world. Lupino Lane.

**oats and barley** *Charlie.* 19 C. This term, which is recorded by Hotten, 1859, and which is now obsolete, is accepted as slang for the masculine given name, Charles; however, no-one named Charles—or 'Charlie'—is ever called or referred to as 'oats and barley'—not even as 'oats'. This (and the other rhyming slang phrases that seem to refer to given names) is suspect. Why should not all, or many instead of two or three only, names be rendered in rhyming slang?

It is likely that 'Charlie' is, in this setting, not meant for a name, but for a slang term. To make a Charlie of a person is to make a fool of him—a victim or a cats-paw. In mid-19 C. a Charlie was a small pointed beard. In early 19 C. a Charlie was a night-watchman (superseded by Robert Peel's Police Force—the 'Bobbies').

If the first years of rhyming slang overlapped the last years of the Charlies, then OATS AND BARLEY probably refers to a night-watchman.

Further, a CHARLEY RONCE is a ponce, and the term is invariably reduced to 'Charley'. Perhaps John Camden Hotten missed the inference, or his 'informant' was too modest to make the meaning so brutally clear. Ponce is the most likely meaning.

**oats and chaff** *A footpath.* 19 C. Recorded by Ducange Anglicus, 1857, now obsolete.

**Obadiah** *A fire.* 20 C. Seldom used. Cf. ANNA . . .

**ocean pearl** *A girl.* 20 C. (Cf. MOTHER O' . . .) This term has very little currency in England. Recorded in *John o' London's Weekly,* 9 June 1934; and in U.S.A. by Chicago May, 1928.

**ocean wave** *Shave.* 20 C. This term in England is far less popular than DIG . . . (q.v.). It may be more popular in America, where its use is recorded by Maurer and Baker, 1944.

**Oh heck** *Neck.* American, Pacific Coast. Recorded by

Maurer and Baker, 1944. Sometimes rendered as OH BY HECK.

**Oh my dear** *Beer.* Early 20 C., but never so popular as PIG'S . . . (q.v.). In use in America, recorded by Chicago May, 1928, and by Maurer and Baker, 1944.

**Oh my God,** see MY GOD.

**oily rag** *A fag* (cigarette). 20 C., used chiefly by workmen, and probably having reference to the soiled state of a cigarette when smokers are employed in a 'dirty-hand' trade, such as engineering.

**old-iron and brass** *A pass.* 20 C. Current in the army during the 1914–18 war. It refers to a 'chit' (or document) permitting a soldier to stay out of barracks later than the normal hour of return. Now obsolete in civilian life, but still having some usage in the army.

**old King Cole** *The dole.* 20 C. and not earlier than *c.* 1925.

**old nag** *Fag* (cigarette). 20 C. Current in the army during the 1914–18 war, now obsolete. Eric Partridge, *Dictionary of Slang* . . .

**old pot and pan** *Old man.* 19 C. The term primarily refers to the father of the family, and is heavily worked by adolescent boys (and girls), who sometimes reduce it to 'the old pot': secondarily it refers to one's husband, and very rarely to a stranger: when it does, the usage is friendly and jocular and the word 'old' pertains to age and is not, in this setting, a term of affection. In American usage it appears to refer to any man, and is so glossed by Maurer and Baker, 1944.

**Oliver Cromwell** *Tumble* (to understand). 20 C. To 'tumble to it', to understand suddenly either that which is being verbally explained, or the implication of incidents. It is now obsolescent. See *Dictionary of Slang* . . . Eric Partridge.

**Oliver Twist** *Fist.* Recorded by Augustus Mayhew in *Paved with Gold,* 1857. In the reduced form *Oliver* it is still in use.

**'oller boys 'oller,** see HOLLER

**on the floor** *Poor.* 20 C. This term is not used to describe chronic pauperism, but acute pennilessness of a temporary character. It is a very widely used term which has gone up in the world, being heard in the suburbs on Thursday when housewives have not 'managed' too well. Because of this, the Cockneys are beginning to extend RORY O'MORE (q.v.) to cover this meaning as well as its own time-honoured one.

**on the mozzle and . . .** see MOZZLE AND . . .

**on the ooze** *On the booze.* 20 C., post 1914–18 war, the inference is on 'to ooze', or drip liquid due to internal pressure.

**once a week** (1) *Beak* (magistrate), (2) *cheek* (insolence). (1) is of 19 C. usage. In those high Bohemian days many folk did see the 'beak' once a week as the result of Saturday-night revels. (2) is a 20 C. development (indicative of social change) and is generally reduced to 'oncer', as: 'Bligh! Ain't you got a oncer? eh?'

**one and eleven pence three farthing** (pronounce fard'n) *I* *beg your pardon*. Recorded by Michael Harrison in *Reported Safe Arrival*, 1943, but apparently very local. See also GARDEN.

**one and t'other** (1) *Brother*, (2) *Mother*. Both are used chiefly in a jocular setting: 'You seen my young one and t'other? 'E ain't bin 'ome fer ee's dinner yert', and having found him: 'Wot's you bin adoin' of? Rollin' in na mud? Wait till yer one and t'other sees yeh!'

**ones and two** *Shoes*. 20 C. American, Pacific Coast. Recorded by Chicago May, 1928, by Maurer and Baker, 1944, and included in the *American Thesaurus*, 1952.

**orchestra stalls** *Balls* (testicles). 19 C. The term is always reduced to 'orchestras', and is employed as a euphemism at several social levels. Cf. COBBLER'S . . .

**orinoko(er)** *Poker*. 19 C. Recorded by Hotten, 1859, now obsolete. The term is suspect: in addition to the fact that it is untraceable, and apparently meaningless, it is not the kind of word employed by Cockneys or other users of rhyming slang. It probably arises from a mishearing. See also Addenda.

**Oscar Asche** *Cash*. 20 C. Formed on the name of the famous actor (1871–1936). The term is always reduced to Oscar, and is fairly popular at several social levels, but the surname seems to have been forgotten as a part of it —even many Cockneys cannot explain why *Oscar* means 'money'.

**Oscar Hocks** *Socks*. 20 C. American, Pacific Coast. First recorded by Chicago May, 1928. Listed by Maurer and Baker 1944, and the *American Thesaurus*.

**Oscar Joes** *Toes*. 20 C. American, Pacific Coast. Recorded by Chicago May, 1928, also by Maurer and Baker, 1944.

**out and in** *Chin*. 20 C. American. Recorded by Chicago May, 1928.

**over the stile** *Sent for trial*. 19 C. Recorded by Hotten, 1859, and still in use: also used in the same sense in the U.S.A. Recorded by Maurer and Baker, 1944, who define it as 'to stand trial'.

**Owen Nares** *Chairs*. 20 C. Current in the theatrical profession. Lupino Lane.

**Oxford scholar** (1) *Dollar* (5s.), (2) *collar*. (1) is by far the more frequent, generally reduced to 'an Oxford' (see HALF AN . . .). (2) is no longer employed by Cockneys who prefer HOLLER . . ., but is used at a higher social level.

**Oxo cube** *Tube* (railway). 20 C. This term seems to have arisen since the second war, and is probably influenced by the blitz and the resultant decentralization of the working-class population, many of whom now have need to ride by Tube.

# P

**Paddy Quick** (1) *A stick*, (2) *kick*. Recorded by Hotten, 1859, now obsolete.

**pair of braces** *The Races*. 20 C. American, Pacific Coast. Recorded by Maurer and Baker, 1944.

**Pall Mall** *Girl* (rhyming on *gal*). 19 C., and now obsolete. Cockney dialect makes Paow Maow—gaow.

**parlamaree** *Gee*. Early 20 C., used by kerbstone salesmen and buskers to describe the accomplice who, by buying the first article, or donating the first coin, 'gees up' the audience. The term is obviously a mispronunciation of Parlyaree, the language of the Circus. See SCAPA . . .

**Pat and Mick** (1) *Prick* (penis), (2) *lick*. 19 C. (1) is Anglo-Irish. (2) is Australian, but further information is required: is it to lick with the tongue or to beat? E.P. *Dic. of Sl.* (p. 1130) 'lit. and fig.'

**Pat and Mike** *A bike*. 19 C. Recorded in *Dictionary of Slang* . . . . Eric Partridge.

**Pat Malone** *Alone*. 20 C. This term, like JACK JONES (q.v.), refers to isolation in an enterprise, or to superior achievement. It is always reduced to 'Pat'. 'He's all on his Pat', or, 'You're all on your Pat' is as frequent as Jack in the same setting.

**peaches and pears** *Stairs*. 20 C. This is an American Pacific Coast version of APPLES . . . (q.v.). Recorded by Maurer and Baker, 1944.

**peas in the pot** *Hot*. 20 C. This term, which does not refer to the weather, or to the temperature of an object, is nearly always reduced to *peas*, and used in reference to the female's sexual avidity: as 'She's peas'.

**Peckham Rye** *Tie* (necktie). 19 C., and by far the most usual term. See also PIG'S FRY.

**pen and ink** *Stink*. 19 C. Recorded by Hotten. Probably formed on the nursery (?) rhyme:

Inkie pinkie pen and inkie,
Who made that awful stinkie?

Converted in recent times (possible post-second war) to PEN AND INKER, it is rhymed with *stinker*; a person of mean habits, not to be trusted, possibly a 'squealer' (informer). To be 'on the pen and ink', is to be under suspicion of having informed, and therefore ostracized.

**penn'orth o' chalk** *Walk*.

PEAS IN THE POT YESTERDAY
AND POTATOES IN THE MOULD TODAY
IT'S ALL THOSE DERRY AND TOMS THAT DO IT

20 C. An alternative form of BALL OF . . . (q.v.). 'Goo orn—taike a pennuf!' is a very forceful term of dismissal.

**penny-a-mile** (1) *Tile* (hat), (2) *smile.* (1) is very rare, because 'tile' for a hat is obsolete. (2) is the current meaning and in so far as it refers to a false smile it is very appropriate.

**penny a pound** *Ground.* 19 C., still in use, but generally reduced to 'penny'.

**penny bun** *son* or *sun.* See also CURRANT . . . BATH . . .

**penny locket** *Pocket.* 19 C. Recorded by J. Redding Ware in *Passing English*, 1909. This term is now obsolete. See SKY . . .

**Phil MacBee** *A flea.* 19 C., now obsolete.

**photo-finish** *Guinness.* The term is of post-second war origin and it is not yet fully established. It is nearly always reduced to 'photo' and pronounced *foater* —(ex Michael Harrison, private letter, 7 October 1958).

**piccolo and flute** *Suit* (of clothes). 19 C. and still in use. Rendered in the plural (q.v.) it seems to be of recent development, and is not often heard.

**piccolos and flutes** *Boots.* 20 C. A rare, and recently developed alternative for DAISY ROOTS (q.v.). See entry above.

**pick and choose** *Booze.* 20 C. Current in the theatrical world.

**pig and roast** *Toast* (toasted bread). Current in the army during the second war. A sarcastic allusion to the non-luxurious menu of the average 'other ranks' mess. Probably this was the original FIG AND POST (q.v.) being a rhyme on it. Semantics support this supposition.

**pig's ear** *Beer.* 20 C. This is by far the most popular term for beer, and it does not discriminate —ale is included. It is invariably reduced to '*pigs*'.

**pig's face** *Lace* (probably decorative crochet-lace, not a boot or shoe lace). 20 C. American, Pacific Coast, recorded by a one-word definition by Maurer and Baker, 1944.

**pig's fry** *Tie* (necktie). 19 C. Obsolescent: the more general term is PECKHAM . . . (q.v.).

**pillar and post** *Ghost.* 20 C. Current in the theatrical world and probably usually applied in the sense of 'the ghost walks', that is, wages are being paid. Lupino Lane.

**pimple and blotch** *Scotch* (whiskey). 20 C. A most appropriate term, since long indulgence in major quantities has that effect upon the skin.

**pint pot** *A sot* (drunkard). 20 C. American, Pacific Coast. Recorded by Maurer and Baker, 1944.

**pipe your eye** *Cry* (weep). 19 C., and so common that it is seldom recognized as rhyming slang. See: E.P. *Dic. of Sl.* p. 633.

**pitch and fill** *A bill.* 19 C. Recorded (with a capital B) by Hotten, 1859, and glossed by him as 'a vulgar shortening of William'. If this interpretation is correct, then there is justification for the farmer who, on a visit to London, and observing on numerous blank walls a notice saying: 'Bill stickers will be prosecuted', remarked, 'Happen they'll soon take him with all this hue and cry!' There is no reason why William and Charles (see OATS . . .) should be honoured in rhyming slang and Thomas, Richard and Harry be neglected. It is most likely that the 'bill'—with a small 'b'—is a placard or notice; specifically one hooked in the button-hole, pinned to the empty jacket-sleeve, or held modestly before the face, while the other hand extends for view (not for sale!) a box of matches or a pair of bootlaces. If Hotten's interpretation is the correct one, the phrase has phonetic value only: if the suggested alternative is accepted then phonetics and semantics combine. A beggar on a good *pitch*, who has a convincing *bill*, will soon *fill* his collecting box. See also BEECHAM'S . . .

**pitch and toss** *The boss.* 20 C. Current in the theatrical world (Lupino Lane), also in Australia, recorded by Sidney J. Baker in *The Australian Language*, 1945.

**pitch the plod** *Plough the sod.* 20 C. American in both origin and usage. Recorded by Maurer and Baker, 1944.

**plate of ham** *Gam* (itself an abbreviation), *fellatio.*

**plates and dishes** *Missus.* 20 C., one of several forms, any of which may be used. See also: CHEESE . . ., LOVE . . .

**plates of meat** *Feet.* 19 C., recorded by Hotten, 1859, and still in very general use, but invariably reduced to 'Plates'. Ducange Anglicus, 1857, gives the term in the singular, 'plate of . . .' and defines it as *street*, but it is not likely that there were two distinct terms, each with its individual meaning, but merely one term with two meanings, one only of which has survived.

**platters of meat** *Feet.* 20 C., a form of PLATES (q.v.), and not used in Cockney circles. Recorded by J. Manchon in *Le Slang*, 1932.

**pleasure and pain** *Rain.* 20 C. Very appropriate indeed if it means pleasure for gardeners and pain for sufferers from rheumatism.

**plough the deep** *Sleep.* 19 C. Recorded by Hotten, 1859, still in use. American Pacific Coast usage recorded by Maurer and Baker, 1944, where the spelling is *plow.*

**Plymouth cloak** *Oak* (a cudgel). Late 17 C. to 18 C., and therefore of historical importance. See Eric Partridge, *Slang Today and Yesterday*, 3rd ed., 1950, p. 274. Fortuitous rhyme.

**poddy calf** *Half* (a crown). 20 C. Australian—where half a crown is better known as *half a caser*—recorded by Baker. A poddy calf, or lamb, is motherless and being brought up on the bottle, or by a foster-mother.

**Pompey 'ore** *Twenty-four*, in the game of House (Housie-Housie) extensively played in the army, 1914–18. *Pompey* is Portsmouth: *'ore* is whore.

**pony and trap** *Crap* (to defecate). 20 C. The term is much less often used than TOM . . . (q.v.).

**Pope of Rome** *Home*. 19 C. Recorded by Hotten, 1859, and now obsolescent.

**pork and beans** *Portuguese* (person). The term was much used in the army during the 1914–18 war, and was influenced by the tins of pork and beans in which none of the former was ever found (the manufacturers said it went into total solution). The term is still alive, but seldom in use, because the Portuguese nation keeps out of the news, and there is practically no Portuguese population in London. The lack of either rhyme or assonance does not prevent Cockneys accepting it as rhyming slang.

**port and sherry** *I'm Jerry*. 20 C. American, Pacific Coast. Recorded by Maurer and Baker, 1944. This is not a masculine given name, see also OATS . . . and PITCH . . . ; it is a slang term meaning: 'I'm wised up to it': 'I know all about it.' See JERRY CUM MUMBLE.

**Port Melbourne Pier** *Ear*. Recorded by Sidney J. Baker in *The Australian Language*, 1945.

**post and rail** *Fairy tale* (a lie). Recorded by Sidney J. Baker in *The Australian Language*, 1945.

**pot and pan** is the American form of OLD POT AND . . . (q.v.). Recorded by Maurer and Baker, 1944.

**potatoes in the mould** *Cold* (the weather). Late 19 C. or early 20 C., the term fluctuates with the temperature. It is never heard in summer and seldom in a mild winter. Prolonged frost brings it into constant employment but always in its reduced form. Cockneys stamp their feet, flap their arms, blow into their curled hands and repeat at short intervals, 'Coo! Taters! Ain't it?'

**pot of jelly** *Belly*. 20 C. American, Pacific Coast, recorded by Maurer and Baker, 1944. The term may have a reference to pregnancy.

**pot o' glue** *Jew*. 20 C., and less frequently used than the various '. . . to two' rhymes. It has currency on the Pacific Coast of America and is recorded by Maurer and Baker, 1944, and *The American Thesaurus*, 1952.

**poverty point** *A joint*. 20 C. American, recorded by Maurer and Baker, 1944, but a one-word definition is not enough—does it refer to a joint of meat, being a form of sarcasm; or to a place, a club, or pub? The latter is probable, as in Australia it is a theatrical term for an actor's rendezvous.

**pride and joy** *Boy*. 20 C. First recorded in *Detective Fiction Weekly*, 21 April 1934, also given by Maurer and Baker, 1944. Cf. SANTOY.

**Prussian Guard** *A card*. Used during the 1914–18 war in the invitation to join a game of 'House'. See also BLADDER . . . SIX . . .

**pudding(s) and pie(s)** *Eye(s)*. 19 C. Recorded by Hotten, 1859, and now obsolescent in England, but it has currency on the Pacific Coast of America. Recorded by

Maurer and Baker, 1944. See also MINCE . . .

**puff and dart** *Start* (the commencement). 20 C., first recorded in *The Evening Standard*, 19 August 1931.

**pull down the shutter** *Butter*. 20 C. One of the numerous phrases rhyming on butter, the general use of which is for bread and butter.

**push in the truck** *F——*. 20 C. Coitus. Cf. TROLLEY AND . . . The term has great currency among long distance lorry drivers.

**put in the boot** *Shoot*. 20 C. Popular in the army, 1914–18, now obsolete.

# Q

**Quaker oat(s)** *Coat(s)*. 20 C. Not commonly used: see I'M AFLOAT.

**quarter pot** *A sot* (drunkard). 20 C. American, Pacific Coast. Recorded by Maurer and Baker, 1944. Probably a verbal extension of quart, see PINT POT.

**quarter to two** *Jew.* 20 C. One of a number of terms ending in 'two', and perhaps the least used of them all: see TEN TO . . .; FIVE TO . . .; FOUR BY . . .

# R

**rabbit and pork** *Talk.* 20 C. Reduced to *rabbit* the term is used chiefly in relation to public men and affairs; it is likely, therefore, to be much heard before a General Election: 'They've all got a lot o' rabbit, but they don't do nuffink when they gi:: in', or, 'If them Yanks didn't 'ave so much rabbit no one wouldn't know 'ow many Sputniks they've busted.'

**rank and riches** *Breeches* (riding). 19 C. Recorded by George R. Sims, 1887. The term is very apt, since in the 19 C. only those possessed of rank and riches wore riding breeches.

**raspberry tart** (1) *Heart*, (2) *fart.* (1) had a fair currency in the 19 C., but (2), which was contemporaneous, killed it. The term applied to the actual breaking of wind but that, now, only secondarily: an oral sound of the same character, and expressing disapproval, is generally accepted as a 'raspberry'. It is probably of theatrical origin, with reference to 'the bird', and is often reduced to *razz*, or to *razzer.* A further extension of meaning to any expression of disapproval has put the word in wide currency, and out of the category of rhyming slang. Polite people, who would not care to use so vulgar a medium of expression as rhyming slang, and who would never even think so robust a word as fart, will use the word raspberry to describe a mild admonition, or gentle expression of disapproval: 'The Vicar gave us all a bit of a raspberry, about the way we hadn't done anything yet about the jumble sale.'

**rat and mouse** *House.* 19 C. An appropriate term, since the urbanized rodents need houses—either domestic dwelling-houses or warehouses—for their survival. Its American use is recorded in *Detective Fiction Weekly*, 21 April 1943. It is also included in *The American Thesaurus*, 1952.

**rats and mice** *Dice.* 19 C. The appearance of dice rolling is suggestive of rodents running: also used in America, on the Pacific Coast, and is recorded by Maurer and Baker, 1944.

**rattle and hiss** *Piss* (to urinate). Recorded by Maurer and Baker, 1944, as current on the Pacific Coast of America, but clearly influenced by Australian SNAKES . . . (q.v.).

**rattle and jar** *A car.* 20 C. American, Pacific Coast. It may be applied to a streetcar or (with contempt) to an automobile (as the term *heap*, short for 'heap of junk', is applied). Recorded by Chicago May, 1928.

**raw and ripe** *Pipe.* 20 C. American, Pacific Coast, and recorded by Maurer and Baker, 1944, but the word 'ripe' to describe a 'sweet' pipe is British, and probably as old as pipe smoking.

**razz-ma-tazz** *Jazz* (music (!) and dancing). The term came in with, and went out with, the epidemic.

**read and write** *Fight.* 19 C. First recorded by Ducange Anglicus, 1857, and listed by Hotten, 1859. It is probable that the addition of the suffix 'er' personalized the term from the beginning, and being taken for granted (as 'ing' would be) was not set down in print, hence, it must be given a separate entry. Another meaning, 'flight' (the only definition given by Ducange Anglicus) is unconvincing. He probably mis-heard.

**reader and writer** *A fighter* (professional (?) boxer). 20 C. American, Pacific Coast. Recorded by Maurer and Baker, 1944.

**read of tripe** *Transportation for life.* This is recorded by Hotten, 1859, as rhyming slang, but it is unconvincing, and there is no one left who has heard the term used, as transportation is a thing of the rather long past.

**red-hot cinder** *Window* (pronounced *winder*). 20 C. Recorded by Maurer and Baker, 1944, as current on the American Pacific Coast: it is a changed form of BURNT . . . (q.v.).

**red-shirt** *Skirt* (a woman or women in general). 20 C. American, Pacific Coast. Recorded by Maurer and Baker, 1944.

**red steer** *Beer.* 20 C. American, Pacific Coast. Recorded by Maurer and Baker, 1944.

**rhubarb** (pronounced *Rhubub*). (1) *Sub* (an advance of wages), (2) *sub* (abbreviation of suburbs). (1) is the older meaning and has been current among workmen certainly from the first decade of 20 C., and probably existed in the late 19 C. (2) is a comparatively late development, influenced by the electrification of local railway lines, and the consequent decentralization of population. In this meaning the word is given a final 's', and it has been adopted in the U.S.A.

**rhubarb pill** *A bill* (for payment). Late 19 C. The inference is that both necessitate an outpouring.

**Richard the Third** *The 'bird'.* 19 C. Theatrical in origin, but extended to include a feathered bird, and often applied to the flocks of sparrows, pigeons and gulls demanding to be fed—a large percentage of bread bought by Cockneys is fed to the 'Richard the Thirds'.

**ride plush** *To hush.* 20 C. American, Pacific Coast. Recorded by Maurer and Baker, 1944.

**rip and tear** *Swear.* 19 C. Cockneys are of course proud of their proficiency in the use of 'bad language'; but often when they talk of 'cursing and swearing' they are being jocular either by exaggeration, or by inversion, for example, the baby, muttering inarticulate good-temper, may be asked: ''Ere—'oo you cursing an' swearing at?'; or a preacher denouncing drink (or the use of profane language) may be described as 'cursing and swearing like anything!' The term, in its reduced form, *Rip*, is so widely employed, and has gone so far up in the world, that it is barely recognizable as rhyming slang: 'Gad! did the Pater let rip about it!'

**ripsey rousers** *Trousers.* 20 C. American, recorded first in *Detective Fiction Weekly*, 21 April 1934, and by Maurer and Baker, 1944. See ROUND THE . . .

**rise and shine** *Wine.* 20 C. American, Pacific Coast. Recorded by Chicago May, 1928. In a non-rhyming setting it is (and has been for generations) the early-morning jocular cry in the army of men coming off guard-duty, who are feeling very wide-awake and cheerful.

**Riverina** *Deaner* (shilling). Recorded by Sidney J. Baker in *The Australian Language*, 1945. See also DOG'S DINNER.

**River Lea** (1) *Tea,* (2) the *sea.* (1) is recorded by Hotten, and is now obsolescent. (2) by Farmer and Henley in *Slang and its Analogues* (Seven volumes), 1896, and is now obsolete.

**River Ouse** *Booze.* 19 C. Used mainly in the sense of to be on the booze—engaged in a serious drinking bout. See Eric Partridge, *Dictionary of Slang* . . .

**R. J. Knowles** *Holes.* 19 C. to 20 C. He was described as 'the very peculiar Comedian', and he appeared, during the week ending Saturday, 5 November 1892, at the Royal Trocadero Music Hall (now the famous Restaurant), sharing the 'bill' with Miss Marie Lloyd, Mr. T. E. Dunville, and Sandow (the strong-man). The term is still current in the world of the theatre. Lupino Lane.

**roaring horsetails** *Aurora Australis.* Recorded by Sidney J. Baker in *The Australian Language*, 1945.

**Roary O'Moore** is American spelling (recorded by Maurer and Baker, 1944) of RORY O' . . . (q.v.).

**roast pork** (1) *Talk,* (2) *fork.* (1) is the older meaning *c.* 1914. Generally reduced to 'Roast(ing)' as ''Ere—wotsher roastin' abaht?' (2) was current in the army during the second war, and perhaps a little earlier. The reference is to a table fork.

**roasty roast** *Post* (winning). 20 C. American, Pacific Coast. Recorded by Maurer and Baker, 1944.

**Robertson and Moffatt** *Profit.* 20 C. Generally reduced to *Robertson.* Formed on the name of a Melbourne trading house, and recorded by Sidney J. Baker in *The Australian Language*, 1945.

**Robin Hood** *Good.* Late 19 C., and now obsolete. See NO . . .

**Robinson & Cleaver** *Fever.*

19 C. London's annual epidemic of typhoid came to an end after 1860 when Bazelgette's Sewage System separated the main drain from the main drinking water supply, but 'scarlet fever' is still a child's complaint, and the term is therefore still in use.

**Robinson Crusoe** *Do so.* The term seems to be derived from a late 19 C. pantomime song:

Mr. Robinson Crusoe—
You dirty old man to do so.

It is now obsolescent.

**rob my pal** *Gal* (girl). A modern variant of BOB(S) MY . . . (q.v.).

**Rob Roy** *Boy.* Late 19 C. This term, which seems to have been anything but popular, is now obsolete.

**rock of ages** *Wages.* 20 C. The term, which is invariably reduced to 'Rocks', is employed largely by factory workers. Cf. GREENGAGES.

**rocks and boulders** *Shoulders.* 20 C. American, Pacific Coast, recorded by Maurer and Baker, 1944, and in *The American Thesaurus*, 1952.

**rogue and dillon** *Shilling.* 19 C., an alternative form of:

**rogue and villain** *Shilling* (pronounced shillun). 19 C. Recorded by Ducange Anglicus, 1857, and by Hotten, 1859. Now obsolete.

**rolley roar** *Floor.* 20 C. American, Pacific Coast. Recorded by Maurer and Baker, 1944. It is probably a development of RORY . . . (q.v.).

**roll me in the dirt** *Shirt.* 19 C. Recorded by Hotten, 1859, now obsolescent. See DICKY . . .

**roll me in the gutter** *Butter.* Recorded by Fraser and Gibbons in *Soldiers' and Sailors' Words and Phrases*, 1925, but this, like others that rhyme on *butter*, was probably used for bread and butter. It is now obsolescent.

**Rolls Royce** *Voice.* 20 C. Current in the theatrical world, and probably applied only to a voice of the first quality. Lupino Lane.

**Ronson** *Ponce.* A weak rhyme and an unusual form: intensely modern, it proclaims the power of print and the impact of advertising, but perhaps the Company whose name is thus taken in vain, does not consider it good value or sound 'Public Relations'. It has come into use certainly after the second war, and probably within the last few years: that is, since 1955.

**roots** *Boots.* 20 C. American, Pacific Coast. Recorded by Maurer and Baker, 1944. Cf. DAISY . . .

**Rory O' More** (1) *Whore,* (2) *floor,* (3) *door.* 19 C. (1) and (2) are given by Ducange Anglicus, 1857, and Hotten, 1859, but before the end of the 19 C. (3) had come to be the major meaning and so it has remained up to the present time, but a change is now taking place: the term is used as a substitute for ON THE FLOOR (q.v.). In America, on the Pacific Coast, the sole meaning is (3). Recorded by Maurer and Baker, 1944, and *The American Thesaurus*, 1952. 'O'Moore' is merely an alternative spelling, entirely incorrect.

**rosebuds** *Spuds* (potatoes). This term was much used in the army during the 1914–18 war, and is still occasionally in use. See Eric Partridge, *Dictionary of Slang* . . .

**roses red** *Bed.* 20 C. This term is American in usage and is so recorded by Maurer and Baker, 1944. The latter disowns it as of Australian origin, and the former assumes it to be of Cockney origin, but the Cockneys themselves disown it both in origin and use. (See UNCLE NED.) Hence it is reasonable to assume that it was born in Ireland.

**Rosy Lea** *Tea.* Early 20 C. Recorded by Fraser and Gibbons in *Soldiers' and Sailors' Words and Phrases*, the term is in more frequent use than RIVER . . . (q.v.) but less than YOU AND . . . (q.v.). Used in Dublin.

**Rosy Loader** *Whisky and soda.* 20 C., and apparently of recent development. It has but a restricted usage.

**Rosy O'Moore** *Door.* 20 C. An American development of RORY (q.v.) recorded in *The American Thesaurus.*

**round and square** *Everywhere.* 20 C., and very seldom to be heard.

**round me houses,** erroneous: see ROUND THE HOUSES.

**round the hay-stack** *Round the back.* 20 C. This may mean simply what it says, or it may mean a visit to the W.C. The lorry driver who says '. . . so I draws up right in front o' the building after an argument with a copper, then I finds I got to go round the hay-stack', means to the back of the building: but to put down one's glass saying, ''Arf a mo. I'm jus' goin' roun' the hay-stack', means to the W.C. 'The back' is a Cockney euphemism for the W.C.

**round the houses** *Trousers* (pronounced *trouses*). 19 C. This is recorded by both Ducange Anglicus, 1857, and by Hotten, 1859. It is still in constant use, and is generally reduced to ROUND ME'S. This has created the impression that there is an alternative term, ROUND ME HOUSES, but there is not. Cockney pronunciation makes of it: 'Reahn ne ahsiz', and in its reduction the journey from 'n' to 'm' is so short that it will not be noticed. In America the reduction takes a different form: ROUNDS. The term —in full—is recorded by Maurer and Baker, 1944.

**Roy Sleuce** *Deuce* (or a Jack in cards). Recorded by Sidney J. Baker in *The Australian Language*, 1945. It is formed by a combination of Roy Rene, and Harry Van Der Sluice, respectively the stage- and proper-names of an Australian comedian.

**rub-a-dub-dub** (1*a* and *b*) *Club*, (2) *pub*, (3) *sub.* (1*a*) A night-club or drinking club. (1*b*) The club in the game of Crown and Anchor. (2) requires no comment. (3) An advance on wages. Cf. RHUBARB. An alternative form is RUB-A-DI-DUB. Evolved from the nursery rhyme,

'Rub-a-dub-dub, three men in a tub . . .' (1*a*) is Australian.

**rubbity rub** (1) *Pub*, (2) *tub*. American, Pacific Coast, recorded by Maurer and Baker, 1944, and apparently formed out of Australian RUB-A-DUB-DUB (q.v.).

**ruby red** *Head*. 20 C. Recorded by Fraser and Gibbons in *Soldiers' and Sailors' Words and Phrases*, 1925, now obsolete.

**ruby rose** *Nose*. 20 C. American. Recorded in *The American Thesaurus*, 1952. The term might, on some occasions, be very appropriate.

**rumble and shock** *Knock* (on the door). American, Pacific Coast, and very appropriate. Recorded by Maurer and Baker, 1944.

**rumpty dollar** *Holler*. 20 C. American, Pacific Coast usage, and of American origin. Recorded by Maurer and Baker, 1944.

**Russian duck** *Muck*. 20 C. Recorded by J. Manchon in *Le Slang*, 1932, now obsolete.

# S

**saint and sinner** *Dinner.* 19 C. This is in the same category as GLORIOUS . . . (q.v.), but it develops the theme of the self-righteous critic.

**St. Martins-le-Grand,** see MARTIN . . . .

**St. Peter's the Beast** *St. Peter's in the East* (St. Peter-le-Bailey). 19 C. Highly specialized, and confined in usage to Oxford University.

**salmon and trout** (1) *Mouth,* (2) *gout,* (3) *snout,* (4) *tout,* (5) *stout.* 19 C. Hotten, who omitted the 'and' in his 1st edition, gives (1). This meaning is now extinct. (2) is wholly unconvincing: rhyming slang users neither suffer from, nor discuss, the disease. In all probability it is a mis-hearing (or mis-spelling?) of *gelt*—money. (3) is seldom used—*beezer* generally describes the nose, but see I SUPPOSE. (4) is current in the racing world and refers to a bookmaker's tout. (5) is the best-known meaning, and refers to the dark-brown liquid that is either 'good for you', or 'Oatmeal'. See IN AND OUT, and PHOTO . . .

**salvation** *Station.* 19 C. Recorded by Charles Bent in *Criminal Life,* 1891, now obsolete.

**Sammy Hall** (rhyming on *ball*) of a unitesticular horse. 20 C. Used in Australia. It is based on the parody:

My name it is Sam Hall,
And I've only got one ball
But it's better'n none at all
Damn yeh eyes.

The true version, entitled 'Captain Sam Hall', was itself a tough pirate song, a Music Hall 'hit' of late 19 C.

**sandy blight** *Dead right.* 20 C. In American usage it is rhyming slang as defined, but in Australia it refers to an eye disease. Recorded by Maurer and Baker, 1944.

**Sandy MacNab** *A cab.* 20 C. This is a post-second war formation, and its use is still spreading.

**San Toy** *Boy.* Early 20 C. and formed on the title of the pseudo-Japanese stage-play that took London by storm in the pre-1914 period. The term is specialized in usage, meaning not just any boy, but 'one o' da boyce'; a crony in the coterie (or gang).

**satin and silk** *Milk.* 20 C. American, Pacific Coast, recorded by Maurer and Baker, 1944.

Suggestive of this liquid food's smoothness.

**saucepan lid** (1) *Quid* (£1), (2) *Yid*, (3*a*) *kid*, (3*b*) *kid*. Late 19 C. (1) is still in use, but not in a strong position. It began to decline when gold coinage was abandoned, because other, more topical terms, came in with the one-pound note. (2) is still in use, but less likely than any of the 'TO TWO' rhymes on *jew*. (3*a*) a child, used extensively and always jocularly. (3*b*) refers to a mild, friendly, and often exaggerative falsehood. The 'ing' suffix is frequently added: '. . . and there he was, saucepan lidding me that he'd bought a new T.V.!'

**Scapa Flow** *Go*. 20 C., after 1914–18 war. It is always used in the sense of going *from*, even when the context might suggest *going to*, as 'You'll 'ave teh give young Jackie a thick ear-'ole when 'e comes in. I sent 'im 'aht to do an errin' and 'e scarpers off to the Pitchers!' Jackie did not scapa *to* the Pictures: he scarpaed *from* the errand. This term is of great interest since it is a superstructure on, and a rationalization of, a far older word; *scarper*, Parlyaree, or the language of the Circus, from Italian *scappare*, to escape, to run away. For this reason, the word is applied to soft, easy footwear, in which one can run (away): escape (from the Police). Since *scarper* and *scapa* (the reduced form of SCAPA FLOW) are both pronounced the same, it is difficult to say with certainty which word is current in the theatrical world, where it means either to desert a play, or to bilk a landlady. See Eric Partridge, *Slang, Today and Yesterday*; Wilfred Granville, *A Dictionary of Theatrical Terms*.

**scarlet pips** *Lips*. American, Pacific Coast. Recorded by Maurer and Baker, 1944. Cf. SHERRY . . .

**scone,** see HOT . . .

**Scotch peg** *Leg*. 19 C. Recorded by Hotten, 1859, and still current, but experiencing severe competition from DUTCH PEG (q.v.). The definition 'egg' is probably either a mis-hearing or a misprint—it is certainly a mistake.

**scream and holler** *Dollar* ($ not 5s.). American, Pacific Coast. Recorded by Maurer and Baker, 1944.

**see the shine** *Give a dime*. 20 C. American, Pacific Coast. Recorded by Maurer and Baker, 1944. This meaning seems as though it might itself be rhyming slang for something else (?).

**seldom see** *B.V.D.('s.)* (The three letters no doubt convey a meaning to an American citizen—they have some reference to feminine under-garments!) 20 C. Recorded by Chicago May, 1928. (British readers are warned of the danger of confusing with B.D.V., a brand of tobacco!) See Addenda.

**seldom seen** *A limousine*. 20 C. American in origin and in use, recorded by Maurer and Baker, 1944, and in *The American Thesaurus*, 1952, the term, if known in England, is apparently never used.

**Sexton Blake** *Cake*. Early 20 C., when S.B., the great detective; Tinker, his youthful assistant; and Pedro, his faithful and amazingly intelligent blood-hound, were thrilling the errand-boys each week. S.B. was Sherlock Holmes debased to 'Penny-blood' level. There are now no errand-boys, no 'S.B. Weekly Library', and the term is obsolescent.

**shake and shiver** *River*. 20 C. Current in the theatrical world. Lupino Lane.

**sharp and blunt** *C——*. 19 C. This is anatomical only.

**sharper's tools** *Fools*. 19 C. This is from a Standard English term for dice.

**shepherd's plaid** *Bad*. 19 C. This term does not seem very well authenticated. It may have been influenced by the grazing of sheep (Scottish flock?) in the London parks, but the custom is in abeyance and the term with it. See SORRY . . .

**sherry flips** *Lips*. 20 C. American, Pacific Coast. Recorded by Maurer and Baker, 1944, and in the *American Thesaurus*, 1952.

**ship in full sail** *A pint of ale*. 19 C. Recorded by Ducange Anglicus, 1857, and by Hotten, 1859. The term, in its reduced form, *a ship*, is still in use, and many of the users wonder why a pint is called a ship. The American form is SHIP IN SAIL, recorded by Maurer and Baker, 1944.

**ship under sail** *Tale*. 20 C. The tale as told by con-men, beggars and others seeking to impose. Recorded by Jim Phelan, *In the Can*, 1939. Cf. BINNIE . . .; DAILY . . .

**shirt and collar** *Dollar* (5s. not $). Recorded in *Everyman*, 26 March 1931, but overshadowed heavily by an OXFORD . . . (q.v.).

**short of a sheet** *In the street*. Probably implying penniless and unable to obtain a bed. American, Pacific Coast. Recorded by Maurer and Baker, 1944.

**shovel and broom** *A room*. 20 C. Does not seem to ante-date the 1914–18 war, and now obsolete in England, but in U.S.A. its use is recorded by Chicago May, 1928; in *Detective Fiction Weekly*, 23 April 1938; by Maurer and Baker, 1944; and in *The American Thesaurus*, 1952. Employed by Damon Runyon, 1930–40.

**shower bath** *Half* (a sovereign, 10s.). 20 C., after second war. It is invariably reduced to *showers*, and has currency on the dog-racing tracks, where 'shahs to a shillin'' means odds of ten to one.

**sighs and tears** *Ears*. 20 C. American, Pacific Coast. Recorded by Maurer and Baker, 1944, who suspect it of having an English origin, which it has not. It may be Irish. It is also recorded in the *American Thesaurus*, 1952.

**Silas Hocking** *Stocking*. 20 C. Current in the theatrical profession, and formed on the name of the author. Lupino Lane.

**silk and top.** *Cop* (policeman). American, Pacific Coast. Recorded by Maurer and Baker, 1944. Cf. SPINNING . . .

**silk and twine** *Wine*. 20 C.

American, Pacific Coast, recorded by Maurer and Baker, 1944. Cf. STRING AND . . .

**Simple Simon.** *A diamond.* 20 C. American, Pacific Coast. Recorded by Maurer and Baker, 1944. Employed by Damon Runyon, 1930–40.

**Sindbad the Sailor** *Tailor.* Late 19 C. The term is seldom heard, but like a number of others, is inclined to be brought out of storage occasionally. (Pronounce, *Simbad.*)

**Sir Berkeley Hunt,** see BERKELEY.

**Sir Walter Scott** *Pot* (of beer). 19 C. Recorded by both Ducange Anglicus, 1857, and Hotten, 1859, now seldom heard. In America the meaning is 'chamber-pot', and it implies no dislike of Sir W. S.'s works. Recorded by Maurer and Baker, 1944.

**six months' hard** *A card.* 20 C. Used during the 1914–18 war in the invitation to join the game of 'House'. See also BLADDER . . ., PRUSSIAN . . . It is, of course, a colloquialism for hard-labour in prison.

**six to four** *Whore.* 20 C. Recorded by James Curtis in *What Immortal Hand*, 1939.

**skein of thread** *Bed.* 19 C. The term is seldom heard. See UNCLE NED.

**skin and blister** *Sister.* 19 C. This is the term that is most often used, and it is one of the few rhyming slang phrases that is never employed in a reduced form, the reason being that to refer to women and girls as 'skin', or as a 'bit o' skin', is highly disrespectful, implying a laxity of morals and, of course, no man's own sister, at any social level, is admittedly unchaste.

**sky rocket** *Pocket.* 19 C. First recorded in *Macmillan's Magazine*, October 1879, and still in frequent use, but nearly always reduced to 'sky'. The usage has travelled up the social scale, and over the Atlantic: its use on the Pacific Coast of America being recorded by Maurer and Baker, 1944.

**sky the wipe** *Hype* (hypodermic syringe). 20 C. American, Pacific Coast. Recorded by Maurer and Baker, 1944.

**slice of ham** An alternative form of PLATE OF . . . (q.v.).

**slick and sleeth** *Teeth.* American, Pacific Coast. Recorded by Maurer and Baker, 1944.

**slim dilly** *Filly* (a girl). 20 C. American, Pacific Coast. Recorded by Maurer and Baker, 1944.

**slip in the gutter** *Butter.* Early 20 C., and like the other terms rhyming on butter, used for bread and butter, not for butter alone.

**sloop of war** *A whore.* 19 C. This term is now totally obsolete in England, but is current on the Pacific Coast of America and is recorded by Maurer and Baker.

**slosh and mud** *A stud.* This one-word definition is unsatisfactory. The term is current in the theatrical profession (Lupino Lane), hence it probably refers to a collar-stud, in which case it has phonetic value only. If, however, it has been transferred to collar-stud from stud-farm it has also a semantic justification: a Cockney cannot conceive of any farm, and more especially a stud-farm, that is not knee-deep in slosh and mud.

**slum of slops** *Hops.* This is recorded by Maurer and Baker, 1944, as of American currency. It is glossed by them as 'tea'. 'Slops' is an obsolescent English slang word for 'tea' and also for low-grade liquor. Slum of Slops is unknown in England, but if it ever was in use it is far more likely to have been applied to beer than to tea.

**smack in the eye** *A pie.* American, Pacific Coast. Recorded by Maurer and Baker, 1944.

**smart and simple** *A dimple.* American, Pacific Coast. Recorded by Maurer and Baker, 1944, and so true—the fair sex must gnash its pearly teeth on reflecting that they cannot be bought by the bottle or the box.

**smear and smudge** *A judge.* American, Pacific Coast. Recorded by Maurer and Baker, 1944.

**smell burn** *Melbourne* (City of, Australia). Recorded by Sidney J. Baker in *The Australian Language*, 1945. It is more of a pun than rhyming slang.

**smog** *Fog.* 20 C. after second war. A totally unnecessary portmanteau word, 'smoke—fog', invented in U.S.A. and popularized by the British Press so that 'naice refayned' people now think it 'voolgah' to say 'fog'. Cockneys despise the word.

**smooth and coarse** *A horse.* American, Pacific Coast, recorded by Maurer and Baker, 1944. Cf. CHARING . . .

**smooth and rough** *On the cuff*, that is, on credit, a starched cuff being a handy note-book. American, Pacific Coast. Recorded by Maurer and Baker, 1944.

**snake in the grass** *Looking-glass.* 19 C. Recorded by Hotten, 1859, and now obsolete. It has all the flavour of the Victorian homolizing attitude of mind which pervaded (in appropriate proportion) all classes of society.

**snake's hiss** *Piss.* Early 20 C. Australian, referring to urine, and to the act of urination.

**snow and rain** *A train.* 20 C. American in both origin and usage. Recorded by Maurer and Baker, 1944.

**soap and water** *Daughter.* Recorded by Fraser and Gibbons in 1925, now obsolescent.

**soldier bold** *A cold.* 19 C., now obsolete.

**song and dance** (1) *Nance* (shortened form of 'Nancy', a homosexual), (2) *pants.* (1) Came into use during the 1914 war, and survived, with the word 'Nancy' up to the second war when 'queer' became popular. See BRIGHTON PIER, GINGER BEER and KING LEAR. (2) is American usage, hence 'trousers', not undergarments: first recorded in *Detective Fiction Weekly*, 21 April 1934, and also by Maurer and Baker, 1944.

**song of the thrush** *Brush.* Communicated by Mr C. H. Dickson, among 'some which my father used', hence, early 20 C.

*The Star*, 30 September 1958. Probably meaning the utensil, but later may have been extended to the sense 'give him the brush (off)', that is, indicate that he is unwelcome.

**song(s) and sigh(s)** *Thigh(s)*. American, recorded by Chicago May, 1928.

**sorrowful tale** *Three months in jail*. 19 C. Recorded by Hotten, 1859, and now obsolete.

**sorry and sad** *Bad*. 19 C. So very apt that it is almost synonymous.

**soup and gravy** *The Navy*. 20 C., and current before 1914, now seldom heard.

**south of the equator** *Elevator*. Probably a lift, but it could refer to a heel-wedge worn to give short people an appearance of height. Both are called elevators in U.S.A. where this term is in use. Recorded by Maurer and Baker, 1944.

**Spanish guitar** *Cigar*. 20 C. Originated in the English theatrical profession and still current—recorded by Wilfred Granville in *A Dictionary of Theatrical Terms*. In America it is current on the Pacific Coast and is recorded by Maurer and Baker, 1944, and *The American Thesaurus*, 1952.

**spinning top** *Cop* (policeman). American, Pacific Coast. Recorded by Maurer and Baker, 1944.

**split asunder** *Costermonger*. 19 C. Recorded by Hotten, 1859, now obsolete.

**split pea** *Tea*. 19 C. Recorded by Ducange Anglicus, and now totally extinct.

**sport and win** *Jim*. 19 C. Recorded by Hotten, 1859, but almost certainly an error due to mis-hearing or to mis-spelling. He was himself aware of this danger: in recording DAISY RECROOTS he adds, 'so spelt by my informant of Seven Dials; he means, doubtless, *Recruits*'. His informant for this term, doubtless either said or wrote 'Jim' meaning *Gem*: which was underworld slang for a gold ring. Any rhyming slang term glossed to mean a person's given name must be viewed with suspicion: see OATS AND . . .; PITCH AND . . . Why are not all personal names rendered in rhyming slang? Why are those that seem to be, so wide open to another meaning?

**stammer and stutter** *Butter*. 20 C. Current in the theatrical profession (Lupino Lane). This, like the other phrases that rhyme on 'butter', is probably used most often in connection with bread and butter.

**stand an ale** *Go bail* (for). American, Pacific Coast. Recorded by Maurer and Baker, 1944.

**stand at ease** (1) *Fleas*, (2) *cheese*. This term in both its meanings was in use in the army during the 1914–18 war, and is still current. (1) is rather humorous: who will stand, sit, or lie at ease if bitten? Recorded by Fraser and Gibbons in *Soldiers' and Sailors' Words and Phrases*, 1928.

**stand from under** *Thunder*. 20 C. Current in the theatrical profession. The term is very apt since it is the standard cry in the

Navy (hence, in the London Fire Brigade), when a heavy object is to be dropped from above. Many ex-sailors become scene-shifters. Lupino Lane.

**steak and kidney** *Sydney* (City of, Australia). Recorded by Sidney J. Baker in *The Australian Language*, 1945.

**steak and kidney pie** *Eye.* Current in the theatrical profession, but rare in other circles. See MINCE . . . Lupino Lane.

**steam packet** *Jacket.* 19 C. Recorded by Ducange Anglicus, 1857, and by Hotten, 1859, but now obsolete.

**steam tug(s)** (1) *Bug(s)*, (2) *mug(s)*. Generally in its reduced form, *steamer(s)*, (1) was, during the late 19 C. and early 20 C., the principal meaning now, thanks to the Sanitary Inspector (who rarely gets, but richly deserves, our thanks), there is little or no need for it, and (2) has come to the fore. A mug is a simpleton—a person for exploiting and fleecing.

**Steele Rudds** *Spuds* (potatoes). 20 C. Recorded by Sidney J. Baker in *The Australian Language*, 1945. (Name of popular author.)

**Steve Hart** *Start* (begin). 20 C. Generally referring to the start of a horse-race, but is also applied to any commencement. American, recorded in *The American Thesaurus*, 1952.

**stewed prune** *Tune.* 19 C. Not in the sense 'that is a pretty stewed prune', but, to the man with the mouth-organ, 'Give us a stewed prune.' The term is now dead because it is usual to say 'turn on the wireless'.

**stick slingers** *Fingers* (the 'g' is evidently hard). 20 C. American, Pacific Coast. Recorded by Maurer and Baker, 1944.

**stop thief** *Beef.* 19 C. Recorded by Ducange Anglicus, 1857, and by Hotten, 1859. It was a term of a semi-derisive character applied only to a stolen piece of beef, never to a bought piece. The term became extinct before the modern term to 'beef', to 'complain' became popular, or it might have been transferred.

**storm and strife** *Wife.* American form of English TROUBLE . . . (q.v.). Recorded by Ernest Booth in *The American Mercury*, May 1928; by Maurer and Baker, 1944; and by *The American Thesaurus*, 1952.

**Stormy Dick** *Prick* (penis). American, Pacific Coast, recorded by Maurer and Baker, 1944. Cf. HAMPTON . . . and UNCLE DICK.

**strike me dead** *Bread.* 20 C. Current in the world of the theatre, and recorded by Gerald Kersh, *Night in the City*, 1938.

**string and top** *Cop* (policeman). American. Recorded in *The American Thesaurus*, 1952.

**string and twine** *Wine.* 20 C. American, Pacific Coast. Recorded by Maurer and Baker, 1944.

**string of beads** *Leeds* (City of, Yorkshire, England), but possibly also for Leeds, a village near Maidstone, Kent. This term, which is used by railwaymen, was recorded in *The Daily Herald*, 5 August 1936.

**strong and thin** *Gin*. 20 C. American, Pacific Coast. Recorded by Maurer and Baker, 1944

**struggle and strain** *Train*. 20 C. Popular in the army during the 1914–18 war, it refers to a railway train, not to training, though for this it would be apt indeed. With the one meaning only it is apt enough, for with the 'full-pack' of the period, plus greatcoat, kit-bag and rifle, a battalion experienced sufficient struggle and strain when travelling by rail, especially on the Continent.

**struggle and strife** *Wife*. 20 C. An alternative form of TROUBLE . . . (q.v.), but seldom employed.

**stump the chalk** *Walk*. 20 C. American. Stumps, on both sides of the Atlantic, are legs. Quoted by J. F. Fishman, in *Startling Detective*, 1947.

**sugar and honey** *Money*. 19 C., recorded by Hotten, 1859, and still widely used in its reduced form. Many people who call money 'sugar' are not aware that it has a rhyming element to follow.

**sugar basin** *A marble mason*. 20 C. Current in the building trade. It carries a double inference: the appearance of rough white marble is similar to that of lump sugar, and being a soft stone it is easy to work—not a bitter struggle to chip, therefore sweet, therefore sugar.

**sugar candy** (1) *Brandy*, (2) *handy*. (1) is recorded by Hotten, 1859 and is still in use; (2) which is a later formation, is generally used in an inverted sense: 'That's sugar-candy, that is', means the situation is disagreeable.

**Sunday best** *Vest*. 20 C. American. Recorded by Chicago May, 1928. In American usage the major meaning of *vest* is 'waistcoat', not undershirt, as in British usage. This can be admitted as rhyming slang only if it refers to any and every waistcoat—not actually to the wearer's Sunday best.

**sunny south** *Mouth*. 19 C. First recorded in *The Referee*, 7 November 1887, it was transitional between EAST AND SOUTH (q.v.) and NORTH AND SOUTH (q.v.).

**suppose,** see I SUPPOSE.

**swallow and sigh** *Collar and tie*. 20 C. Current in the world of the theatre, probably not later in origin than early 20 C. Wilfred Granville suggests it is formed on the fact that a tight collar and tie cause one to do both. See *A Dictionary of Theatrical Terms*.

**swear and cuss** *Bus*. 20 C. Recorded by Len Ortzen in *Down Donkey Row*, 1938. It is a very apt term for even mild, long-suffering folk do so while waiting.

**Sweeny Todd** *The Flying Squad*. 20 C., mentioned in the *Daily Express*, 25 March 1938; in *Sharpe of the Flying Squad* by F. D. Sharpe, 1938; and in *What Immortal Hand* by James Curtis, 1939. From Sweeny Todd the demon barber of Fleet Street, who cut his customers' throats and sold the bodies to a pie-maker. The term is often reduced to 'the Sweenies'. (See p. 164.)

**sweet Margaret** *A cigarette.* 20 C. American, Pacific Coast. Recorded by Maurer and Baker, 1944, with alternative SWEET MARGUERITE, which, though it loses rhyme may refer ironically to the smell, as suggested by Eric Partridge, *Dictionary of the Underworld.*

**swiftly flowing** *Going.* Late 19 C. Recorded in *Sydney Bulletin,* 18 January 1902, quoted by Sidney J. Baker in *The Australian Language,* 1945.

**switch and bone** *Telephone.* American, Pacific Coast. Recorded by Maurer and Baker, 1944.

**Sydney Harbour** *A barber.* 20 C. Recorded by Chicago May, 1928, and by Maurer and Baker, 1944. Clearly of Australian origin.

# T

**take a cook,** see GIVE A . . .

**take a fright** *Night.* 19 C. Recorded by Hotten, 1859, and now obsolete. Psychologists who are interested in the infantile neurosis called *Pavor nocturnis* should make a note of this term.

**take and give** *Live* (with a woman, as man and wife). 19 C. Recorded by J. Redding Ware in *Passing English,* 1909. Now obsolete.

**tale of two cities** *Titties* (breasts). 20 C. This is generally employed in a jocular setting, and is frequently Spoonerized: *Sale of two . . .*

**tamtart** *Sweetheart.* A girl, probably a mutilated form of JAM TART (q.v.). 19 C., now obsolete.

**tar and feather** *Weather.* 20 C. American, Pacific Coast. Recorded by Maurer and Baker, 1944.

**tarry rope** *Dope* (not drugs, but a 'dopey', or stupid person). American, Pacific Coast. Recorded by Maurer and Baker, 1944.

**tartan banner** *Tanner* (sixpence). This term was evolved during the 1914–18 war and had currency in the army. It is now obsolescent.

**taters in the mould,** see POTATOES . . .

**tatters in the mould** A misspelling of TATERS IN THE . . . (q.v.).

**tea and cocoa,** see COFFEE.

**tea and tattle** *Battle.* 20 C. American, Pacific Coast, recorded by Maurer and Baker, 1944, probably referring to an engagement between rival gangs.

**tea and toast** *Post* (winning post). 20 C. American, Pacific Coast. Recorded by Maurer and Baker, 1944.

**tea for two and a bloater** *Motor.* The term, which arose in the first decade of 20 C. and is now obsolescent, was applied to a private, not to a commercial, vehicle, and was derisive. It was in the category of 'If you can't afford a motor, buy the hat',—the stiff peaked cap that all motorists wore.

**tea-leaf(ing)** *A thief; thieving.* 19 C. Charles Booth, in *Life and Labour of the People in London,* says, ' "Tea-leaf" is for some inexplicable reason, the name used by the police for pickpockets.' Charles Booth was, and is, accepted as an 'authority'!

**tea-pot lid** is an alternative form of SAUCEPAN LID (q.v.).

**tears and cheers** *Ears.* 20 C. American, Pacific Coast. Recorded by Maurer and Baker, 1944.

**ten to two** *Jew.* 20 C. As one among several 'to two' rhymes, all having the same meaning, this enjoys a reasonably wide currency.

**the Binnie Hale,** see BINNIE HALE.

**the Daily Mail,** see DAILY . . .

**there first** *Thirst.* 20 C. This term, which was in use in the army 1914–18, implies the wild rush to the pub (or canteen) when they open. It is now obsolete.

**there you are** *Bar* (public-house). 19 C. It is expressive both of satisfaction at getting there one's self, and of there finding one's friends.

**these and those** (1) *Nose,* (2) *toes,* (3) *clothes.* 20 C. (1) and (2) are Australian. (2) and (3) are American, recorded in *The American Thesaurus,* 1952.

**thick and dense** *Expense.* 20 C. American. Recorded by Ernest Booth in *The American Mercury,* May 1928.

**thick and thin** (1) *Gin,* (2) *chin.* 20 C. American. (1) is recorded by Chicago May, 1928. (2) appears in *The American Thesaurus.*

**thimble and thumb** *Rum.* 20 C. Recorded in *Weekly Telegraph,* 6 April 1946. Probably a misspelling of FINGER AND . . . (q.v.).

**this(es) and that(s)** (1) *Hat,* (2) *spats.* (1) in the singular, is American, Pacific Coast, recorded by Maurer and Baker, 1944. (2) in the plural is early 20 C. Cockney: now obsolescent because spats are no longer worn. (1) is to be heard in Australia.

**Thomas Tilling** *A shilling.* 19 C. T.T. was famous for his service of horses and horse-drawn vehicles. He supplied the magnificent horses to The London Fire Brigade; those that drew the Royal Mail vans, and others. He also ran buses, coaches, and the like. The term is now obsolete, but is used by Michael Harrison in *All the Trees were Green,* 1936.

**thousand pities** *Titties* (breasts). Late 19 C., and now obsolete.

**three by two** *Jew.* This term arose after the 1914–18 war, and was probably a civilian's perversion of FOUR BY TWO (q.v.). It is now obsolete.

**three or four** *Door.* 20 C. American, Pacific Coast. Recorded by Maurer and Baker, 1944. Cf. RORY . . .

**three quarters of a peck** *Neck.* 19 C. Recorded by Ducange Anglicus, 1857, and by Hotten, 1859, who adds that it is written simply as '$\frac{3}{4}$'. It has now fallen into oblivion, as such long phrases must.

**throw me in the dirt** *Shirt.* 19 C., recorded by Ducange Anglicus, 1857, now obsolete. A phrase containing five words obviously had no survival value from its birth.

**tick tack** *The track* (racing). Thus recorded as of American usage by Maurer and Baker, 1944, who add 'or TIC TAC signals to a bookmaker'. See TIN TACK.

**tiddley wink** is the American form of TIDDLY WINK (q.v.) (Maurer and Baker, 1944).

**tiddler's bait** *Late.* 20 C. Many a child has been late for afternoon school through fishing in the park. 'Tiddler' is slang for the stickleback (a small fish of the genus *gasterosteus*) with which London Park ornamental waters are well stocked—in fact, both tiddlers and sparrows may themselves fairly claim to be Cockneys.

**tiddly wink** *A drink* (alcoholic). 19 C. The term appeared in *Punch* in 1895. Generally used in its reduced form: 'Come and have a tiddly' and often preceded by 'little'. It is applied more frequently to 'shorts' (short drinks, wines and spirits), than to beer. To be 'tiddly' is to be drunk, in which meaning it is used far beyond the normal range of rhyming slang, and has become almost a euphemism.

**Tilbury Docks** *Socks.* 19 C. This term seems to be sacred to the Navy, hence it had a vogue in the London Fire Brigade before the second war. It is now obsolescent. (Tilbury Docks, built 1886.)

**Tilly Bates** A mis-spelling of TIDDLER'S BAIT (q.v.). Tilly is (or was) a popular Cockney girl's name: Matilda became 'Tilda, 'Tilda became 'Till, 'Till became Tilly. The surname Bates is very frequently met with among Cockneys: it is a diminutive of Bartholomew.

**tillywink,** see TIDDLY WINK.

**ting-a-ling** *Ring* (finger ring). American, Pacific Coast. Recorded by Maurer and Baker, 1944.

**tin-lid** *Yid.* 20 C. Recorded by Michael Harrison in *Reported Safe Arrival*, 1943.

**tin-plate** *Mate.* A form of CHINA (q.v.) employed by troops from New Zealand during the 1914–18 war.

**tin-tack(s)** (1) *Fact(s)*, (2) *track* (racing), (3) *the sack* (dismissal). When polite society annexed BRASS TACKS (q.v.) the Cockney abandoned it, and evolved TIN TACKS, which is used in all the settings that suit BRASS TACKS. Cockney dialect makes *fack(s)* of 'fact(s)', and the combination of *tin* and *tack* slips more easily from the tongue if *tin* is softened too, hence, *tin-tack* becomes *tick-tack* or *tictac.* In racing circles the man who signals the 'facts' of change of odds to the Bookmakers is the tic-tac man, hence any kind of signalling becomes 'tic-tac' as: 'I guessed he'd slip orf without paying ees round—I see 'ees bleet'n' misses give 'im the tic-tac.' (2) is American, and refers to a horse-racing track. Recorded by Maurer and Baker, 1944. (3) is not of frequent occurrence—'the sack' seems to be sufficiently slangy in itself.

**tin tank** *Bank.* Chiefly Post Office Savings Bank, or other banking house dealing with savings accounts, but may be applied to any bank. It is of early 20 C. origin and has a fair currency but is inferior to IRON TANK (q.v.).

**tip and tap** *Cap* (head gear). 20 C. American, Pacific Coast. Recorded by Maurer and Baker, 1944, and in *The American Thesaurus*, 1952.

**tisket** *Bastard.* Evolved during the second war and heavily overworked in the Civil Defence Services, particularly in the National Fire Service. It is forged out of a popular song containing the words:

A tisket a tasket,
A little yellow basket.

The word 'basket' is euphemistic for *bastard*, and the apparently very innocent ditty had as a second meaning the Japanese who were universally described as 'little yellow bastards'. *Tisket* served all the shades of meaning of bastard (see *The Cockney*, Julian Franklyn), and is now abandoned.

**tit for tat** *Hat.* Early 20 C. The word 'for' in Cockney, dialect, becomes *feh*, hence 'tit feh tat' which, in its reduced form, becomes 'tit feh'. This, understood as one word *titfa*, has, like several other rhyming slang terms, became detached from its environment, and is used over a wide social field.

**tit willow** *Pillow.* 20 C. This term is seldom heard because there is little reason for its use. Any one of the other terms for sleep or bed is more likely to occur, but now and then a Cockney talks of getting his head on the old tit willow.

**toad in a hole** *A roll* (of currency notes). American, Pacific Coast. Recorded by Maurer and Baker, 1944.

**Tod Sloan** *Alone.* This term, when employed, is generally reduced to Tod, but either PAT MALONE (q.v.) or JACK JONES (q.v.) is far more likely to be used.

**Tom and funny** *Money.* 20 C. Recorded by J. Redding Ware in *Passing English*, 1909. Now obsolete.

**Tom, Harry and Dick** *Sick* (unwell, on the sick list). London Transport workers, chiefly busmen. 20 C. An ingenious rearrangement of the three hypothetical 'average men'.

**tomfoolery** *Jewellery.* Late 19 C., and still in use. Quoted by Michael Harrison in *Reported Safe Arrival*, 1943. Reduced form, TOM.

**Tom Mix** *Six* (score in playing darts). Recorded in the *Evening News*, 2 July 1937. (Tom Mix, a film actor.)

**Tommy Dodd** (1) *Odd*, (2) *rod* (a revolver), (3) *sod*. (1) is 19 C. usage and is derived from a coin-tossing term; *c.* 1863 there was a Music Hall song 'Heads or Tails are sure to win, Tommy Dodd, Tommy Dodd'. At about the same period it was a euphemism for God, particularly in 'Tommy Dodd knows'. It is now obsolete in England but is enjoying a new lease of life on the Pacific Coast of America where it refers to (2). Recorded by Maurer and Baker, 1944. (3) is merely a playful euphemism—'You old Tommy Dodd, you!'

**Tommy O'Rann** *Scran* (food). 19 C. Recorded by Hotten,

1859, and still in use. It is employed chiefly by workmen.

**Tommy Rabbit** *Pomegranate.* This term was common in the first decade of 20 C., when a pomegranate cost a half-penny; it was recorded in *Passing English* by J. Redding Ware, in 1909, and it has now passed: so has the pomegranate, except from the 'luxury' shops.

**Tommy Rocks** *Socks.* 20 C. The American version of ALMOND (q.v.). Recorded by Maurer and Baker, 1944.

**Tommy Roller** *Collar.* 19 C. Recorded by C. Bent in *Criminal Life*, 1891. Cf. HOLLER . . .

**Tommy Toy** *Boy.* 20 C. American. Probably comparable with British SANTOY (q.v.). Recorded in *The American Thesaurus*, 1952.

**Tommy Tucker** *Supper.* Late 19 C. A poor rhyme not helped by semantics, yet the term survives. It is probably based on the nursery rhyme:

Little Tommy Tucker
Sang for his supper.

**Tom Noddy** *The body.* 20 C. American, recorded in the *American Thesaurus*, 1952.

**Tom Right** *Night.* 19 C. Recorded by Ducange Anglicus and suggestive of the night-time being more suitable for some criminal activities than is the day. Compare TAKE A FRIGHT. Now obsolete.

**Tom Tart** (1) *Fart*, (2) *girl* (sweetheart). (1) is American usage recorded by Maurer and Baker, 1944. (2) is Australian. Cf. JAM TART, and TAMTART.

**Tom Thacker** *Bacca* (tobacco). Late 19 C. Recorded by Eric Partridge. Now obsolescent. Cf. NOSER MY . . .

**Tom Thumb** *Rum.* 20 C. Recorded by Fraser and Gibbons in *Soldiers' and Sailors' Words and Phrases*, 1925. The term was never very popular among soldiers who preferred backslang *mur* to all other terms. Now obsolescent.

**Tom Tit** *Shit* (to defecate). Early 20 C. This term is used far more often than any other with an equivalent meaning. It is never reduced, but the first word is invariably stressed. 'E'yar mate: you git on tapeing up them ends while I go an' 'ave a *Tom* tit.' Industrialists, Economists, Sociologists, and others might have a shock if they could compute the number of man-hours wasted behind those words, for visitors in genuine need find every cubicle occupied by smokers, by talkers, and by forty-winkers, all of whom have departed from the bench behind the immunity afforded by the formula.

**Tom Tripe** *Pipe* (tobacco). 19 C. Recorded by Hotten, 1859. Now obsolete. See CHERRY . . .

**Tom Tug** (1) *Mug* (simpleton), (2) *thug* (gangster). (1) was originally Cockney and is recorded by Hotten, 1859. It is now obsolete in Britain (see STEAM TUG) but has currency in U.S.A. where it is recorded by Ernest Booth in *The American Mercury*, 1928; and also by Maurer and Baker, 1944. (2) is also American, and is included in the *American Thesaurus*, 1952.

**too Irish stew** *Too true.* 20 C., used largely in the army 1914–18. It is invariably reduced to *too Irish,* and very frequently garnished with an intrusive 'bloody': 'too bloody Irish'. This last, in wide use, was not recognized as altered rhyming slang until the connection was discovered by the late Gerald Bullett.

**Tooting Bec** *Peck* (food, something to peck at). 19 C., still heard, but uncommon. It is, when used, generally reduced to *Tooting*. 'Let's have a speck of Tooting.'

**top joint** *A pint* (of beer). 19 C. Recorded by Ducange Anglicus, 1857, and by Hotten, 1859. It is now obsolete, but in its day it was pronounced 'top jint', no longer a form of Cockney dialect.

**top of Rome** *Home*. 19 C. Recorded by Ducange Anglicus, 1857, and now obsolete. Cf. POPE . . .

**torn thumb** *Rum*. This is a rare degenerative form of TOM THUMB (q.v.).

**total wreck** *Cheque*. 20 C. American, Pacific Coast. Recorded by Maurer and Baker, 1944. Indiscriminate payment by cheque can make a total wreck of a banking account. Eight pounds is a most dangerous sum, requiring only a 'y' on the word and an 'o' on the figure. The term is also in use in Australia.

**touch me on the knob** *A bob* (shilling). 20 C. Invariably reduced to *touch me,* this term has a great deal of use for its humorous association. To *touch* is to 'borrow', hence 'she'll touch me for a touch me' is a catch-phrase which can often be used in connection with shilling-in-the-slot gas meters. Cf. THOMAS TILLING.

**towns and cities** *Titties* (breasts). 20 C., now obsolete.

**toy** *A boy*. 20 C. American, and thus glossed by Maurer and Baker, 1944, but does it mean mother's little darling, or one of the gang? The latter is probable. Cf. SANTOY.

**train wreck** *Neck*. 20 C. American, Pacific Coast. Recorded by Chicago May, 1928.

**trap and mouse** *House*. 20 C. The American form of CAT AND . . . (q.v.). Recorded by Maurer and Baker, 1944.

**trolley and truck** *F——*. 20 C. Reference to coitus, never as an expletive.

**trollywags** *Bags* (trousers). 19 C., and now obsolete.

**trot and pace** *Face*. 20 C. American, Pacific Coast. Recorded by Maurer and Baker, 1944.

**trouble and strife** *Wife*. Early 20 C., and by far the most widely used of all 'wife' (or missus) rhymes. It is generally jocular. Sometimes, *life*.

**true till death** *Breath*. 20 C. A very apt phrase, used in the world of the theatre. Lupino Lane.

**tumble and trip(s)** *Lip(s)*. 20 C. Lips, when one is under police interrogation, are inclined to tumble and trip. The term is American, and is recorded by Chicago May, 1928.

YOU GET ON MY WEST HAM RESERVES
OH, SHUT YOUR GLASS CASE

**tumble down the sink** *A drink.* 19 C., and still very popular. It possesses a semantic as well as a phonetic strength, nevertheless, it is generally reduced to *tumble.*

**Turpentine** *Serpentine* (Lake—Hyde Park, London). 20 C. This is used at various different social levels, and is invariably jocular. Sometimes reduced to *Turps.*

**turtle doves** *Gloves.* 19 C. Recorded by Ducange Anglicus, 1857, and by Hotten, 1859. It is still used here, and has a currency on the Pacific Coast of America. Recorded by Maurer and Baker, 1944.

**twist and twirl** *Girl.* 20 C. American. Recorded by Ernest Booth in *The American Mercury,* 1928; by Maurer and Baker, 1944, and the *American Thesaurus,* 1952. See also WINDS . . .

**two and eight** *State* (of nervous tension). This seems to be a 1914–18 war formation, but it does not appear to be destined to obliterate HARRY TATE (q.v.).

**two by four** *Whore.* 20 C. American, Pacific Coast. Recorded by Maurer and Baker, 1944.

**two-foot rule** *Fool.* 19 C. Recorded by Ducange Anglicus, 1857, and by Hotten, 1859. It is now obsolescent.

**two-thirty** *Dirty.* Late 19 C., still used occasionally. It refers to grime, not to behaviour: 'He's that two-thirty you don't like to go near him', but not 'he did me a two-thirty trick'.

**typewriter** *A fighter.* 20 C. Although not very popular, it is not obsolete. It refers to the amount of fight in a person, not to a quarrelsome nature: 'Jack's the boy for the shop-steward's job—he's a typewriter, he is.' It may also be applied to one who can 'use his dooks'.

# U

**umble-cum-stumble** An alternative from of UNDER . . . (q.v.).

**Uncle Ben** *Ten.* Score on the game of House (Housie-Housie), extensively played in the army, 1914–18.

**Uncle Dick** (1) *Prick* (penis), (2) *sick.* (1) is less popular than HAMPTON (q.v.). (2) refers to any illness, not only to vomiting. Both are early 20 C. in origin and still in use. (2) Reduced to 'dickey' is widely applied, particularly to children when they are not well: 'That boy seems very dickey. Better get the doctor.'

**Uncle Fred** *Bread.* 20 C. This is used chiefly by, and to, children.

**Uncle Ned** *Bed.* 19 C., and very popular. It refers to the article of furniture itself, and to the act of going there. Also used, but very rarely, for *head.*

**uncles and aunts** *Pants* (trousers). 20 C. American. Recorded by Chicago May, 1928, and by Maurer and Baker, 1944. This rhyme suggests the pronunciation 'ants' for *aunts*: in 1672 Matthew Brisbane, M.D., receiving a coat-of-arms, had for his crest a 'hillocks eme of aunts—' ants were intended.

**Uncle Willy** *Silly.* Early 20 C., and still applied to a simple-minded person who is deserving more of sympathy than contempt. In Australia the term has become inverted: 'he's auntie', means 'he's uncle' short for Uncle Willy.

**under beneaths** An alternative form of UPPERS (or UNDERS) (q.v.). Recorded by Chicago May, 1928.

**under-con-stumble** (1) *Tumble,* (2) *rumble.* This is the modern version of an 18 C. term, JERRY-CUM-MUMBLE (q.v.) which is itself not quite dead. (1) means to understand suddenly, (2) is to find out.

**unders and beneath** *Teeth.* 20 C. American. Recorded in *The American Thesaurus,* 1952; see also UPPER.

**upper deck** *Neck.* 20 C. American, Pacific Coast. Maurer and Baker, 1944.

**uppers and beneath** *Teeth.* 20 C. American. Recorded by Chicago May, 1928, and by Maurer and Baker, 1944. See also UNDERS . . .

# V

**Vera Lynn** *Gin.* 20 C. Has currency in the theatrical profession, based on the name of the actress. Recorded by Wilfred Granville in *A Dictionary of Theatrical Terms.*

**very best** *Chest.* 20 C. American, Pacific Coast. Recorded by Maurer and Baker, 1944, and in *The American Thesaurus*, 1952. Might apply either to the thorax, or to a box.

**Vicar of Bray** *Tray.* 20 C. Current in the theatrical profession and so defined by Lupino Lane. It may apply either to a utensil for carrying objects, or to the number three.

**Victor Trumper** *Bumper* (a cigarette end). Recorded by Sidney J. Baker in *The Australian Language*, 1945. Based on the name of the Australian cricketer. Cf. *bumper* as a cricket term.

**Victoria Monk** Alternative, or a mistaken, form of MARIA . . . (q.v.). Victoria Monks (note the final 's') was a famous Music Hall star of the late 19 C. Her most popular song was 'Won't you come home, Bill Bailey?'

**virgin bride** *Ride.* Recorded in *Sydney Bulletin*, 18 January 1902, and quoted by Sidney J. Baker in *The Australian Language*, 1945.

# W

**war and strife** *Wife.* 20 C. This version of TROUBLE AND . . . came into use during the 1914–18 war, but is now seldom heard.

**Warwick farms** *Arms.* Recorded by Sidney J. Baker in *The Australian Language*, 1945. Cf. CHALK FARM.

**waterbury watch** *Scotch* (whisky). Late 19 C. or early 20 C., but not very popular.

**Wee Georgie Wood** *Good.* 20 C. Australian. Generally reduced to *Wee Georgie*, and preceded by *any*. Sidney J. Baker, *Australian Slang*, 1942. Wee Georgie Wood was a popular Music Hall 'turn'.

**weep and wail** *Tale.* 19 C., now obsolescent, used exclusively for a beggar's 'tale' and generally reduced to 'weep'. 'He's got such a lovely weep that he can trap lolly from the copper who tells him to take a penn'arf!'

**weeping willow** *Pillow.* 20 C. This term seems to have been evolved and used in the army during the 1914–18 war. It is now of infrequent occurrence in Britain (Cf. TIT WILLOW), but is current in U.S.A., where its use is recorded by Chicago May, 1928; by Maurer and Baker, 1944 (they date it 1900); and in the *American Thesaurus*, 1952.

**Westminster Abbey** *Shabby.* 20 C. This is a theatrical term, and is probably influenced by the antiquity of the Abbey.

**whale and gale** *Jail.* 20 C. American. Recorded in *Detective Fiction Weekly*, 21 April 1934, and by Maurer and Baker, 1944.

**what am** *Ham.* 20 C. American, Pacific Coast. Recorded by Maurer and Baker, 1944.

**whip and lash** *Moustache.* 20 C. American, Pacific Coast. Recorded by Maurer and Baker, 1944.

**whip and slash** *Moustache.* 20 C. American, and merely a version of WHIP AND LASH (q.v.).

**whistle and flute** *Suit* (of clothes). 19 C., and still the most popular term for clothes. Often reduced to *whistle.*

**widow's mite** *A light.* 20 C. The term does not refer to luminosity, but to ignition: a 'light' for pipe or cigarette—a small thing, but of great value when without a box of matches or with a dry petrol-lighter.

**Wilkie Baird** Alternative spelling of:

**Wilkie Bard** *Card.* 20 C.,

might be late 19 C. It may be applied to any and every card, but it refers specifically to an actor's professional card which will admit him, or any person to whom he gives it, to a theatre. This is extended to the free-pass given by Theatres and Music Halls (probably also Cinemas) to shopkeepers who display advertising bills. Within the theatrical profession, given a final 's' it refers to playing-cards. Based on the name of the Music Hall artiste.

**wind(s) do whirl** *Girl.* 19 C. Now obsolete in England but current in America where its use is recorded by Maurer and Baker, 1944. WINDS DO TWIRL is an alternative form. See also TWIST AND . . .

**wind up** *Pinned up.* Taut, stretched tight, on edge; hence in a state of fear. The term has become so common that its rhyming slang association is lost. First recorded by Raymond (son of Sir Oliver) Lodge, who specifically mentions its rhyme, and printed among his letters under the date 20 May 1915.

**wish me luck** *Duck* (to dodge, or escape). American, Pacific Coast. Recorded by Maurer and Baker, 1944.

**woolly west** *Breast or chest.* 20 C. Thus glossed by Chicago May, 1928, meaning, probably, that the term may be applied to either sex.

**worry and strife** *Wife.* An alternative form of TROUBLE AND . . . Recorded by Len Ortzen in *Down Donkey Row*, 1938.

# Y

**yard of tripe** *Pipe* (tobacco). 19 C. Recorded by Henry Mayhew in *London Labour and the London Poor*. Now obsolete. See CHERRY RIPE.

**Yarmouth bloater** *A motor* (car). 20 C. Merely a contracted and less derisive form of TEA FOR TWO AND . . . (q.v.).

**Yorkshire tyke** *Mike* (microphone). Used by radio technicians and others connected with broadcasting. Evolved *c.* 1945.

**you and me** (1) *Tea,* (2) *pee* (urination). 19 C. (1) is still popular, probably on account of its friendly inference. (2) is Australian, also *pea.*

**you know** *Snow* (cocaine). 20 C. American, Pacific Coast. Recorded by Maurer and Baker, 1944.

**you must** *Crust* (of bread). 20 C. This is very little used, except to children.

**yours and hours** *Flowers,* but is merely a mis-hearing and consequent mis-spelling. The Cockney who, on the stage and in literature, drops every 'h', in real life uses many an intrusive one. 'Yours and ours' (q.v.) would normally be pronounced *Yawsenas* —asked to elucidate, any Cockney would fall into the intrusive 'h'.

**yours and ours** *Flowers.* 20 C. The term is employed chiefly by Covent Garden porters and street-vendors of flowers.

# ADDENDA

*Additional Abbreviations*

| | |
|---|---|
| * | precedes a term which has been recorded in the Glossary. |
| B.S. | indicates a term employed by A. K. Brice's father (or grandfather) before 1945. |
| B-RAF | indicates a term acquired by Mr Brice while in the Royal Air Force. |
| B | indicates a term used by Mr Brice between the wars. |
| B-ES | indicates terms acquired by Mr Brice senior while working at Ealing Studios. |

*Dict. Am. Und. Lingo: Dictionary of American Underworld Lingo*, by H. E. Goldin (and others).

## A

**Abergavenny** *Penny*. 20 C., but probably not before 1918. It is uncommon, and may be regarded as obsolescent, if not as quite obsolete.

***Adam and Eve** (2) *Leave*. The implication is a hurried departure. Printed in *The Evening Despatch* (Birmingham), 19 July 1937.

**alderman's eyes** *Flies* (house flies). 19 C. The term was current during the last decade of 19 C. and is now seldom heard. (B.S.)

**Alderman's nail** *Tail* (particularly dog's). 19 C. Reduced to *Alderman*: 'Does he wag his Alderman then?' or, when not addressing the dog himself, 'Happy as a dog with two Aldermen.' (B.S.)

***Allacompain** A sweetmeat so called was obtainable in the 19 C. but it is doubtful whether it was cheap enough to be indulged in at Cockney level, and it is not likely, therefore, to have influenced the term. See *Passionate Kensington*, Rachel Ferguson.

**Alma Gray** *Tray* (three). 20 C. a threepenny piece. Exclusively Australian, and recorded by Sidney J. Baker in *Australian Slang* (1942).

**anti-wank** *Anti-tank*. 20 C. The term was evolved in the Army during the second war. It was an adjectival phrase, for example, 'anti-wank gun'.

**'apenny dip** *Ship.* 19 C. Cockney and Merchant Navy usage. Appears to have been in currency as early as 1860; now obsolescent, but heard occasionally in Dockland.

**apple and pip** *Sip.* 20 C. (possibly 19 C.) to urinate. 'Sip' is backslang.

***apples and pairs** is an error for APPLES AND PEARS (q.v.).

**army tank(s)** *Yank(s).* Specifically American soldiers: used among prisoners of war in the Far East, 1942–5. Quoted by Sidney J. Baker in *Australia Speaks*, 1953, from an article in *The Sydney Sun*, 22 September 1945.

**artful fox** An alternative form of CHARLES JAMES (q.v.).

**Auntie Ella** *Umbrella.* 20 C. This term, which seems to have come into being since the second war, is used almost exclusively by women, at the suburban-Cockney level. Cockney working-class women do not seem to favour the use of umbrellas: men in that social stratum most certainly view them with contempt.

**Auntie Nellie** *Belly.* 20 C. Cockney, generally with reference to digestive disturbances: for example, 'No mate. I won't 'ave no more—me ole Auntie Nellie's playin' me up.'

**Aunt Maria** An alternative form of ANNA . . . (q.v.).

# B

**baby's cries** *Eyes.* 20 C., a rare alternative for MINCE (q.v.) recorded by A. Hyder, *Black Girl, White Lady*, 1934.

**ball and chain** *Jane.* This is not rhyming slang, although it is believed to be by its Cockney users. The rhyme is fortuitous, and the association occasioned by similarity of meaning, but the disparity in age makes it no true marriage. *Ball and chain* is old slang (early to mid-19 C.) for a woman to whom one is attached, particularly one's legal wife—from the fetters once used in Britain, and still used in the Southern and Western States of U.S.A. to secure convicts who work at road-mending. *Jane* is modern slang, being a general term for women and girls. It is a comparatively recent (*c.* 1930) import from U.S.A. to which country it travelled from Australia where now *a Sheila* has taken over its duties. Cf. old British *Judy*, which originated in the Army, and a *Party*, which is exclusive to the Navy.

***balloon car** was used in U.S.A. where it was not rhyming slang. It referred to a street-car having an oval body that swivelled round on a fixed undercarriage, thus reversing on a single track. It may not even have been slang: perhaps trade-jargon, or a technical term.

**Balmy Breeze** *Cheese.* 20 C. Seldom heard in England, but reported to have a moderate currency in New York.

**bark and growl** *Trowel.* 19 C. bricklayers, particularly those engaged on railway construction. D. W. Barrett, *Navvies*, 1880.

**Barney Dillon** An alternative form of JOHN DILLON (q.v.—addenda).

**barrel of fat** *Hat.* 20 C. Australian, and quite an apt phrase to describe an old and greasy one. (B.)

**bear's paw** *A saw.* 20 C. Used generally by workmen: not confined to any particular type of saw, or to any specific trade.

***Beecham's Pill** (3) *Dill* (a dupe or simpleton). Used in Australian underworld since about 1925. Quoted by Sidney J. Baker in *Australia Speaks*, 1953.

**Betty Lee** *Tea.* 20 C. Probably originally merely an altered form of ROSY LEA, but it was recorded with the *Lee* spelling by John Lardner in *Newsweek*, 21 November 1949.

**Billy (O') Gorman** *Foreman.* 19 C. This term was in use among the navvies and is recorded by D. W. Barrett (*Navvies*, 1880). It has fallen into disuse in Britain and has been lost sight of, but JERRY O'G. (q.v.) is likely to have been derived from it, and re-applied to its American, and subsequent British use. It might have been carried to the U.S.A. by Irish navvies.

**Billy Prescot** *Waistcoat.* 20 C., a variant of CHARLIE P . . . (q.v.). See also COLONEL P.

**biscuits and cheese** *Knees.* 20 C. Used in the Royal Air Force during the second war. 'Get off your biscuits.' (B-RAF.)

**bits and bats** *Knick-knacks.* 20 C. An underworld term, referring to assorted, not very valuable, pieces of jewellery.

**blackbird and thrush** *Brush.* 19 C., of which SONG OF THE . . . (q.v.) is an altered form, and possibly has a specialized application as this has: it is *to brush*, particularly one's boots; in which connection the *black* is important. Very little brown footwear was worn before 1914, hence any unfortunate child (generally schoolgirl) provided with brown shoes (shoes, too, were uncommon) and stockings was sure to attract attention from the street boys who called 'Dipped yeh leg in na musterd pot!' The term is recorded by D. W. Barrett in *Life and Work Among the Navvies* (1880).

***blue moon** is first recorded in *Life in St. George's Fields*, (1821) J. Burrows. This is rather early for rhyming slang.

**blue o'clock** *Two o'clock* (in the morning). 19 C., meaning very late at night, as in '. . . and I got to bed about blue o'clock'. Now obsolete, probably never very popular, and certainly not true rhyming slang.

**Bob Squash** *Wash.* 20 C. This is now an underworld term only, having reference to the lavatory division of a public convenience. A pickpocket is said to be 'working the Bob' when he specializes in removing wallets from the jackets of people washing their hands. (See also LEMON AND DASH.) During the 1914–18 war, used in the Army, it meant simply to wash oneself.

**boracic lint** *Skint* (penniless). 20 C. This term, which seems to be as recent as post-second war, is invariably reduced to *boracic* (pronounced *brassic*). 'No good to ask him—he's boracic.' (See also PINK . . .)

***bottle and glass** (2) Specialized in use by pickpockets in the phrase 'off the bottle' meaning a wallet removed from a rear trousers pocket. See also JEER.

**bottle of beer** *Ear.* 20 C. Generally used in a jocular setting. For example, 'Just a word in your bottle o' beer mate—I'm going 'ome—got to go to work in the morning.'

**bow and quiver,** see CHEERFUL GIVER.

**bread and honey** A rare alternative form of BEES AND (q.v.).

**bread and lard** *Hard.* 20 C. Cockney. Often used to express lack of sympathy. After listening to some tale of woe, the comment, 'Gor blimey! ain't that bread an' lard, eh?' means the complainant is held to be making an unnecessary fuss.

**brewer's bung** *Tongue.* 20 C. Uncommon, probably a Covent Garden porter's exclusive. (B.)

**bride and groom** (1) a *broom*, (2) a *room.* 19 C. An apt phrase since both a room and a broom are necessary to a bride and groom, but now obsolete.

**Brigg's rest,** alternative spelling of:

**Brig's rest** *A vest.* 20 C., used mostly by convicts to describe the rough woollen undergarment supplied to them—so irritant that it permits no rest.

**Brighton sands** *Hands.* 20 C. Seldom heard. Probably used more in the underworld than elsewhere.

***Brussels sprout** (2) In racing circles it is transferred to *a tout*, and that famous commentator upon Racing, who contributes to the Press under the pseudonym of 'The Scout', is referred to as 'The Brússel'. Communicated by Mr Clive Graham.

***bubble and squeak** (3) *Beak* (magistrate). See ONCE A WEEK, GARDEN GATE. (4) *Squeak.* To squeak is to inform, or betray, hence 'to put the bubble in'. (There may be a secondary rhyming quality between *squeak* and *speak*, the former being itself rhyming slang for the latter.)

**bucket and pail** *Jail.* 20 C. Cockney, but has its greatest currency among stevedores and other river-side workers.

**bug and flea** *Tea.* 20 C. Commonly used in the Army, particularly among Cockney troops, during the 1914–18 war. Now obsolete. Communicated by Mr S. A. Cleal.

**bull ants,** see BULL'S AUNTS.

**bully beef** (1) *Chief* (warder), 20 C. (2) *deaf.* (1) probably since 1920. Used by prisoners and 'old lags'. Given by Frank Norman in *Bang to Rights*, 1948. Cf. CHUNK OF . . . (2) is amusing, depending for rhyme on a Scottish accent, *deef.* Probably from Glasgow, mid-20 C.

***burnt cinder** In the underworld often reduced to *burnt.* 'A stiff burnt' is a plate-glass window.

**butter and beer** An erroneous form of:

**bottle of . . .** (q.v.).

## C

***candle-sconce** In the underworld it is inclined to be reduced to *Candle*.

**can of oil** *Boil* (septic focus). 20 C. Generally condensed to 'canov': as ' 'e's gorra lovely canov on 'e's nick, ain' 'e?'

***Cape of Good Hope** may be heard in the reduced form 'Cape' particularly in the underworld.

**Captain Running-board** *Captain Ford* (waterfront ephemeral). A dock superintendent. A 'running-board' is not, as one might expect, the 'door-step' of a motor-car; it is a wooden platform used in erecting staging for working: particularly in the meat-ships, where the hind- and fore-quarters have to be run up to vans awaiting loading.

**car park** *Nark* (informer). Mid-20 C., but accept with caution. It emerged during an argument between two 'informants' following an enquiry concerning the correct form of GRASS IN THE PARK. One said it was the same as *grass park*, the other that it meant 'snake in the grass'. 'Waow, wazza diffruns?' 'Diffruns! Bloimey! 'Ere—ahr-baht caw-pawk?' 'Ain't tawkin' abaht it.'

**cash and carried** *Married*. 20 C. A degenerative form of CUT AND . . . (q.v.). The inference is more mundane than romantic. It originated early in the second war, when U.S.A. offered to supply munitions on a cash and carry basis.

**cattle truck** *F——*. 20 C. Always reduced to Cattle(d) and used in all senses of the unprintable except, perhaps, violent expletive. The workman who hits his thumb with a hammer doesn't fool around with euphemisms: if only moderately irritated he might say: 'I rec'on the bloke wot designed this 'ere engine ought to get cattled', or, 'I backed a winner wot came in nowhere and I was prop'ly cattled', and, of course, 'H'm—wouldn't moind cattling *'er*.'

***cellar flap:** sense (1) sometimes reduced to *Cellar*.

**chain and crank** *Bank*. 20 C. This term would be very apt had it been influenced by 'the machinery of finance', but such a rationalization is totally unjustified. It is not very popular. See IRON . . .

**Charlie Frisky** *Whisky*. 19 C. The term, contemporary with I'M SO . . . (q.v.), seems to have been used by workmen. It is now obsolete.

**Charlie Hunt** is a rare alternative form of JOE HUNT (q.v.). It is not popular because in truncation it is apt to mislead: 'That bloke's a Charley!' might be mistaken for CHARLEY RONCE (q.v.).

**Charlie Randy** *Brandy*. 19 C. In the 19 C. spirits were cheap, and labouring men often indulged: the stimulant may have been beneficial when long hours and prodigious exertion were normal. D. W. Barrett, *Navvies* (1880).

**cheap and nasty** *A pasty.* 20 C. Australian. See Eric Partridge, *Supplement* to *A Dictionary of Slang* . . .

**cheerful giver** *Liver.* 20 C. This term, which is now obsolescent, was from *c.* 1930–40 very popular among the Covent Garden Market porters who, in a loud and semi-sing-song tone would retort, 'The Lord loves a Cheerful Giver!' when a foreman, or other official, displayed irritability. They would refer to the condition when in conversation as 'bow and quiver'. For example, 'The gaffer's got a bow and quiver this morning, ain't he—eh?'

***china plate** (2) *Mate.* Occasionally used in the Merchant Navy with reference to the First Officer. See also HARRY TATE.

**chitney pace** *The face.* American usage only. Quoted by 'Convict 1269' in *Detective Fiction Weekly*, April 1938.

**chow** *A cow.* 20 C. Australian. It does not refer to cattle, but to people of either sex, and to inanimate objects or conditions that are unpleasing or unfavourable. When specialistically applied to a Chinaman (a usage also Australian) it may have some connection with Chinese food which is popular there.

**cob-o'-coal** *Dole.* 20 C. Since 'the dole' has been promoted to 'National Unemployment Insurance Benefit', the term has fallen into disuse. See BEGGAR MY . . .

**coffee stalls** *Balls.* 20 C. Less common than ORCHESTRA STALLS (q.v.) and apparently used in full. (B.)

**coke frame** *Dame* (woman). 20 C. The term is unknown in England, but is reported from New York.

**come a clover** *Tumble over.* 20 C. Communicated by Mr S. A. Cleal who first heard it in 1925, from a relation who served with a London regiment in the 1914–18 war, hence it is reasonable to assume it was then in use. It is now unknown.

**Cousin Sis** (on the) *Piss* (on the). 20 C. To be engaged on a drinking bout. Recorded by Gerald Kersh, *The Nine Lives of Bill Nelson* (1942).

**cow's lick** *Nick(er)* (£1). This is an underworld term, and seems to be rhyming slang; the final 'er' of *nicker* might easily be abandoned in order to force a rhyme.

**Crimea** *Beer.* 19 C. Used chiefly in the Army, and obsolete before 1914.

**crowded space** *Suitcase.* An underworld term. Very appropriate since suitcases 'lifted' from railway stations during the holiday-season are generally very tightly packed, and the station is a most crowded space.

# D

**Daily Distress** *Daily Express.* 20 C. From about 1930 and now obsolescent. All newspapers received nicknames at that period largely because they were behaving in an undignified manner, but not all of the names were rhyming slang: for example, *The Crocodile* for *The Chronicle*.

**Daily Growl** *Daily Mail.* 20 C. This, with most of the other nicknames for daily papers, was evolved about 1930 (see above). In Cockney dialect 'mail' and 'growl' are phonetically very close together. The term is now obsolescent.

***Daily Mail(s)** (4) *Nail(s).* 20 C. Used by joiners, and by 'rough carpenters' in the building trade. (B.S.)

**Daily Wail** *Daily Mail.* 20 C. This seems to be among the older nicknames for this paper—it may even have been its first *c.* 1910.

***daisy beaters** *Creepers* (the feet). 19 C. This is probably the original rhyme which, although poor, is superior to 'feet'.

***Darby and Joan** (2) *'Phone.* 20 C. (See MAGGIE . . ., SWITCH AND . . .) This usage is uncommon: 'the blower' ante-dates the electro-telephone, and is still paramount.

**Darky Cox** *A box.* 20 C. It refers to a box at the theatre, but it is rarely heard even in the theatrical world.

**Davy Crockett** *Pocket.* 20 C., evolved *c.* 1956 in the theatrical profession. Not in general use. See also SKY . . .

**Davy Large** *A barge* (waterfront ephemeral). Davy Large was a dock-worker employed by Scruttons Ltd., 'Stevedores and Master Porters'. He later became a Trade Union Official.

**dibs and dabs** *Crabs* (crab-lice). 20 C. See also BEATTIE . . .

**Dicky Diaper** *Linendraper.* 19 C. Now obsolete. It was, in the late 19 C., a very appropriate example of rhyming slang. In those days women and girls were modest, and such articles were not advertised blatantly as they now are: further, it was to the Linendraper, not the 'Chemist', that purchasers went. The rhyme is better than it appears to be. Cockney pronunciation is 'dryper'.

**Dicky dirk** *A shirt.* So spelt, probably a misprint, in *Detective Fiction Weekly*, April 1938. See DICKY DIRT.

***dickory dock** (2) *Cock* (penis). In this sense perhaps not before 20 C. It may, too, be formative of juvenile 'dicky', the penis. See also DICKY DIDDLE.

**didn't ought ter** (did not ought to) *Water.* Late 19 C., had some minor currency during the first decade of 20 C., but was a 1914–18 war casualty—has not been heard of since. See also DIDN'T OUGHT.

**ding dong bell** *Hell.* 20 C. This term was popular in the R.A.F. during the second war: 'What the ding dong bell does he think he's playing at?' (B-RAF.)

**dink** *Chink* (a Chinaman). 20 C. Australian. There seems to be a tendency for modern Australian rhyming slang to abandon the rhythm and employ one-word rhymes.

**dirty daughter** *Water.* 20 C.,

popular with the troops during the 1914–18 war but now obsolescent. In so far as it is still employed, it is by old soldiers only, and particularly when fighting their battles over again which, in spite of the second war, they still do.

**do as you like** *Bike.* 20 C. (See also MAD . . ., PADDY . . .) It is often the boast of ostentatious youth—'I can do as I like on this 'ere ole' grid—you watch me!' He will then perform acrobatic feats that, merely to witness, almost induces a heart attack in sober age.

***do me good** is sometimes used by carpenters and other workmen for wood (timber).

**do my dags** *Fags.* 19 C. The phrase lived on into the 20 C., but became obsolete before 1925. *Do my dags* itself, meaning 'copy my tricks', or 'follow my lead' in a game, became obsolete about that time.

**Doctor Crippen** *Dripping.* 20 C. (*c.* 1910). It referred to edible dripping, the gravy-impregnated fusible fat from meat, which Cockneys regarded as not only something of a delicacy when spread on bread and more particularly on toast, but as a means of effecting economy in housekeeping. Before 1914 the big West End restaurants would give dripping (and also giblets) to people calling at the kitchen entrance.

**dog and bone** *'Phone.* 20 C. This term seems to have been evolved since the second war, probably partly due to the increase in the number of telephones installed.

**Dona Highland Flingers** *Music Hall singers.* 19 C. Generally of a serio-comic singer—obsolete. Given by J. Redding Ware in *Passing English.*

**door-knob** *Bob* (a shilling). 19 C., now obsolete.

**dot and carried** *Married.* 19 C. This phrase was in use during the last quarter of the 19 C., but before the end of the first quarter of 20 C. CUT AND . . . (q.v.) had taken its place. The change may have been influenced by the two strip-cartoon typists, Dot (Dorothy)—she was the one who could spell—and Carry (Caroline). These ladies began their newspaper career during the 1914–18 war. Later, Aubrey the office-boy (who showed a marked preference for Dot), was thrown in for good measure. In non-rhyming slang 'dot and carry one' is a term of reference to a person who walks with a limp.

**Dublin tricks** *Bricks.* 19 C. Used particularly by bricklayers engaged on railway construction. D. W. Barrett, *Life and Work Among the Navvies* (1880). Many bricklayers' labourers were Irishmen.

**Duchess of Fife** *Wife.* 19 C. Invariably reduced to *Dutch* (my old Dutch). It was the inspiration for Albert Chevalier's song of that title and is by that immortalized.

**dustbin lid(s)** *Kid(s)* (children). 20 C. This term is inclined to be used when the children have created a formidable amount of litter.

# E

**earwig** *Twig*. 20 C. Not in use before the 1914–18 war, and probably then influenced by a popular song, *Twiggy-vous?* which was taken over from Kipling, *Stalkey & Co.* To 'twig', to understand, was in use in 18 C.

**eau de Cologne** *The 'phone*. 20 C. This term reduced to 'Eau de', and pronounced Odour, is used almost exclusively in racing circles. Communicated by Mr Clive Graham.

**Elkie Clark,** see L. K. CLARK.

**engineer's spanner** *Tanner* (sixpence). 20 C., probably since 1930. Used chiefly in the Merchant Navy.

**Enoch Arden** *Garden*. 20 C. Used by Australian prisoners of war in the Far East; recorded in *The Sun* (Sydney newspaper), 22 September 1945, quoted by Sidney J. Baker in *Australia Speaks*, 1953.

**Errol Flynn** *Chin* (particularly in the sense of 'on the chin', to take punishment), the term is used in the underworld, and especially in prison. It cannot have been evolved much before, say, 1938; and by 1950 it was falling into disuse. It was probably suggested by the 'tough guy' parts Errol Flynn played in his films.

**eyes of blue** *True*. Never employed without the prefixed *Two*, hence q.v.

# F

**family tree, the** *Lavatory*. 20 C. (before 1939), used in the armed forces and now obsolete. Recorded in *A Dictionary of Forces Slang 1939–1945* (published 1948), Partridge, Granville and Roberts.

**feather plucker** *F——er*. 20 C. City of London business man's term to describe a person he does not like or trust. See PHEASANT PLUCKER.

**fellow feeling** *Ceiling*. 19 C., now obsolete.

***finger and thumb** (3) *Chum*. An uncommon usage, generally jocular.

**fire-alarms** *Arms*. 20 C. Current in the Army and having reference to one's upper limbs, and to 'small arms' (rifles). In this latter sense it is rather appropriate. It should be noted, for the enlightenment of the young, that before the second war objects known as Fire Alarms were to be seen at frequent intervals along the streets of the Metropolis. By their means a direct call was transmitted to the nearest Fire Station. The abolition of these safety devices on the assumption that everyone has a telephone may be as much a cause of the frequent loss of life from fire since the war, as is the increased use of oil heating stoves.

***five to two(s)** (2) *Shoes*. 20 C. This use of the term might be expected to enjoy a far greater currency than it actually does, since shoes have become the general footwear, almost entirely replacing boots, as worn before 1914; nevertheless, the old term DAISY ROOTS (q.v.) holds its own and, strangely enough, includes shoes.

**fleas (-) and (-) itchers** *Pictures* (the Cinema). 20 C. (since 1945). Australian Juvenile. (Pronounce *Pitchers*.) Recorded in *Australia Speaks*, 1953, Sidney J. Baker.

**flour mixer** *Shixa* (a non-Jewish girl). 20 C. This is an interesting example of rhyming slang employed by Cockney Jews. The English phrase has a Yiddish meaning. This process in reverse—a Yiddish phrase having an English meaning—is not uncommon. See MOZZLE AND BROCHA. The rhyme seems to be simply a rhyme with no reference to the housewifely function: it may even be *Flower*, which again probably has no reference to either domestic art, or to menstruation.

**fly-by-night** *Tight* (drunk). 20 C. This term, which is now obsolete, was in use in the Army during the 1914–18 war. See also ELEPHANT'S . . .

**fourpenny pit** *Fourpenny bit.* 19 C., recorded in *Passing English* by J. Redding Ware, but to classify it as rhyming slang is to pay it a compliment—it is merely slovenly pronunciation. The suggestion that it was a true term based on the fact that the entrance fee to the pit of a Music Hall was fourpence is unacceptable: the groat (4d. piece) was then out of circulation.

***France and Spain** London taxi drivers reduce it to Frarney.

**frisk and frolic** *Carbolic.* This term which is late 19 C. to early 20 C. is now obsolescent. Up to the 1914–18 war, 'Carbolic' (not Phenol, but a semi-viscous black liquor that turned white in water) was a 'line' successfully hawked by the itinerant vendor who poured pennyworths from a large stone jar. In these days of 'Pine'—of antibiotics and questionable synthetics, so crude a disinfectant—in spite of its pleasant, clean, tarry smell—would be scorned. Recorded by A. J. Brooker in *The Tablet*, 12 March 1960.

**frock and frill** (1) *chill*, (2) *ill.* The 'chill' referred to is the common cold. (2) is seldom if ever applied to a case of serious illness, but only to minor megrims to which excuses for a restful day the term BEECHAM'S PILL (q.v.) is sometimes applied.

***frog and toad** In the American underworld 'on the heel and toe' refers to running. It is exemplified as follows in *Dict. Am. Und. Lingo*: 'Old Jim was slow on the heel and toe (running) so he hit the deck and the bull (policeman) thought he popped (shot) him and stayed hot on my tail (pursuing me) . . .'

**frog-skin** *Sov'rin* (£1). 19 C. Australian in both origin and use. Now quite forgotten as rhyming slang, but as a naturalized American it means a dollar bill.

**frying pans** *Hands.* 20 C. The upper extremities—not workers, or assistants. 'Git yeh fryin' pans aht o' yeh pockets!' *Pans* and *Hands* are a true rhyme in Cockney, the latter being pronounced *'an's*. The term is now obsolescent.

**Fulham and Chelsea** *Mr Kelsey* (waterfront ephemeral). A foreman in the docks: it was invariably reduced to 'Fulham', and clearly influenced by the titles of football teams.

***full as an egg** is general slang for exceedingly drunk. One in that condition is inclined to fall and make no effort to rise. A person shot through the head does likewise, and that seems to be the sole association.

**fusilier** *Beer*. 19 C. Used in the Army, and obsolete by 1914.

## G

**Gah-damn** *Jam*. 19 C., now obsolete. It may be spelt *Gor* or *Gaw*, and is the Cockney rendering of God. It is most commonly met preceding *blimey*, when it may also take the forms *caw* and *coo*.

***garden gate** (2) *Mate*. 20 C. Merchant Navy, but of infrequent occurrence, with reference to the First Officer. See also HARRY TATE. (3) *Eight*. A 20 C. development employed chiefly in the underworld.

**gasp and grunt** An alternative form of GRUMBLE AND . . . (q.v.).

**gay and hearty** *A party*. 20 C. The term is descriptive of what such a social gathering should be, and generally is, without becoming 'wild'; but see also DING-DONG.

**George the Third** An occasional alternative for RICHARD THE THIRD (q.v.).

***ginger pop,** occurs in *Tottie*, a Dagonet Ballad, by George R. Sims and was printed in *The Referee*, 7 November 1887.

**Glasgow Rangers** *Strangers*. 20 C. Used by the look-out men to pass the warning that people whom they suspect of being plain-clothes policemen are present at a mock-auction, or any of the various modern versions of thimble-rigging, such as picking out the packet containing a petrol-lighter wrapped in a pound-note.

**glass of beer** *Ear*. 20 C. Generally jocular: 'I must whisper in your glass of beer', means the speaker must retire to urinate. It arises from a Victorian smoking-room story. A little boy, having said 'in company', 'Mama, I want to wee-wee', was scolded, and ordered to say under those circumstances, in future, 'I want to whisper.' Some time later, when in charge of a maiden aunt, the circumstances arose—'Do you? Well, whisper in my ear, dear,' said the lady, bending down.

**goddamus** *Mandamus* (a writ of). 20 C. American underworld. Perhaps not quite admissible as rhyming slang, but a border-line case that seems to merit the benefit of the doubt. Such a writ is probably of fairly common occurrence in U.S.A. due to State autonomy: in Britain it would be difficult to find an underworld character who had so much as heard the word.

**golliwogs, the** *Dogs, the.* i.e. Greyhound Races. ''e done 'is dough on da gollies!'—he lost his money on the dog-racing track.

***goose and duck** (2) *Truck.* 20 C. This use (and no other) is occasionally employed by dock-workers.

**goose's neck** *Cheque.* 20 C. Does not seem to ante-date 1950. Employed by Cockneys and often reduced to goose's: 'Can you sausage me a goose's?' Can you cash a cheque for me?

**Gor-damn** Alternative spelling of *Gah-damn* (q.v.).

**gowler** *Howler.* 19 C., now obsolete. It was always applied to a dog that howled—not to a human baby equally proficient in the art of annoying the neighbours.

**grasp and grunt** An alternative form of GRUMBLE AND . . . (q.v.).

***grasshopper** Doubt of the authenticity of this term on the assumption that the insect is beyond Cockney ken is ill-founded. The creature figures in London legend: Gresham's grasshopper is as familiar as Whittington's cat.

**grass in the park** *Nark* (informer). 20 C. Reduced to 'grass', it has as much likelihood of being in the mind of a speaker as has GRASSHOPPER (q.v.), although the latter is the older term. On Friday, 16 December 1960, the following appeared in *The Evening News* and is reprinted here by kind permission of the Editor: 'The origin of the criminals' slang term "To Grass" (it means to inform upon) was discussed at Middlesex Sessions today. "Rhyming slang for Grasshopper, tell a copper," said Mr R. J. Lowry, counsel. The Chairman, the Hon. Ewen Montagu, Q.C. disagreed: "From 'whispering grass'," he suggested.' From this, one might conclude that the Hon. Ewen Montagu's judgement was false though poetic: he is, however, too shrewd a judge to make an injudicious pronouncement; too sound a seaman to get under way without an anchor.

His remark was prefaced with the words, 'I've always been brought up in the tradition that it came . . .' In a private letter (23 December 1960) he says: 'In my younger days at the Bar, that was the derivation of which I was told by Police of all ranks . . . I have a vague recollection of a popular [Music Hall?] song which brought in "whispering grass" . . . "someone's been whispering—someone's grassed".'

**grass park** A contracted form of the previous entry (q.v.) and see also CAR PARK.

**groan and grunt** An alternative form of GRUMBLE AND . . . (q.v.).

**growl and grunt** An alternative form of GRUMBLE AND . . . (q.v.).

**Gunga Din** *Gin.* 20 C. Australian, generally in combination 'Gunga Din and Squatter's daughter', Gin and water. (B.)

## H

**half stamp** *A tramp.* 20 C. An underworld term. The world of tramps and the underworld overlap, but are not the same thing.

**ham shank** *Yank.* 20 C. about 1943. Employed in the Merchant Navy in relation to both American ships and men. Communicated by Charles Bowness. By 1944 the Americans had themselves adopted it, and grafted it on to the New York collection.

**hammer and nail** *Tail* or *Trail* (to follow). 20 C. An underworld term, generally shortened to 'hammer'. 'I hammered him all the way down Oxford Street, and when he went down the gents for a strain-off I got his frog and feather off the bottle!'

***Hampstead Heath**—often reduced to *'amps.*

**Handley Page** *The Stage.* 20 C. Mainly theatrical, and hardly likely to have been in use before the 1914–18 war.

**ha'penny dip** *Ship.* 20 C. This term is current in the Docks, and among other waterfront workers. It arises from the old London back-street sweetstuff shops' custom of organizing a bran-tub on Saturdays. (The 'bran' was invariably sawdust, as used on the shop floor during wet weather.)

**Hardwicke Grange** *Change* (waterfront ephemeral). Name of a ship carrying cargo from Argentina to Tidal Basin, Victoria Docks. Owners—Furness-Houlden. She was in service up to at least the second war. All ships of this line end their names in 'Grange': *Royston Grange*: *Dunster Grange.*

**Harry Nash** *Cash* (waterfront ephemeral). Harry Nash was, strangely enough, actually a çashier by profession in the employ of Scruttons Ltd., 'Stevedores and Master Porters'.

***Harry Randall** Rachel Ferguson, in *Passionate Kensington* (1939), says:
' "And to dear old Harry Randall
No one else can hold a candle"
is a line from a fellow comedian that I carry away with me from about 1909; while Musical Comedies of *The Dairymaid* vintage were often billed [at the *Coronet Theatre*, Notting Hill Gate].'

***Harry Tate** *Mate.* (First Officer) employed in the Merchant Navy, and never applied to a second (or lesser) officer. Communicated by Charles Bowness, who first heard it in 1941.

**has beens** *Greens* (vegetables). 20 C. The term is employed by convicts, and seems itself to be a prisoner since it is not used elsewhere.

**heap of saucepan lids** See SAUCEPAN . . .

**hearth-rug(s)** (1) *Bug(s)*, (2) *Mug(s)*. 20 C. This term, which is now obsolescent, never was so popular as STEAM-TUGS (q.v.).

**heaven** *Seven* or *Eleven.* A good example of a one-word rhyme. It is used by dice-gamblers only—the score is possible with not less than a two-dice throw.

**heavens above** *Love.* 20 C. Cockney, often used in a semi-derisive setting: for example, with reference to 'a bull and cow' (q.v.).

**Hector pecking** *Necking* (making love). 20 C. This term is reported from U.S.A. but does not seem to be known in England.

**helter-skelter** *Air-Raid Shelter*. 20 C. but obsolete with the need to run helter-skelter to an air-raid shelter. Recorded in *New Statesman*, 30 August 1941.

**Henry Meville** *Devil*. 19 C. '. . . what the Henry Meville
Do you think you're doing there?'
from *Tottie*, a Dagonet Ballad by George R. Sims, printed in *The Referee*, 7 November 1887.

**hens and bitches** *Bends and hitches*. 20 C. Used chiefly among R.N.V.R. men during the 1914–18 war. To some few people the making of correct 'knots'—that is, in naval parlance, bends and hitches—'comes natural-like' after their having been shown how once. To others the process remains forever a scatter of hens and a barking of bitches. It will be observed that the phrase is an imperfect Spoonerism originating, probably, from a perfect specimen, hen*d*s and bitches. Recorded by Gordon S. Maxwell in *The Motor Launch Patrol*, 1920.

***here and there** (2) *Hair*. Australian usage.

**hickey(-)hockey** *A jockey*. 20 C. Australian racing slang since about 1920. Recorded by Lawson Glassop in *Lucky Palmer*, 1949.

**high as a kite** *Tight* (drunk). 20 C. A rhyming slang rationalization of the word which was first recorded as a term for intoxication in 1627 (May, *Lucan*—O.E.D.). The word fell into desuetude in England but survived in the U.S.A. It was re-imported towards the end of the 19 C., and converted into rhyming slang before 1914.

***high-stepper** Not American origin. Current in the Army 1914–18. Recorded in *A Dictionary of Forces Slang*, Partridge, Granville and Roberts.

**hill and dale, the** *Tale, the*. 20 C. This is one of a number of terms all referring to 'the tale' as told by con-men, professional scroungers, and others in, or on the fringe of the underworld. This (and others) recorded by Jim Phelan in *The Underworld*, 1953. See also BINNIE . . . DAILY . . . and SHIP.

**hock** *Cock*. 20 C. usage is largely confined to the underworld. The reference is to the active member in a homosexual relationship.

**hod lot** *A Police-patrol car*. This is an unusual form in which the first, not the last word, makes the rhyme: *hod* rhymes with 'Squad', and the reference is to the Flying Squad. 'Lot' is the usual British underworld term for a car, and is equivalent to the American term 'heap' (i.e. a heap of junk). The term does not seem to have been in use when the Flying Squad, led by Inspector Sharpe, was something of a novelty—see SWEENY TODD—but to have been evolved about 1950.

**holy nail** *Bail*. 20 C. This term is employed by thieves and other underworld characters in whose lives the subject of legal bail is one of paramount importance. See also ROYAL MAIL.

**hopping-pot** *The lot* (all). 20 C. It generally precedes a list that ends with 'the lot!' as 'So they charges 'im with the hoppin'-pot: causing obstruction on the carriage-way, causing obstruction to foot-passengers, trading without a licence, resisting the police—the lot!'

**hot and cold** *Gold*. 20 C. There may be a reference here to 'hot', recently stolen hence, avidly sought after by the police.

# I

***if and and** may refer to the metallic clatter made by a tinsmith, hence appropriate to describe a modern 'band': from, 'If "ifs" and "ands" [correctly, "an's"] were pots and pans, there'd be no work for the tinkers to do.'

**I'll be there** *A chair*. 20 C. This term is underworld, or semi-underworld. Cf. I DON'T CARE.

***in and out** (4) *Tout* (bookmaker's). 20 C. vide Eric Partridge, *Dict. Slang. Addenda*.

**Irish rose** *Nose*. 20 C. An alternative form of RUBY . . . (q.v.) but rather less popular.

**iron-hoop** *Soup*. 20 C., now obsolete. Iron-hoops (and indeed all forms of hoops) have, with the increase of motor-traffic, become impossible toys to use in the streets, and they always were frowned upon by adults in parks.

# J

**jack-up** *Pack-up* (to finish, to depart). 19 C. First recorded by D. W. Barrett, *Life and Work Among the Navvies* (1880).

**Jamaica,** see OLD JAMAICA.

***Jane Shore** Mr A. J. Brooker, in a letter, says: 'Ed. VI's mistress, and the notorious heroine of a barnstorming play which kept her history well before the average Londoner, so that it was natural enough for her name to be adopted as the rhyming slang for a street-walker . . . nobody ever spelt Shoreditch, which London legend holds was so named because Jane's dead body was dredged out of it (*not* from Shore, a sewer) Shawditch.'

Mr Brewster, writing on the same matter, calls attention to *The Ingoldsby Legends*:

'While Louis Quatorze kept about him, in scores,
What the Noblesse, in courtesy, term'd his "Jane Shores",
—They were called by a much coarser name out-of-doors.'
(Second Series—*The Black Mousquetaire. A Legend of France.*)

This, however, does not invalidate the term's connection with the Navy.

**J. Arthur Rank** *Bank*. The term was evolved when Mr Rank was making both films and news. It is invariably employed in its reduced form. 'You may as well wait: 'e won't be long: 'e's gawn rahn na Jay Arfer!'

**jeer** An alternative spelling of:

**jere** *A queer* (homosexual male). Often mis-spelt *jeer*, but it is a 17 C. word defined as 'a turd'. In 18 and 19 C. it was showman's slang for the posteriors, but its 20 C. use is deliberate (not simply fortuitous) rhyming slang. In the combination 'off the jeer' (jere) *off the rear*, it is mid-20 C. pick-pocket's slang for a wallet removed from the victim's rear trousers pocket. See also BOTTLE AND GLASS.

**Jerusalem artichoke** *Moke* (donkey). Late 19 C. to early 20 C. Donkeys, who were well-cared for and never over-worked, were often named 'Jerusalem'. The term is now obsolete, and since a sane man can feel no love for a lorry, the coster's transport is no longer affectionately nicknamed, but on occasions of ill-timed breakdown it may be called anything except a van.

**Jim Brown** *Town*. 19 C. It probably referred to the West End of London, but is now obsolete.

**Jimmy** *Immi* (immigrant). Australian rhyming slang applied to a newcomer. Recorded by Sidney J. Baker in *The Drum*, 1959. See JIMMY GRANT.

***Jimmy Britts** was a boxer who flourished in early 20 C.

**Jimmy Grant** *An emigrant*. 19 C. The term, used in some respects exactly like a nickname, was applied to people about to 'go out to the Colonies'—particularly to Australia, to which country the term was carried and there inverted in its meaning and only the first element was retained. See JIMMY.

**Jimmy Rollocks** An alternative form of TOMMY . . . (q.v.).

***Joe Blake** (4) pluralized, to rhyme with 'snakes', it may be used for 'the D.T.s' (Delirium Tremens).

***Joe Rook(s)** *The books*, meaning the bookmakers, particularly those who attend meetings and set up their stand on the course.

**Joe Soap** *Dope* (a 'dopey', i.e. foolish, person). 20 C. Cockney, generally reduced to 'a Joey'. It was a very widely used term in the R.A.F. during the second war.

**John Dillon** *Shilling*. 20 C. Used in New Zealand, and not before *c*. 1930. From the name of a famous race-horse.

**Johnny Rann** Alternative form of TOMMY O'RANN (q.v.).

**Johnnie Rollocks** Alternative form of TOMMY . . . (q.v.).

**John Sperl** *File* (abrasive tool). 20 C. American underworld, given in *Dict. Am. Und. Lingo* by H. E. Goldin, but it may not be rhyming slang. It depends on the pronunciation *ferl* for 'file', and such a pronunciation, though Brooklynese in Britain, may not be in Brooklyn.

**Jonah's Whale** *Tail*. 19 C. Printed in *Tottie*, one of George R. Sims' Dagonet Ballads. *The Referee*, 7 November 1887.

**jug and pail** *Jail*. 20 C. The word 'jug', a prison, is not a reduced form of this term: on the other hand, the term may have been forged out of BUCKET AND

PAIL simply because 'jug' was a familiar word. It is from 'Fr[ench] *joug*, a yoke, via ob[solete] Scots *joug(s)*, a pillory'. (Partridge, *A Dictionary of Slang*, p. 446.)

**Jumbo's trunk** A once popular, but now rare, alternative for ELEPHANT'S . . . (q.v.). Jumbo was the name of an elephant at the London Zoo. When he was sold, in 1882, to the American Circus Master—Barnham—it was not only the Cockneys who raised a furious protest. The elephant was so popular that the Elephant and Castle Public House (Southwark, London, S.E.1) was often referred to as 'Jumbo'. Printed in *The Referee*, 7 November 1887, from *Tottie*, a Dagonet Ballad by George R. Sims.

## K

***kangaroo** (2) *Screw* (a prison warder). Current in the Australian underworld since about 1920. It is a one-word rhyme only superficially. Kangaroo is apprehended as a compound: Kangerroo, in relation to the species Walla-roo. Generally shortened to 'Kanga'.

***Kate Karney** was re-animated during the second war. 'He's in the Kate.'

**Kate and Sidney** *Steak and kidney* (pudding). 20 C. This term is hybrid between rhyming slang and a Spoonerism, but savours rather more of the former. The term, which was very common before (say) 1920, when it was everyday cook-shop slang, is less commonly used now that there are no cook-shops, and even our daily bread is Americanized; but it is not obsolete, and is still the most likely slang term for steak and kidney pudding, but as such good fare is now obtainable only in the home, the slang is not often to be heard.

**Kennington Lane** *Pain.* 20 C. There is many another Lane in London that would supply an adequate rhyme, but none would display the same wit of application. It is generally used in conjunction: 'A Kennington Lane in the Newington Butts', and that is topographically correct. Kennington Lane branches off to the right as one goes southward along Newington Butts, London, S.E.1. (That Kennington Lane has an 'upper' and a 'lower' is generally ignored, as is Bond Street's 'old' and 'new'.)

**Kentish Town** A rare alternative form of CAMDEN . . . (q.v.).

**kettle on the hob** (1) *Bob* (a shilling. (2) *Bob* (the diminutive of the masculine given-name Robert). 20 C. The term was current among the plasterers working at Ealing Studios (1946–52), (B-ES), but it is almost certainly a child of the first decade 20 C. This term does not really transgress the apparent rule that rhyming slang does not come into use for personal names: (2) is not really a second meaning, but is a jocular transposition. Both are normally reduced: 'Oi, Kettle! Gis za loan of a kettle, will yeh?'

**King Dick(s)** *Bricks*. 20 C. Used only in the building trade.

**King Dicky** *Bricky*. 20 C. A 'bricky' is, in the building trade, the name used for a bricklayer.

**King's Proctor** *Doctor*. 20 C. (possibly late 19 C.). Never popular, and now obsolescent.

**kitchen stoves** *Cloves*. 20 C. Australian, generally in combination: 'Tom Thumb and kitchen stoves', Rum and cloves. (B.) Both kitchen stoves and cloves are hot and black.

## L

**l.b.w.** (leg before wicket) *Ticket*. 20 C. Generally in the sense of 'That's the l.b.w.'—that's the ticket—something pleasing and satisfying, often of an unexpected character. (When the best batsman is out l.b.w. it is unexpected, and highly amusing and pleasing to the supporters of the opposing Cricket Club.)

**L. K. Clark** *Mark* (position). An underworld term implying a place (and time) of starting: 'We get off the L. K. at nine . . .' Mr Brice gives it as 'Elkie Clark', and has heard it used in the same sense in Glasgow.

**lace curtain** *Burton* (beer). 20 C. Since 1930 generally reduced to 'lace' and extended in meaning to include all beer and ale.

**Lal Brough** *Snuff*. 20 C. The term, which is uncommon, seems to have greater currency among female than male snuff-takers. In Holloway [women's] Prison, London, snuff is called *Lally*, and up to the time of the 1914–18 war, 'Lally' was sometimes used as a general nickname for an old woman: the inference was that elderly women were snuff-takers. (Lal, Lally, is a Cockney diminutive of the feminine given-name Alice.)

**Lancashire lasses** *Glasses* (spectacles). 20 C. This term is rarely used by Cockneys who have a rooted objection to pronouncing 'glasses' as rhyming with 'lasses': the latter remains as it is, the former becomes 'glawses'. In the singular—lass—it refers, with the same reservations, to a drinking glass.

**Land of Hope** An alternative form of CAPE OF GOOD . . . (q.v.).

***laugh and joke** 19 C. Recorded by D. W. Barrett, *Life and Work Among the Navvies* (1880).

**laughed and sang** *Slang* (particularly rhyming slang). This should be accepted with caution. It is not used by Cockneys. Though recorded in *Newsweek* (21 November 1949) which is generally reliable, this term does not seem to be well authenticated: it might have been the spontaneous creation of an 'informant'.

**left and right** An alternative form of READ AND WRITE (q.v.).

**lemon and dash** *Wash* (*c*. 1950). 'Wash', in this setting, does not refer to the act of ablution, but to the place: to the wash-room in a public convenience. It is a modern pickpocket's term—'Jack's doin' alright on the old lemon lark'—means that Jack is successfully picking the pockets of jackets hanging on the pegs provided in public wash-rooms. Cf. BOB SQUASH and LEMON SQUASH. Perhaps a key to some mysteries of semantics.

**lemon squash.** *Wash.* 20 C. This seems to have emerged about 1920, and to have had a vogue up to the second war, but it is now rarely, if ever, employed: it has, however, been revitalized in an altered form—LEMON AND DASH (q.v.).

**liffey water** *Porter.* 20 C. Before 1914, chiefly Irish in usage. Cf. the story of the famous Irish brewer who, accused of filling bottles with Liffey water replied, 'We make our beer with brains—not water.' The term is extended to mean any kind of beer.

***Lilley and Skinner** (2) *Beginner.* 20 C. Used throughout the retail trade, and referring to one learning to be a shop-assistant. (B.)

**Lincoln's Inn** (1) *Finn,* (2) *Fin,* (3) *Gin.* All three 19 C. (1) is early 19 C. racing slang for a £5 note, from *finnif,* ex *fümf,* Yiddish: (2) is less orthodox and refers to the hand (also sometimes called a flipper), as, ' 'Ullo! ole choina! Gis yeh Lincoln's Inn! Ain't seen yeh fer years!' (3) Had a growing popularity in the first decade of 20 C. but it lost ground under the impact of the song *Father O'Flinn* (see BRIAN O'LINN) and has never recovered.

***Little Bo-Peep** is an alternative form of BO-PEEP (q.v.) but the term is seldom so prefixed.

**Little Grey Home in the West** *Vest.* 20 C. This term, now obsolete, was very common among the troops at the time of the 1914–18 war. It was the title of a popular song which was itself parodied to 'Little grey louse (or flea) in my vest'.

**loop the loop** *Soup.* 20 C. The term may be influenced by a late 19 C. exhibition of daring in which a performer, strapped to a wheel, whizzed round on a coiled track. The description is also applied to acrobatic aeronautics, in which the machine is flown through a similar intorsion.

**Lord Russell** Alternative form of LORD JOHN . . . (q.v.).

**lump of school** *A fool.* 19 C. Compulsory education (such as it was) was not popular when it was introduced. The coster's idea was that the sooner a boy gained practical experience out with the barrow in the market the better, and that going to school and getting 'book-learning' dulled the natural wits. There might be something in it.

# M

***Mac Gimp** In *Dic. Am. Und. Lingo* it is defined as *pimp,* but no reference is made to its rhyming quality. Emphasis is laid on its reduced form 'Mac', with a note, 'this word is often prefixed to any fictitious name . . . as MacGimp, MacGluke, Mackife, Mackoozey'. It is rarely used in Britain, but when it is, the reduction to 'Mac' is very much inclined to be again lengthened to *Mackerel* or even to *Macaroni*.

***MacIntire and Heath** were not dentists. They were what the Americans call 'a Vaudeville team' and the British style, 'a Music Hall turn'. In *The Old Time Saloon* (1931) George Ade says: 'It was Tom Heath . . . who was chased out of the Irish [Saloon] on St Patrick's Day because he ate the shamrocks on the bar, thinking they were watercress. He always insisted that they were very good with mustard.'

***Major Loder** from Major Eustace Loder (b. 1867), owner of the famous racehorse Pretty Polly who won twenty-two races out of the twenty-four which she entered, and on the two occasions of failure was a very close second. (I am indebted to W. P. J. Flood-Murphy—a veritable encyclopaedia of the turf—for this information.)

**Manchester City** *Titty*. 20 C. An alternative form (later?) of BRISTOL . . . (q.v.).

**Mary-Lou** *Blue*, but always in the phrase 'bet on the Mary Lou' (bet on the blue). Australian racing slang for 'to bet on credit', blue or black indicating credit, red indicating debit. 20 C., perhaps about 1920. Recorded by Lawson Glassop in *Lucky Palmer* (1949).

**merry-go-round** *Pound*. 20 C. One pound sterling. Cockney usage. Possibly influenced by the oft repeated adage, 'money was made round to go round'—which is a kind of conscience salve when spending heavily.

**Mick O'Dwyer** *Fire*. 20 C. An uncommon variant of ANNA MARIA (q.v.).

**Micky Bliss** An alternative form of the next:

**Mike Bliss** *Piss* (to urinate). 20 C., hence to deflate the bladder, thus 'to take the Mike (or the Micky) out of . . .', to deflate (or humiliate), also 'to take the piss out of . . .', to insult.

**milk jug** *Mug* (a dupe or simpleton). Current in the Australian underworld since about 1920. Often reduced to *Milkie*. Recorded by Sidney J. Baker in *Australia Speaks*, 1953.

**milkman's horse** *Cross* (angry). 20 C. A mild form of warning used mostly by mothers to children, for example: 'If I 'ave to tell yeh agin I'll git milkman's awce I will, so stop it when yeh told!'

***mince pies** is sometimes reduced to *mincers*.

**Miss Fitch** *Bitch*. 20 C. Referring, not to the female of the *canine* race, but to the more aggressive, disagreeable, spiteful and unpleasant females of the *homo sapiens* race.

**mogadored** *Floored* (beaten). 20 C. This should be accepted with caution. Mogador (or mogadored) is a word that seems to have sprung into being during the 1920s without antecedents. If its only meaning was 'floored' it might be rhyming slang of waterfront origin, based on the name of a ship, but more often it means deceived, confused, bewildered, puzzled. Examples: 'By the time he'd downed a couple of I'm sos, and swallowed my rabbit with it, I'd got him properly mogadored and he parted with a quid!' or: 'Coo blimey, I don't know. He's told me one yarn, and she's told me the opposite. It's got me properly mogadored. I don't know what to think.'

**monkey's tail(s)** *Nail(s)* (ironmongery). 20 C. Current among the carpenters and joiners, and other workmen at Ealing Studios (1935–9). (B-ES.)

**Moody and Sankey** *Hanky-panky* (itself slang for the handkerchief, with which the conjurer employing the quick hand deceives an observing eye). As rhyming slang it is applied specially to verbal legerdemain, and invariably reduced to *Moody*. 'Don't try that old Moody on me—I know all the answers!' Communicated by F. A. Allen, Esq.

**Moreton Bay fig** *Gig* (short for fizz-gig). An informer. Current in the Australian underworld since about 1940—communicated to Sidney J. Baker by an ex-prisoner, quoted in *Australia Speaks*, 1953. Often reduced to 'Moreton Bay'.

***mother and daughter** (2) *Quarter*-(post) (which is itself usually abbreviated to 'quarter'). Probably 19 C., but certainly before 1914. Used by Thames watermen with reference to the posts along London's river frontage at which a tug, a lighter, or other craft may be tied up.

**Mozart and Liszt** *Pissed* (intoxicated). Generally shortened to Mozart. Communicated by Mr Clive Graham. Perhaps the B.B.C. is responsible in part, for those who had heard of Mozart and Liszt did not use rhyming slang, and those who did use it had not heard of them before radio took culture down the Borough, and broadcast rhyming slang to Mayfair. See SCOTCH, ELEPHANTS.

**mud-in-the-eye** *Tie* (necktie). 20 C. Recorded in *The New Statesman*, 29 November 1941, as rhyming slang with this meaning, now obsolete; but as one of the convivial and meaningless 'toasts' that topers utter out of habit it existed long before that date, and is still extant.

**mumble and thumb** *Rum*. Recorded in the *Weekly Telegraph*, 6 April 1946, but almost certainly an error. See THIMBLE AND . . . also FINGER AND . . .

**mutton flaps** *Japs* (Japanese prisoners of war). Used by Australian servicemen in the Far East, 1942–5, and subsequently by Australian civilians with reference to any Japanese. Quoted by Sidney J. Baker in *Australia Speaks*, 1953.

# N

**Naughton and Gold** *Cold* (inflammation of the mucous membrane). 20 C. 'Caw bloimey—I got anuvver bleedin' Naughton and Gold a-comin'!' From the famous Music Hall artists.

**Navasota** *Motor*(car). (Waterfront ephemeral.) Name of a refrigerated meat ship (between Argentina and London—see *Hardwicke Grange*). Owners—Royal Mail Line.

**Nellie Duff** *Puff* (life). 20 C. Always in the setting: 'Not on your Nellie Duff!' (or 'Your Nellie': or 'Your Nell'). The term was printed in *The New Statesman*, 30 August 1941, when it was about ten years old. It seems to have been imported from U.S.A.

**Nervo and Knox** *Socks*. 20 C. Not in general use; probably more popular in the theatrical world than elsewhere. Formed on the names of the well-known entertainers.

**Newton Heath** *Teeth*. A local (Manchester) form of HAMPSTEAD . . . (q.v.).

**nine-shillings** *Nonchalance*. 19 C. This is given, without comment, by Farmer and Henley in *Slang and Its Analogues*. It is now totally obsolete, and the word 'nonchalance' is not one likely to be rendered in rhyming slang, since it is quite beyond the vocabulary of the average user of rhyming slang.

***Noah's Ark** (3) *Dark*. It must have been—very! There were no portholes; however, this usage is rare. (4) *Lark* (fun). 19 C. Printed in *The Referee*, 7 November 1887, from *Tottie*, a Dagonet Ballad, by George R. Sims.

**no soap** *No hope*. It is claimed that *no soap*, the American slang term meaning 'no transaction will take place', is rhyming slang: 'there is *no hope* of a transaction'. Well, it does rhyme, so it might be.

# O

**odour**, see EAU DE . . .

**okey-doke** *A poke* (wallet). 20 C. This is an underworld term, generally reduced to 'okey', as: 'Yeh—I done the lemon squashes and got four okeys.' From O.K.

**old bag** *Old hag*. 19 C. Generally applied to an elderly and ill-conditioned prostitute, but may refer to a comparatively young one, or even to a non-prostitute who is unpopular.

**Old Jamaica Rum** *The sun*. 19 C. Employed only in the Navy and now obsolescent. Invariably reduced to 'the old Jamaica'.

***old King Cole** In recent times the 'old' tends to be replaced with 'Nat', from the name of the popular vocalist, Nat King Cole. In usage it becomes 'on the Nat'.

**one and eight** *A plate*. 20 C. This term is seldom used, but may have greater currency in the underworld, than in other spheres.

**one for his knob** *Bob*. 20 C. This term is used by street traders as (when possible) part of their 'cry'—it helps to attract attention, and to be an amusing fellow influences sales.

***orinoko(er)** (2) *Tobacco*. This term for tobacco was in Cockney use as far back as 1703 (see Partridge, *A Dictionary of Slang* . . .). The date makes it either a fortuitous rhyme, or a forerunner, indicating the Cockney tendency. There is, however, a sounder reason for this second entry than an extra meaning and an earlier date.

Both Mr A. J. Brooker, and Mr H. A. Jones (Principal of the City Literary Institute) call attention to the blind spot displayed in the first edition. 'Orinoko' is a misspelling of *Oroonoko: or, The Royal Slave. A true history* by (Mrs) Alphra Behn (1688). This novel in its ninth edition suffered a spelling change, becoming 'Oronooko' (1759). In that year, too, the stage version by Thomas Southerne (first produced at Drury Lane in 1696), was altered by Hawkesworth, and it ran till 1829.

Mr Jones says: 'Truncated and mutilated versions . . . were done at Penny Gaffs . . . in the early 19 C. and were very popular since the tragic leading role was "a part to tear a cat in".'

There can be no doubt that Cockneys were very familiar with the word, hence its inclusion in early rhyming slang.

## P

**Paddy Rammer** *A hammer*. 20 C. Used by workmen, never very popular, now obsolescent, but printed in *John o' London's Weekly*, 9 June 1934.

**panorama** *A hammer*. 19 C. Particularly a navvy's hammer. The term has not survived; and strangely enough there seems to be no strongly established rhyming slang for a hammer.

**pen'orth o' bread** *Head*. 19 C., now obsolete. See CRUST, LOAF.

**penny-come-quick** *Trick*. 19 C. In its chief usage it referred to a confidence trick and was appropriate: a successful confidence trick caused a penny (money) to come quick. In its extension it referred to any trick—a conjuring trick, a balancing trick. It is now obsolete.

**peppermint rocks** *Socks*. 20 C. An alternative form of ALMOND . . . (q.v.).

**pheasant plucker** *Pleasant f——er*. 20 C. Primarily a Spoonerism, it is, perhaps, not fully admitted to the status of rhyming slang, but in its altered form—FEATHER PLUCKER (q.v.) it qualifies. It is generally (if not always) intended to be reversed in meaning as well as its form: 'You are [or he *is*] a pheasant plucker, I *must* say!' means—you are, or he is, a very unpleasant person.

**pickled pork** *Talk*. 20 C. Recorded in *The Evening Despatch* (Birmingham), 19 July 1937. Uncommon in London. Cf. RABBIT . . .

**pie and one** *Son*. 20 C. Seldom heard, and probably applicable also to 'sun'. See BATH BUN, etc.

**pie(s)** *Eye(s)*. 20 C. American listed by Wentworth and Flexner, but its inclusion is an act of generosity since it has no individual existence, being merely *mince*, or *kidney pies* reduced in the wrong direction.

***pig's ear** is defined as 'an unlicensed liquor store' by H. W.

Shoemaker in *Thirteen Hundred Old Time Words* (1930), all of which survived in Pennsylvania at the time of his publication.

**pimple and wart** (1) *Quart*, (2) *Port* (wine). This term, which had a run of popular usage among public-house frequenters in the early years of 20 C. is now virtually obsolete in both senses.

**pineapple chunk** *Bunk*. 20 C. Before 1914, and still current. Used by merchant seamen, particularly Cockneys, and largely on the P. & O. Line. Generally reduced to *pineapple*. From the tinned variety of the fruit cut into cubes measuring about an inch. Communicated by Charles Bowness.

**pink lint** *Skint* (penniless). 20 C. This term is particularly favoured in racing circles, where to be 'pink lint' at the conclusion of a race meeting is not a matter so rare as to excite comment. Communicated by Mr Clive Graham. (See also BORACIC . . .)

**plain and gravy** *The Navy*. 20 C. An alternative form of SOUP AND . . . (q.v.). The 'plain' referred to is plain (as distinct from plum) dough (duff): in short, a Norfolk dumpling.

**plain and jam** *Tram*(car). 20 C. (See also BAA-LAMB, BREAD AND . . ., JAM-JAR, JAR OF . . .) The 'plain' refers to plain suet roll, a slice of which, with jam, was a popular cook-shop 'after'.

**plasterer's trowel** *A fowl*. 19 C. Obsolescent, but heard occasionally. J. Redding Ware, in *Passing English*, gives 'Plasterer's trowel and seringapatam' for 'fowl and ham'.

***plate(s) of meat** In the U.S.A. underworld the term is applied to the *street*: an interesting transposition.

**plink plonk** *Vin Blanc*. 20 C. This term had a vogue during the 1914–18 war, and was particularly favoured by Australian troops. It may be related to the term 'dirty water', a general slang term for alcoholic beverages. 'Plonk' was a 1914–18 term for mud—perhaps suggested by the noise made when shovelling it out of a trench, or when walking in it.

**Polly Flinder(s)** *Window(s)*. 20 C. before 1914. During the first war it was a favourite with the troops, and seemed to have replaced BURNT CINDER but the latter has come into its own again, and the former is seldom used.

**polone** *Pony*. Circus and theatrical. In the latter, a similar word, not rhyming slang, *paloney*, means 'a girl'. Cf. Spanish *paloma*, a dove. In Standard English, *polony*—a sausage of semi-cooked pork. Communicated by Charles Bowness.

**post and rail** *Fairy tale* (a lie). 20 C. Australian. Sidney J. Baker who places it on record dates it *c*. 1910.

**potash and perlmutter** *Butter*. 20 C. This in common with other rhymes on 'butter', is generally applied to bread and butter. The late W. Macqueen Pope told me that the play (*Potash and Perlmutter*) which came from U.S.A.—author: Montague Glass

—was first produced in London at *The Queen's Theatre*, Shaftesbury Avenue, on 14 April 1914. The play was a huge success and the term may have come into use even before 1915. It is now obsolescent.

**potato-peeling** (pronounce '*tater pillin*) *Shilling*. 20 C. Not a very popular term, and seldom used except in the greengrocery trade.

**pot of honey** *Money*. 20 C. Alternative form of BEES AND . . . (q.v.). In its reduced form it becomes *honey* (not pot), but the reduced form of BEES AND . . . is invariably *bees*.

**pound of lead** (often reduced to 'pound') is an alternative form of LUMP OF LEAD (q.v.).

**powdered chalk** *Walk*. 20 C. (See also PENN'ORTH, BALL OF . . .) Generally in the sense 'to take a walk', to go away. Mr F. C. Wright is of the opinion that the American expression 'take a powder' is derived from a diminutive but Eric Partridge gives (*Dict. of Slang*, p. 655) 'Powder. To rush: Coll[oquial] and dial[ect] . . . ex the rapid explosiveness of [gun]-powder.' This usage can be traced back to 1632. There is no justification for the assumption that 'he took a powder' suggests an aperient powder, hence the rapid departure.

**press and scratch** An alternative form of CUTS AND . . . (q.v.).

**pudding and gravy** *Navy*. 20 C. Applied only to the Royal Navy. It is the modern development of SOUP AND GRAVY (q.v.).

***puff and dart** (2) *Heart*. 19 C. 'Heart' is the earliest meaning dating from about 1860. Recorded in *Old-Soldier Sahib*, Frank Richards, 1936.

## Q

**Queen's Park Ranger(s)** *Stranger(s)*. 20 C. From the Cup-contending Association Football Team. Its use ranges from a proud father's announcement that the baby has arrived, to an underworld warning that restraint in conversation is indicated.

## R

**rabbit's paw** *Jaw* (talk). 20 C. Recorded by Frank Norman in *Stand On Me* (1959). It can hardly be described as an alternative form of RABBIT AND PORK (q.v.) because the rhyming element is so very different, notwithstanding that the meaning is the same and the first word is the same, hence when reduced to 'Rabbit', the hearer does not know which phrase the speaker has in mind. It might be correct to describe 'Rabbit's paw' as a version of 'Rabbit and Pork'.

**raffle and crank** *Bank*. This seems to be a ghost term containing the spook of *rattle and clank*, and *chain and crank*. The off-spring of faulty hearing, slovenly speaking, and Raffles the gentleman burglar.

**Ranjitiki** *Tricky* (waterfront

ephemeral). Name of a ship owned by The New Zealand Shipping Co. She was (is?) a refrigerated meat boat and had hold-room for a cargo of wool. Her London berth was No. 33 Shed, Royal Albert Dock.

**Rajputana** *Banana* (waterfront ephemeral). Name of a ship carrying general cargo between London (King George V Dock) and the Far East. She was in service up to at least the second war. Owners: P. & O.

**Rank, J. Arthur,** see J. ARTHUR.

***rat and mouse** (2) *Louse.* This is an occasional usage in the underworld where it has reference to a person—generally an informer.

**ratcatcher's daughter** is a rare variant of FISHERMAN'S . . . (q.v.).

**rattle and clank** *Bank.* 20 C. Suggestive of the busy handling of many coins, hence more descriptive of the pre-wages day banking scene before 1914 when gold coinage was in circulation.

**raughty** *Naughty* (troublesome). 20 C. Apparently of naval origin, and having reference to a quarrelsome person—one who seeks to fight when drunk. It is also used in the Army. Cockneys use the word 'raught', either for a quarrel, or a vociferous complaint.

**Rawalpindi** *Windy* (waterfront ephemeral). Name of a P. & O. general-cargo ship: King George V Dock to the Far East. She was afloat up to at least the second war.

***Richard the Third** (2) *Turd,* it is, however, seldom employed in this sense, and even less frequently as (3) *word.*

**ridgy-dite** *All right.* 20 C. Australian usage. Recorded by Kylie Tennant, in *The Joyful Condemned,* 1953, quoted by Eric Partridge in *Dictionary of Slang,* 6th Edn. supp.

**rip-rap** *Tap* (to borrow money). 20 C. Generally in the sense 'on the rip-rap'.

**roach and dace** *Face.* 20 C. This is rare, and may be used only by those 'sportsmen' who go fishing.

**Robert E. Lee** *Quay.* 20 C. Current among dock workers and Cockney seamen. It is unlikely to have been imported 'solo' from the U.S.A., but has probably been 'lifted' from the song of American origin:

'Waiting on the levee,
. . . I said on the levee,
Waiting for the Robert E. Lee.'

which had reference, not to the historic character, but to a pleasure boat named after him. The song was 'popular' in Britain *c.* 1910.

**rollick** *Ballock.* 20 C. This barely qualifies as rhyming slang. Were it an anatomical expression only it would be merely a euphemism, as *ruddy* is for 'bloody' (see p. 1): it has, however, a second meaning—to Rollick (or to ballock) is to reprimand: to give (or get) a rollicking, hence the term may have some small claim to inclusion: particularly as rude boys often retort 'Rollicks!' when subjected to a rollicking.

**rolling billow(s)** *Pillow(s)*. 19 C. This term, which was commonly used by workmen in 19 C. is now virtually obsolete, but some of the older Covent Garden porters claim to know it, and they assert it is still employed in Boro' Market. (The Borough Market, Southwark, London, S.E.1, handles chiefly potatoes.)

**Rotten Row** *Bow*. 19 C. Recorded in *Passing English*, by J. Redding Ware. Bow is an East London district. The term is now obsolete.

**row-de-dow** *A row* (riot). Irish. Printed in *The Referee*, 9 March 1895. J. Redding Ware, in *Passing English*, says it is derived from the chorus of *The British Grenadiers*.

***Roy Sleuce:** the name may be spelt *Sluys*.

**Royal Mail** *Bail*. 20 C. An underworld term in frequent use, but seldom heard outside thieves' society. See also HOLY NAIL.

***Russian duck** (2) *f*—— (coitus). The term, which had become obsolescent with meaning (1), seems to be experiencing a renaissance with this one.

**Russian-Turk** *Work*. 19 C. The term was employed to describe the particular undertaking on which the workman was engaged, not, apparently, his activity. For example, a bricklayer was on the Russian-Turk at (say) Kentish Town, but his occupation was that of a 'bricky'.

# S

**sailors on the sea** *Tea*. 20 C. Uncommon, possibly local. Mr K. S. Brice says (letter 11 November 1960): '. . . heard during 1958 while in hospital at Barnet. All the patients were from Finchley and Southgate area, but I had never before heard it: one would say, "I'll be glad when the sailors comes round" and at length I had to display my ignorance by asking, "Who are the sailors?" Had it not been that I had myself used *you and me* all my life I would have put two and two together, I expect!'

**Salford Docks** *Rocks*. 20 C. A term used in the Merchant Navy and by coastwise sailors. Probably both originated and popularized by men from Manchester. Salford is on the Ship Canal.

**Sam Cory** *A story* (waterfront ephemeral). Sam Cory was a dock-worker employed by Scruttons Ltd., 'Stevedores and Master Porters'.

***Sammy Hall** Mr A. J. Brooker says in *The Tablet* (12 March 1960) '. . . another actor, Ross, [was] the original Sam Hall the Chimneysweep . . . "Sam Hall, and I hates ye one and all" with its cursing chorus was based on the lugubrious old ballad of Captain Kidd, as he sailed, as he sailed . . .'

***Sandy MacNab** (2) *Scab* (an objectionable person, particularly an untrustworthy one—an informer). 20 C. Australian underworld. Recorded by Sidney J. Baker in *Australia Speaks*, 1953.

***saucepan lids, heap of** *Dibs, heap of*. 19 C. Plenty of money.

**sausage and mash** (1) *Cash*, (2) *crash or smash* (a collision). (1) is 19 C., *c.* 1870 and in its reduced form, 'a sausage', has spread so far and so wide that the majority of people who declare '. . . and I hadn't a sausage!', meaning 'I was without money', are unaware that it is truncated rhyming slang. (2) is of mid-20 C. —contemporary—and is not yet fully established. First heard in August 1959 used by a taxi-driver, it has been tried on others of that brotherhood, and only about half of those interrogated claimed knowledge of it.

**Sausage Roll** *A Pole*. 20 C. London's underworld is at present (mid-1960) suffering from an influx of Polish thieves who are employing new techniques in picking pockets. The matter is often under discussion, and conversation is thickly studded with reference to 'them blee'n' Sausage Rolls . . .' It seems they employ a nasty foreign method which the underworld cannot regard as honest thieving.

**Saveloy** *Boy*. 20 C. Cockney. The term seems to be employed to describe the juvenile male, rather than the adult crony, but see SAN TOY, etc. Saveloys are a form of ready cooked sausages, and a favourite Cockney relish.

**Scotch mist** *Pissed* (intoxicated). 20 C. A very appropriate term of recent origin, but one not strong enough to uproot ELEPHANTS (q.v.).

***seldom see** B.V.D. is the 'Nation-wide' trade mark of the most popular American brand of *masculine* underclothing. It is sometimes printed as *Beeveedee*.

**Seringapatam** *Ham*. 19 C. now obsolete. Mentioned by J. Redding Ware in *Passing English*.

**sham** (or **shaun**) **spadah** *Motor*(car). 20 C. Evolved since 1918, never very popular, and now obsolete. Probably from *Spad*, a single-seat biplane, being the initial letters of *S*ociété *P*our *A*viation et ses *D*érivés (see Eric Partridge, *Dictionary of Slang*, p. 804). On the other hand it might be a London waterfront term formed on the name of a ship.

***short of a sheet** may be one of America's importations from Australia, in which country there is a term 'short of a sheet of Bark'. In England it is sometimes used to mean mentally dull.

**shovel and tank** *Bank*. 20 C. The term is not so unconnected as it seems. Before 1914, when gold coinage was handled, every bank-teller was supplied with a 'shovel'. The few that survive are symbols rather than tools.

**silver spoon** *Hoon* (a procurer). Hoon is an old-established term in the Australian underworld, where the rhyming slang equivalent, which is of more recent origin, is also employed. Recorded by Sidney J. Baker in *Australia Speaks*, 1953.

***sky the wipe** Mr A. J. Brooker, writing in *The Tablet*

(12 March 1960), says, 'What a pity that the vivid Australian "sky the wipe", or throw in the towel, should be Americanized to do duty as rhyming slang for a hype, or hypodermic syringe.'

**slither and dodge** *Lodge.* Early 20 C. (perhaps late 19 C.). The Lodge referred to is a local branch of a Friendly Society. It is frequently reduced to *slither.* Printed in *The New Statesman,* 29 November 1941.

**smoked haddock** *The Paddock.* Used only in racing circles, and always in full. Communicated by Mr Clive Graham.

**soaks** *Folks.* 20 C. A convivial rhyme on 'soak', a drunkard. The potman, at closing time, if absolutely certain that only cronies and regulars are present, might shout 'Time—please—soaks'—instead of 'gentlemen'.

**soap and lather** *Father.* 20 C. This is far less likely to be heard than is OLD POT . . . (q.v.).

***song of the thrush**: first recorded by Rev. D. W. Barrett in *Life and Work Among the Navvies* (1880), see also BLACKBIRD AND . . .

**South of France** *Dance.* 20 C. The term is applied to both the social function of 'a dance', and the physical action (? artistic expression) of dancing.

**spit and drag** *Fag.* 20 C. Often '*a* spit and *a* drag'; it generally refers to the act of smoking rather than the cigarettes, and very often to clandestine smoking: ' 'Ere, use yeh loaf old choina, I'm goin' rahn' ne 'ay stack fer a spit 'n' a drag.' The rhyming quality of the phrase is obscured when it is rendered, 'a spit and a draw'.

**squabbling bleeder** *Squadron Leader.* A humorous and friendly term of reference used in the R.A.F. during the second war. (B-RAF.)

**Squad, halt** *Salt.* 19 C. The term was, and remains, exclusively military. It was not brought out into 'civvy street' after the 1914–18 war as so many other army terms were. Probably no one had happy recollections of squad-drill.

**squatter's daughter** *Water.* 20 C. The Australian form of FISHERMAN'S (q.v.).

**stand and freeze** *Stand at ease.* 20 C. (? late 19 C.). Obviously military in both origin and use. It was flourishing during the 1914–18 war, but seems to have expired, leaving no trace, before the second war. The motorization of the army might account for the loss, foot-drill having shrunk in importance.

**stand to attention** *Pension.* 20 C. (but perhaps late 19 C.). Probably of military origin, and having reference to a time-serving (retired) soldier's pension. It is not employed to describe the Welfare State's Old Age Pension.

**star's nap** *Tap* (to 'borrow'). Theatrical. The connection is vague but not quite invisible: *stars* leading actors, *nap* (q.v.) a slap.

**stone jug** *Mug* (a fool). 19 C., less popular than STEAM TUG (q.v.). Cf. MILK JUG.

**sweet pea** *Tea.* 20 C. Recorded in *Newsweek,* 21 November 1949, but it is not a popular form. See YOU AND ME.

# T

**'tater pillin**, see POTATO.

**taxicabs** *Crabs* (crablice). 20 C. Recorded by Frank Norman in *Stand on Me,* 1959. See also BEATTIE AND . . .

**tea grout** *Boy Scout.* See BRUSSELS . . . which is the more popular phrase. *Grout* is a S.E. word meaning 'grain' but it is descending towards slang. Tea, or coffee grouts means the residue after the infusion is used. Tea-leaves. Coffee grounds.

**teddy bear** *Lair* (a flashily dressed youth, perhaps derived from *Larrikin,* also Australian). Used in Australian underworld from about 1930. Communicated by Sidney J. Baker, and recorded in *Australia Speaks,* 1953.

**tent peg(s)** *Egg(s).* 19 C. Originally tramps' slang, and as such recorded by Jim Phelan in *We Follow the Roads* (1949); it has crept in 20 C. upward into Cockney usage, but is not frequently heard.

**that and this** *Piss* (to urinate). 20 C. 'Keep your mince on my pig's. I'm going round the haystack for a that and this.' Cf. MRS CHANT.

**thirty-first of May** *Gay* (a simpleton or dupe). Australian underworld since about 1925. Recorded by Sidney J. Baker in *Australia Speaks,* 1953.

***this and that** (3) To *Bat* (in the game of Cricket). There is no evidence of its use as a noun—'Whose bat will you carry when you go in to this and that?' Mid-20 C. London street boys.

**threepenny bits** (1) *Shits* (diarrhoea), (2) *Tits* (breasts). 20 C. (1) More likely to be used in the abstract than in the physical sense, as 'Gah blimey! That feller giz me na frupnees 'e do—waie 'e tawks.' (He irritates me by his affected accent—or foolish conversation.) Cockney. Cf. JIMMY BRITTS. (2) Not very popular. See TALE OF . . .

**tickle your fancy** *Nancy* (homosexual). This is a modern term, evolved since the second war, and used in polite society—not in the underworld. (B.)

**to-and-from** *Pom,* short for *Pommie,* an Englishman. Used by Australians (1942–5) in relation to English servicemen, particularly in prisoner-of-war camps in the Far East. Recorded by Sidney J. Baker in *Australia Speaks* (1953).

**tom cat** *Door-mat.* 20 C. Communicated by Wilfred Granville, author of *Sea Slang,* in a private letter dated 21 March 1960: 'I heard "tom cat" as rhyming slang for door-mat, in the following phrase: "Wipe yeh feet on the ol' tom cat an' come right inside." '

***Tom Mix** (2) *Fix* (difficulties). This sense is comparatively new—since 1945. ' 'E won't 'arf git 'isself in a right old Tom Mix wiv that tongue of 'is!' (Mr K. S.

Brice dates this use to a date before the second war.)

**Tommy get out, and let your father in** *Gin.* 19 C. This long and cumbersome phrase, first recorded by D. W. Barrett (*Navvies,* 1880), was probably never very popular. It was contemporaneous with BRIAN O'LINN (q.v.) which he spells *Lin.*

**Tommy Rollocks** *Ballocks* (testicles). Current during the last quarter of the 19 C. and still in use. Generally in the setting: 'Kick up the . . .'

**Tommy Tripe** *Pipe.* According to Farmer and Henley to 'pipe' is to observe, or notice. 'Tommy his plates'—observe (look at) his feet.

**Tom Sawyer** *A lawyer.* 20 C. Cockney. It may refer to a professional lawyer, but is more likely to be applied to a 'sea-lawyer'.

***Tom Tug** (3) *Bug.* Mr A. J. Brooker in *The Tablet* (12 March 1960) says: 'Tom Tug, the jolly young waterman appears in rhyming slang in a sense . . . indicating a wingless insect of the genus *Cimex,* which came over with William the Dutchman with gin and other evils.'

**tracy-bit(s)** *Tit(s)* (female breast(s)). Current in the Australian underworld since about 1920. Communicated to Sidney J. Baker by an ex-prisoner, recorded in *Australia Speaks,* 1953.

**trams** *Gams* (legs). 20 C. This term is underworld and semi-underworld. The word 'gams' for legs, originally cant, has risen to the status of low-slang, but it is not yet employed in even moderately polite society. (Its use in U.S.A. seems a trifle more respectable than in Britain.)

**tray-bit(s)** A debased form of TRACY-BITS (q.v.).

**two eyes of blue** *Too true* (emphatically or unpleasantly true). 20 C. 'Two eyes of blue it is, mate!' London street boys before the second war, and by them bestowed upon the R.A.F.

## U

**Uncle Bert** *Shirt.* 20 C. An uncommon alternative for DINKY . . . (q.v.) but probably having a greater currency in the underworld than elsewhere.

***Uncle Willy** (2) *Chilly* (cold). In use among Cockneys before the second war, and current in the R.A.F.

## V

**Vanity Fair** *Chair.* 19 C. Communicated by Mr K. S. Brice who heard it from his father who, in turn, *may* have heard it from his own: if he did so, it puts the date at mid-19 C.

***Victor Trumper** The word 'bumper' may be an altered form of *dumper,* an old-established Durham term for a cigarette-end.

# W

**Walter Joyce** *Voice.* 19 C. Printed in *The Referee*, 7 November 1887 from *Tottie*, a Dagonet Ballad by George R. Sims.

**Wanstead Flats** *Spats.* 20 C. (early). An alternative form of THIS(ES) (q.v.). Wanstead Flats is a district in North East London, not, as it may appear to be, a modern building. The term went out of vogue with the article.

**warrior(s) bold** *Cold* or *a Cold.* Apparently an alternative form of SOLDIER BOLD (q.v.). Submitted by R. A. Hadrill, Esq., who came upon it (*c.* 1955) in a Turkish bath where it was used by all the attendants with reference to the plunge pool. They in turn had picked it up from a bookmaker.

**West Ham Reserves** *Nerves.* 20 C. Derived from the 'West Ham' unit in the Association Football industry. Generally reduced to 'West Hams': example, 'Waitin' abaht 'ere gits on my West Hams it do, straight.'

**whip, the old** *Ship.* 19 C. This term was exclusive to the Navy where it was employed as early as 1887. Men on shore leave, gathered in a pub reminded each other that it was 'time to get back to the old whip'. It referred only to one's own ship.

**whistle and toot** *Loot* (money). 20 C. Very seldom heard in full, and one of the few examples of the retention of the rhyming word in the shortened form: *Toot*, money, is very commonly used.

**white mice,** *Lice.* 20 C. Used only in Australia. White mice will run up their owner's sleeve—or up anyone else's. K. S. Pritchard, *Kiss on the Lips* (1932).

***Wilkie Bard:** in the racing world it refers to the racecard.

**William Powell** *A towel.* 20 C. This is a term used by convicts, and is seldom heard outside of a prison. (W.P., a film actor.)

**Willy Lee(s)** *Flea(s).* 20 C. Recorded in *Australia Speaks* by Sidney J. Baker, 1953.

**windjammer** *Hammer.* 20 C. Current in Ealing Studios 1935–9. Mr K. S. Brice who submits this, suggests that the workman mentioned on p. 26 was using an altered form of his own making.

**wooden pegs** Alternative for either SCOTCH PEGS (q.v.) or DUTCH PEGS (q.v.).

**wooden shoes** *Jews.* This is barely admissible as rhyming slang. It was a political street-cry during the passage of 'The Jew Bill' (mid-18th century).

> No Jews!
> No wooden shoes!

There is no evidence that it survived the agitation of the period, and it was in all probability 'manufactured' by the agitators—not a specimen of extemporary slang.

**Woolwich and Greenwich** *Spinach* (a green vegetable, *Spinacia Oleracea* of the order *Chenopodiaceae*). 20 C. From *The Times Educational Supplement*, 25 March 1960: 'A Putney greengrocer sold the present reviewer a pound of Woolwich and Greenwich in 1938.'

BIRD LIME
IS NOT ON
OUR SIDE,
HENRY
TOO IRISH STEW,
CYRIL, TOO
IRISH

# Y

**yellow plaster** *Alabaster.* 19 C. The term can be traced back to 1870 when it was in frequent use by monumental masons. Now obsolete.

**yellow silk** *Milk.* 19 C. This term is seldom heard now that the big combines have swallowed the small milkmen, but in the late 19th and early 20th century, the Cockney roundsmen employed by the Welsh dairymen not only used the term, but supplied the commodity by the yard. One yard equalled an imperial pint. Substitution of this kind is a Cockney form of humour: pence are often quoted as pounds.

**yet to be** *Free.* 20 C. generally meaning without cost—a part of the good time coming: but sometimes without restraint, or even release from prison.

**Yid** *Quid* (£1). 20 C. Australian, recorded in Dal Steven's novel *Jimmy Brockett*, 1951.

**Yiddisha fiddle** *Diddle.* 19 C. (minor form of cheating, or of acquisition). Invariably reduced to *fiddle*, and very commonly used over a wide social range.

This is offered as a suggestion only, and should be accepted (if at all) with caution. Eric Partridge, *Dictionary of Slang*, p. 272, gives, '2. to cheat: C. 17–20; S.E. until *c.* 1800, revived by the underworld *c.* 1840. Mayhew.—3. Hence, to make a living from small jobs done on the street.' Its revival in 1840 might be attributable to rhyming influence: its earlier usage could not have been. See also JERRY DIDDLE.

**you and me** (3) *Flea.* 19 C. This sense was familiar to Mr K. S. Brice's father *c.* 1900.

# LIST OF MEANINGS

(INCLUDING ADDENDA)

THE word with which a rhyming slang phrase rhymes is its meaning, thus : *stairs*. The most important phrase for this is 'apples and pears', but those of less note are also given at the same references.

In some cases, however, the meaning out of context is either meaningless or ambiguous. *Spruce*, to many people, refers only to a species of fir tree; hence to assist the searcher such an entry is 'translated', listed in its own alphabetical order, and distinguished by being placed in brackets thus : (deception). There is no phrase that rhymes with 'deception'.

This system is not carried to excess. The word *kid* for example is not translated to (child) but it is entered at (deception).

The same process is involved when a meaning is followed by page numbers both in and out of brackets. Those out of brackets refer to phrases that rhyme with the word, those in brackets to phrases that rhyme with its analogues.

NOTE: The headings on page 183, on page 185, and the top of page 187, as well as that on page 191, are those given to the pieces by their respective authors. The others are my own classifications, and the author's titles appear at the ends of the paragraphs.

# EXAMPLES

Doss Chiderdoss (A. R. Marshall), the 'Pote' of the '*Pink 'Un*', produced, every week, something between a half and a whole column in verse, of wit, wisdom and caustic comment on current affairs. The ability to do that (even without lapsing into rhyming slang) is enough to make a man immortal. Neither 'Doss Chiderdoss' nor the *Pink 'Un* should ever fade from public memory.

*29 October 1892*

## THE RHYME OF THE RUSHER

### (In Appropriate Rhyming Slanguage)

I was out one night on the strict teetote,
'Cause I couldn't afford a drain;
I was wearing a leaky I'm afloat,
And it started to France and Spain.
But a toff was mixed in a bull and cow,
And I helped him to do a bunk;
He had been on the I'm so tap, and now
He was slightly Elephant's Trunk.

He offered to stand me a booze, so I
Took him round to 'The Mug's Retreat';
And my round the houses I tried to dry
By the Anna Maria's heat.
He stuck to the I'm so to drown his cares,
While I went for the far and near,
Until the clock on the apples and pears
Gave the office for us to clear.

Then round at the club we'd another bout,
And I fixed him at nap until
I had turned his skyrockets inside out,
And had managed my own to fill.
Of course I had gone on the half-ounce trick,
And we quarrelled and came to blows;

But I fired him out of the Rory quick,
And he fell on his I suppose.

And he laid there, weighing out prayers for me,
Without hearing the plates of meat
Of a slop who had pinched him for 'd. and d.'
And disturbing a peaceful beat.
And I smiled as I closed my two mince pies,
In my insect promenade;
For out of his nibs I had taken a rise,
And his stay on the spot was barred.

Next morning I brushed up my Barnet Fair,
And got myself up pretty smart,
Then I sallied forth with a careless air,
And contented Raspberry Tart.
At the first big pub I resolved if poss.,
That I'd sample my lucky star;
So I passed a flimsey on to the boss,
Who served drinks at the there you are.

He looked at the note, and the air began
With his language to pen and ink;
For the mug I'd fleeced had been his head man,
And had done him for lots of chink.
I'm blessed if my luck doesn't hum and ha,
For I argued the point with skill;
But the once a week made me go ta-ta
For a month on the can't keep still.

On 30 December 1893 he introduced a line or two terminating in rhyming slang into a Cockney 'poem' entitled 'A High Old Time'. May 19th in the following year finds him employing a refrain line, 'all harbour light' to a 'poem', so entitled which has a headnote addressed to 'Learned Judges, worthy Magistrates, and other innocents' who 'are informed that "all harbour light" is cabby's favourite rhyming slang for "all right"'. (It is sub-titled 'A lay of the Cab Strike'.)

In 'It's a Sad Heart that never Rejoices' Uncle, who threw a party (on 29 December 1894) '. . . squandered the tin, For the girls he had gallons of Brian O'Lynn'.

*Saturday, 4 September 1897*

## 'MEG'S DIVERSION'

### (A sonnet in Slang)

Now, a tear-drop fell from the girl's mince pie,
And her raspberry tart was torn
With anguish; for she had an empty sky,
And she'd nothing to bullock's horn.

But she cooled each mince with a little scent,
And her Barnet arranged with grace;
And then down the apples and pears she went
With a sorrowful Chevy Chase.

And she saw, as she passed her landlord's shed,
That the Rory he'd failed to close;
And the thought came into her loaf of bread,
Just to pop in her I suppose.

And she did and a quick glance round she flung,
The old pot and pan wasn't there;
But a piar of his round the houses hung
At the Anna Maria to air.

She said to herself, 'If they're decent stuff,
It's all harbour, I think they'll do;
I'll half-inch 'em—they're sure to fetch enough
To purchase a Brian or two!'

So she sleeved 'em under her velveteen;
And she hurried her plates once more
Round the Johnny Horner, to where she'd been
Just a birdlime or two before.

Addressing the cove behind the bazaar,
As she stood in the mashkin[1] box,
'How much on these round me's?' she asked him, far
From expecting that she'd get shocks.

But the bushel of coke said, 'Go away;
Why, the half of it's done a bunk.

[1] Obviously the cubicle provided by pawnbrokers to enable business to be transacted in privacy, but why?

**maskin** *Coal*: comparison with a coal-bunker as provided in the old type of 'Buildings' (Peabody); or, **muskin** *a person*. Hardly from **moosh** *the mouth*, and by extension, *the face*, hence to save one's face.

If I lend you on this, the boss will say
That I must be elephant's trunk.

'Your old pot and pan must be half a tree!'
Said the cove; and it flashed on Meg
That her landlord's misfortune was that he
Only boasted of one Scotch peg.

And she'd quite forgotten, when with her mit
She'd annexed the forbidden fruit,
That his slacks were built as one and a bit,
And he'd only one daisy root.

And a tear-drop fell from the girl's mince pie
And her raspberry tart was torn
With anguish; for she had an empty sky,
And the bags wouldn't bullock's horn.

Saturday, 9 May 1908, he published 'Significant Strains' which was partly in rhyming slang. The first verse, which follows, contains rather more than the rest of the rhyme.

Uninvited, we dropped into a suburban rub-a-dub,
After closing time, my old pal Bill and I;
All alone in the bazaar, we helped ourselves to beer and grub,
Then we looked around for oof to fill the sky.
But the tills had all been emptied, and the only likely spot
Where a little bees and honey might be found,
Was the automatic 'tinkler', worked by pennies in the slot,
So we started on it when we'd skirmished round.
All was quiet, not a sound disturbed the stillness of the night;
You could hear a dewdrop drop, or just about;
When, without a moment's warning to our horror and affright,
An accusing strain of melody rang out . . .

*Saturday, 11 July 1908*

The Juvenile Delinquent, whose wrong-doings are attributed by the 'beak' to a predilection for 'penny bloods', conducts his own defence largely in 'titles', but makes use of a little Rhyming Slang. '. . . I shouted, "Your bees, or your trouble and strife," like the hero in *Highwayman Harry*.'

*13 March 1909*

## DAYLIGHT SAVING

He'd divested himself of his daisies below,
And had crawled up the apples and pears;
As if fearful of letting the fork and knife know
He'd got back to his home and his cares.
Then he stood on the landing and blinked all around,
But his bedroom he couldn't well miss;
For the Rory was open, and there, fully gowned,
Was the missis, who asked, 'What means this?
You were due home last night at 10.30 p.m.
Not at dawn on the following day!'
And, though elephant's trunk, he was sobered pro tem.
And explained in a dignified way:
'I assure you its abso-hic-lutely all right,
I'd your own peace and comfort in view;
'Twas for your sake, my darling, I stayed out all night,
I was saving the daylight for you!'

An appended note declares; 'Barbers all over the country approve of the Daylight Shaving Bill.'

## UNDERWORLD

. . . this whistle I got on's a bit different from the old grey one they dish you out with back in the queer place!

'No,' he said, 'She ain't got no ponce. What'd she want a Jo Ronce for . . . ? . . . , what with the steamer she's got for regular . . . she don't do so bad, I should coco.'

Why don't you take off your Gawd forbid? We're passing the Cenotaph.

'. . . he likes me to call him [Biffs]. It was his monicker at Oxford College or some place.'
'The berk.'
'I won't have you using that bad language.'
'You know what it means all right, so don't get all pound-noteish.' [1]

[1] **pound noteish** high hat, up stage and County, putting on the guiver, pretending to superiority.

'You berk. You gone and dropped the bloody glim.'
'Damn the glim. Take a butcher's out o' the cinder.'

'. . . the slops had been turning up at the block of flats just as he was making his get away. Yes, and coming along in a jam jar too. That made them look like Sweenies.'

From *The Gilt Kid*—a novel by James Curtis (Jonathan Cape, 1936)

## COCKNEY LIFE

The street Bookmaker, on the verge of arrest, is enabled to elude the law by the sudden outbreak of a fight, the organizer of which says:

'You must be gettin' old—to go out and get yourself knocked off the first day of the season. It's a good job I'm around, and there's some china plates in the street. And it only cost a pound to start that read and write.'

Charlie and Mr Perks are on their way to the hop-field, the former (in a hurry) to see his best girl, the latter (in none) to see his wife. Their transport is an old tandem-bicycle.

'Hi! come on Perks,' he [Charlie] cried, 'let's get goin'. I want ter see Doris terday.'

Perks got up [from the roadside grass, where they had been resting] slowly, yawning. 'Wait till you've bin married ten years,' he said, 'Yer won't be in such a 'urry then. I ain't eager ter see my ole gooseberry pudden, I kin tell yer. 'Speshully as I ain't got no greengages for 'er.'

Perks and Charlie, continuing the journey, decide to help shovel sand out of a lorry in return for a lift.

'You use yer Lord Lovell on the sand by the tail-board,' Charlie instructed. 'I've gotta keep my mince pies on you. You must 'ave given your mother a shock when you was born.'

'Where yer orf to Charlie?' he [Ginger] enquired.

'Goin' for ball o' chalk down the Lane; comin?' [they push through the crowds in Petticoat Lane: they watch the vendors and the entertainers, which is tiring.]

''Ere, the old currant bun's getting warm; and me plates o' meat ache. . . .'

From *Down Donkey Row* by Len Ortzen (Cresset Press, 1938)

## THE ARMY

Harry was a Jew. In his own phrase: a 'tin-lid'. Otherwise, a 'four-by-two', a 'Kangaroo', or a 'five-to-two' . . . With mock admiration, he murmured: 'Oh, ve-ry nice! Oh ve-ry apples and rice!'

The Professor . . . peered at Harry.

'. . . I beg your pardon!'

'We 'aven't got no garden,' said Harry.

'Garden?' . . .

'One 'n' 'leven-pence three farden.'

'What the hell are you talking about?'

'I was only askin' abaht yer whistle . . . yer whistle-an'-flute!'

Harry pushed a packet of cigarettes across to me. 'Light up China!' He indicated the three gunners with a nod of his head. 'When them blokes begins ter warm up, there's goin' ter be a bit of pen-an'-ink in ere.'

I'll come back, . . . as sure's there's a nose on me duce-an'-ace.

From *Reported Safe Arrival.* (The journal of a voyage to Port 'X'), by Michael Harrison (Rich and Cowan, 1943)

## SUPERIORITY BEHAVIOUR

Gwenda, who has lost her income through the effect of the economic depression, has reached the point at which she has to sell the contents of her flat. Her friend Gerrard, who has himself been one of the three million unemployed so long that he has discovered how to survive, has advised Gwenda not to call in a dealer and has himself introduced an interested consumer: a coster whose son is about to be married. The prospective buyer, feeling awkward, reacts by flight to rhyming slang:

'The customer wore a cloth cap and a choker round his neck. Between these two he had an apparently badly swollen red nose, busy, shrunken eyes, and a pair of cracked, pale-blue lips. His Cockney was of a quality that Gwenda could scarcely understand, and to make matters worse, he chewed match-sticks, and spat splinters all over the place.

'Pressing his gigantic fist into the middle of [the bed] he forced the spring down almost to the floor, remarking: "Yhus, norra bad Uncle Ned; gorra jerry?" and he gave a wheezy laugh.

'"Yhus, movin' aht, are yeh? Norra bed flat. I sees yeh got the fisherman's daughter laid on an' all—where 'e's a-goin' teh, they 'ave teh go dahn two flights er apples and pears: still—do fer 'em fer a star' off! When me an' na misses kicked orf, we didn't 'ave 'arf wot 'e's a-gettin'—blimey! worrer ole potan 'pan I 'ad—bless yer 'eart!—'e knocked me dahn every toime 'e a-seed me—'e did!"'

From *This Gutter Life* by Julian Franklyn (Scholartis Press, 1934)

## PRESS MATTER

*Sydney Mirror*, 14 October 1942

Gurney's Cartoon strip entitled *Bluey and Curley*, quoted by Sidney J. Baker in *The Australian Language*, 1945:

'Struth, a bag of coke comes into the Sydney Harbour for a dig in the grave, and finds the pitch and toss has gone down th' field of wheat. Blimey no Mark Foy is going to give me a dig in the grave. Yer might take me Port Melbourne Pier off.'

*Sydney Bulletin*, 18 January 1902

(Quoted by Sidney J. Baker in *The Australian Language*, 1945)

Me mother's away, as I was swiftly flowing up the field of wheat in the bread-and-jam, a heavenly plan with a big charming mottle of O-my-dear sticking out of his sky-rocket fancy-sashed the girl-abductor on his bundle of socks with it cos he wouldn't let him have a virgin bride for nothing.

*Sydney Truth*, 7 January 1900

(Quoted by Sidney J. Baker in *The Australian Language*, 1945)

I 'ad a brown I'm afloat, a green Jacky Lancashire in me lef-'and sky, and tan daisy roots. When I meets the cheese and kisses and prattled off down the frog and toad, I tell you I was a bit of orl right.

## SHOW OFF

'In a public-house, under normal conditions, a request for a pint of "brown" or of "wallop" will be made; but in the presence of an "observer", when the Cockney uses his rhyming slang excessively and ostentatiously, partly to mystify and partly to establish his own superiority, the request will be for a *Walter Scott* (pot) of *pig's ear* (beer). He may add that he will not get *elephant's trunk*—or he may abbreviate to *elephant's*—(drunk) on it because it is half *fisherman's daughter* (water);

but if he does he can be sure his *trouble and strife* (wife) will soon pick him up off the *Rory O'More* (floor) and get him into *Uncle Ned* (bed).

'If he sees that "someone" is pricking up his ears, he may "look at him a bit old-fashioned like" and continue by telling the potman to put it on the *Cain and Able* (table) same as if he was at the *Pope o' Rome* (home) just for a *Bushey Park* (lark). He may then say when he has got it down his *bushel and peck* (neck) he intends to take a *ball o' chalk* (walk) round the Johnny Horner (corner) to give his *Charing Kraws* (horse) *Tommy O'Rann* (scran—slang for food); if he leaves it much later he rec'ns he ought to be *'arf inched* (pinched—arrested), but he supposes he'd better hand out the *sugar and honey* (money) before leaving.

'If the victim of all this verbal show-off now appears all agog, the Cockney will not be able to withstand the temptation to add a little more to the general effect by saying that after he had his *Rosy Lea* (tea) he took a *Martin-le-Grand* (hand) at *Wilkie Bards* (cards) and lost so heavily that he had to put his *Dicky Dirt* (shirt) in *bullock's horn* (pawn); and in order to keep the *love and kisses* (missis) quiet he'd had to buy her a bottle of *Tom Thumb* (rum). Then, as a parting shot, he may ask for a match to light his *cherry-ripe* (pipe); and for good measure, turning back at the door, inquire if anyone has got a *linen draper* in his *sky-rocket* (newspaper in his pocket); whereupon the interloper is expected to drop, deflated, from the sky-high eminence of his patronizing eavesdropping. If he does not, then the rest of the company continue the good work till the potman, banging on the counter, yells 'Nah den—laidies and gints—*bird-lime*!'

From *The Cockney* by Julian Franklyn (Andre Deutsch, 1953)

## ME AND MY GIRL[1]
### A Musical Comedy
### by
### Lupino Lane

Lord Hareford is dead: but he has left a document in which he confesses to an unfortunate marriage, and expresses his fear that there may be a son and heir.

There is. None other than Mr Bill Snibson, of Lambeth Walk (the part was taken—with distinction—by the author) and the play opens

[1] Produced at the Victoria Palace Theatre, London, it was performed before crowded houses, and was perhaps the greatest success as a musical play since *Chu Chin Chow*.

when the family solicitor, having found Bill, has brought him from London and introduces him to his family and the guests at Hareford Hall.

ACT I—SCENE 1

DUCHESS: I hope you enjoyed your drive.
BILL: Not arf—but I nearly lost me titfa!
ALL: Titfa?
BILL: Me tit for tat.
ALL: Tit for tat?
BILL: My Hat! It was so windy I had to pull it over my gingerbread.
ALL: Gingerbread?
BILL: Me lump o' lead!
ALL: Lump of lead?
BILL: Me Uncle Ned!
ALL: Uncle Ned?
BILL: Oh, me 'ead—the empty part o' me.

BILL: I'm 'ere ter day an' gorne termorrer. I started loife wi nuffink an' I still got it; but when I'm absolutely 'earts—
SIR JOHN: Arts?
BILL: 'earts of Oak.
SIR JOHN: A Building Society?
BILL: Naow! Broke!

BILL: You're not kiddin' me, are yeh? D'you reely mean teh say as Lord Hareford were reely moi ole' pot an' pan?
DUCHESS: Pot and pan?
BILL: I mean—moi ole man. My farver . . . I don't fit in . . . 'Oxton 'stead of Oxford! 'ere, I'm a sport. Gimme da bees an' honey—
ALL: Bees and honey?
BILL: The money—then I'll mizzle.

[*The aristocrats catch the disease*]

ACT I, SCENE 3

JACQUELINE: . . . I'm sick of being Hearts of Oak.
GERALD: Hearts of Oak?
JACQUELINE: Yes—broke. I learned that from His Lordship.
GERALD: There you are! What did I tell you? She's after his bees and honey.

PORCHESTER: So you've got it too! Why, only this morning I found myself asking my man for a bottle of pig's ear.

BILL: (confronted with the morning's mail and being informed of one with the Lambeth post-mark) Oh! Let's have a basinful o' that!

PORCHESTER: Basinful?

BILL: A butcher's.

PORCHESTER: A butcher's?

BILL: A butcher's 'ook.

PORCHESTER: And what is a butcher's hook?

BILL: A look. Don't no-one rahn' 'ere un'nerstan' plain English!

[*Charles, the servant, is helping Bill to dress—*]

BILL: Gimme that 'oller boys 'oller!

CHARLES: 'oller boys 'oller?

BILL: Oxford scholar!

CHARLES: Oxford scholar?

BILL: The arf-a-dollar! (*Charles offers him half-a-crown*) Naow!—the collar! Nahr fer the Peckham Rye.

CHARLES: The Peckham Rye, Sir?

BILL: The tie—and you might get these trousers altered, they're too tight under me arms—like me piccolo and flutes.

CHARLES: Eh—your—?

BILL: My daisy roots.

CHARLES: Daisy roots?

BILL: My boots! They 'urt me plates o' meat. That's me feet. —'Ere—why can't I wear a dickey?

CHARLES: And what is a dickey, sir?

BILL: Shirt wivaht a chassis—gimme my Charlie Prescot—that's my waistcoat—and now my I'm afloat.

CHARLES: The—eh—what sir?

BILL: Quaker oat.

CHARLES: Porridge, sir?

BILL: Naow! Coat. Nah gis me titfa and me turtle doves an' I'll be on me Edna May.

CHARLES: Your—eh—hat—and?

BILL: Me gloves an' I'll be on me way.

# APPENDIX

## A Pained Parson

The following is from an address delivered at Carlisle, in mid-nineteenth century by the Rev. A. Mursell:

'The point to which I have yet to direct attention is manliness in speech. There are many young men who seem to consider it essential to manliness that they should be masters of slang. The sporting world, like its brother, the swell mob, has a language of its own; but this dog-English extends far beyond the sporting world. It comes with its hordes of barbarous words, threatening the entire extinction of genuine English. Now just listen for a moment to our fast young man, or the ape of a fast young man, who thinks that to be a man he must speak in the dark phraseology of slang. If he does anything on his own responsibility, he does it on his own "hook". If he sees anything remarkably good he calls it a "stunner", the superlative of which is a "regular stunner". If a man is requested to pay a tavern bill, he is asked if he will "stand Sam". If he meets a savage looking dog he calls him an "ugly customer". If he meets an eccentric man, he calls him a "rummy old cove". A sensible man is a "chap that is well up to snuff". Our young friend never scolds, but "blows up"; never pays but "stumps up"; never finds it difficult to pay, but is "hard up"; never feels fatigued, but is "used up". He has no hat, but shelters his head beneath a "tile". He wears no neckcloth, but surrounds his throat with a "choker". He lives nowhere, but there is some place where he "hangs out". He never goes away or withdraws, but he "bolts"—he "slopes"—he "mizzles"—he "makes himself scarce" —he "walks his chalks"—he "makes tracks"—he "cuts his stick"—or, what is the same thing, he "cuts his lucky"! The highest compliment you can pay him is to tell him that he is a "regular brick". He does not profess to be brave, but he prides himself on being "plucky". Money is a word which he has forgotten, but he talks a good deal about "tin", and "the needful", "the Rhino", and the "ready". When a man speaks he "spouts"—when he holds his peace he "shuts up"; when he is humiliated, he is "taken down a peg or two", and "made to sing small". Now, a good deal of this slang is harmless; many of the terms are, I think, very expressive; yet there is much in slang that is objectionable. For example, as Archdeacon Hare observes in one of his sermons, the word "governor", as applied to a father, is to be reprehended. I have heard a young man call his father the "relieving officer". Does it not betray on the part of the young men great ignorance of the paternal and filial relationships, or great contempt of them? Their father is to such young men merely a governor—merely the representative of authority. Innocently enough the expression is used by thousands of young men who venerate and love their parents; but only think of it, and I am sure that you will admit that it is a cold, heartless word when thus applied, and one that ought forthwith to be abandoned.'

This was printed, without any paragraph breaks, in *The Times*, 3 April 1858. In the narrow column it is even less easy on the eye.

## A Pained Parent

The following is from a letter to The Editor of the *Daily News* for 25 September 1868. It begins with a long paragraph in praise of the boy's achievements at school—they are almost as good as his achievements out of school—then comes the wail of complaint:

'This morning my Son and I left the Great Western Station in a "privileged cab" for Hampstead, stopping to make some purchases on the way. On dismissing the vehicle, a dispute arose as to the fare, and the cabman was insolent. My son, who had just borrowed what he called "half a skid" from me, promptly took up the cudgels, or, in other words, the coarse language of the streets, and metaphorically smote that cabman hip and thigh. "Were we such a brace of fools," he asked, with indignant fervour, "as to pay showful prices for riding in a blessed growler? Did the driver think to flummox us by his lip because he thought we weren't fly to him? He, the driver, must get up earlier and go to bed without getting buffy, which he hadn't done for a week of Sundays, before he found that little game would draw in the dibs. No more tight than we were, wasn't he?—(with great depth of meaning, this)—then what made him so precious fishy about the gills, if he hadn't been out on the batter the night before?"

'These questions and comments, incomprehensible as they were to me, appeared to give the cabman poignant anguish, and eventually caused him to drive away muttering and discomforted. But sir, at what a price was this triumph obtained? Where did my lad pick up the slang? How did he learn its import and its ready use? Are other schoolboys equal adepts with him? Is "cant" now considered to be a regular branch of learning, and is it included in the curriculum like the modern languages? My son may be exceptionally gifted in this particular, but he laughs *my* questions off, and speaks of the strange words used lightly as "the lingo his pals talk in at school". I therefore feel constrained to appeal, through your columns, to parents and to tutors to explain this monstrous perversion of the Queen's English, and to tell me whether it is common amongst our youth? I am, &c.,

A. FATHER'

Oh come off it, papa! If those awful words were incomprehensible to you, how did you recall them so accurately when writing?

My dear, dead sir, we, your peers, one hundred years (almost) after you, judge you a bit of a liar, and a perfect prig. Today, any father would be proud of a school-boy son who could 'slap down' a taximan so effectively.

## Native or Naturalized

Sir St Vincent Troubridge, writing in *American Speech* (Vol. XXI, No. 1, February 1946) and claiming as his qualification to make a contribution to the literature on the 'nationality' of rhyming slang the fact that from 1914 to 1922 he served as a young officer in a Cockney Regiment, comments on a number of Dr Maurer's suggestions concerning the country of origin of some of the terms recorded by him in the article *Australian Rhyming Argot* . . .[1]

In his introductory paragraph Sir St Vincent says: 'To give one example. Mr Maurer has *red hot cinder* "a winder (window)" noted as origin uncertain, either American or English. Now my Cockneys in those old days would not have dreamed of using anything but *Polly Flinders* (incidentally the name of the heroine of the English Christmas Pantomime of *Robinson Crusoe*; note how many rhyming slang words are derived from the theatre) for window, so I contend that of Mr Maurer's two possibilities, *red hot cinder* is probably of American origin.'

Yes: but only the 'red-hot' element which is an altered form of Cockney *burnt*. 'Burnt cinder(s)' is an older and 'deeper' term than is 'Polly Flinder(s)'. It is generally reduced to *burnt*, and in London's underworld 'a stiff burnt' is a plate-glass window. (See the *Glossary* and the *Addenda* at the appropriate entries.)

There follows a commentary, arranged in alphabetical order, on twenty-nine of the terms recorded by Dr Maurer beginning with *basin crop* which Sir St Vincent rightly declares to be ineligible for inclusion in the category of rhyming slang. One other term dealt with by Sir St Vincent is incontestably Australian and is omitted hereunder where each of the remaining twenty-seven, accompanied by Dr Maurer's suggestion is followed by (*a*) Sir St Vincent's comment and (*b*), our own opinion.

[1] See pages viii, 18.

*Bees and honey*, probably English. (*a*) Almost certainly English. (*b*) Quite certainly English.

*Bonny fair*, probably American. (*a*) This is certainly a mistake. (*b*) Yes—the mistake is that *Bonny* is simply an American corruption of *Barnet*.

*Bowl of chalk*, probably American. (*a*) Agreed. (*b*) The only American thing about it is the word *Bowl* which is a corruption of *Ball*.

*Chevy Chase*, obsolete in England. (*a*) By no means. (*b*) Invariably reduced and pronounced *chivvy*, hence both are, with modification, correct.

*Derby Kelley*, probably American. (*a*) English: probably from some mid-XIX C. individual of criminal fame in Derbyshire. (*b*) Yes, English, but not from any Derbyshire criminal—Derby is the old English given name *Darby*.

*Dip South*, American or English. (*a*) American. (*b*) Yes, *Dip* is probably a corruption of *deep*.

*Duke of Cork*, English. (*a*) English. (*b*) No—Irish.

*East and West*, probably English. (*a*) Probably American. (*b*) A better definition is needed: if it refers to the undervest Dr Maurer is right, but if the waistcoat is indicated, then the victory goes to Sir St Vincent Troubridge.

*Fiddle and flute*, probably English. (*a*) Agreed, but always whistle and . . . (*b*) So the honours are fifty-fifty: *fiddle* is an American prefix.

*Fifteen and two*, probably American. (*a*) Almost certainly American. The English is *five to two*. (*b*) Both the English and the American might be any number to two, and never twice alike.

*Forty-four*, probably American. (*a*) Almost certainly American. The English is *five to four*. (*b*) As above, but substitute *four* for *two*.

*Half a lick*, probably American. (*a*) Agreed. (*b*) Far more likely to be Irish.

*Here and there*, probably English. (*a*) This is doubted. (*b*) Probably American—if it does not turn out to be either Australian or Irish.

*Hickory dock*, American or English. (*a*) Probably American in this form. The English is *Dickory*. (*b*) There is no choice between *Dickory* and *Hickory*: they appear with equal frequency in the nursery rhyme books, so it stands an equal chance of nativity on either side of the Atlantic, but *hickory* is the favoured American form.

*I desire*, English. (*a*) *Anna Maria* is ten times as usual. (*b*) Nevertheless, *I desire* was one of Hotten's crop of terms, so it must be English.

*Johnny Skinner*, probably American. (*a*) Agreed. (*b*) Quite certainly English.

*Kidney pie*, American or English. (*a*) Almost certainly American. (*b*) Almost certainly neither—most likely Irish.

*Lean and Lake*, probably English. (*a*) Very rare if English. (*b*) Hence, it is most likely Irish.

*Mother and daughter*, probably English. (*a*) If English, rare; I have never heard anything but *Ratcatcher's daughter* (from a popular song of the 1850s). (*b*) *Ratcatcher's daughter* is but an inferior version of *Fisherman's daughter*: *Mother and daughter* is a Thames waterman's term, so it is certainly English.

*Ocean wave*, English. (*a*) Rare, if English, (*b*) but nonetheless, English.

*Peaches and Pears*, probably English. (*a*) More probably American. (*b*) Most probably Irish.

*Pot of glue*, American or English. (*a*) More probably American, (*b*) but again most probably Irish.

*Roary O'Moore*, probably American. (*a*) Almost certainly English. (*b*) Rory O'More, being one of the terms recorded by Ducange Anglicus,[1] is most emphatically not of American origin. It has reached U.S.A. via Australia from England where, out along some railway embankment, or canal ditch, it was invented, about a hundred and thirty years ago, by an Irish navvy. All that is American about it is the spelling.

*Shovel and broom*, American or English. (*a*) If English, it is much rarer than *birchbroom*. (*b*) Of the two, the latter is the rarer, but both are English.

*Simple Simon*, probably American. (*a*) More probably English. Simple Simon is an old English Nursery Rhyme. (*b*) American citizens too, in infancy, learn nursery rhymes, and the term is American in its idiom.

*Strong and thin*, probably English. (*a*) Agreed. (*b*) Also agreed!

*Tom Tug*, probably American. (*a*) Almost certainly English. (*b*) Quite certainly English: from Dibden's opera.

## Blazon Atte Bow

A writer in *The Heraldry Gazette* for April 1960, after referring to an exhibition of objects of heraldic interest in the present writer's Collection, and mounted by him at The City Literary Institute, under the auspices of which house of learning courses of public instruction in the subject are held, said:

'It seems a long way "from Heraldry to Cockney Slang", but an article so headed in the City Press (25.3.60) reminds us that our above mentioned member Mr Franklyn, besides being the author of *Shield and Crest*, a forthcoming book on heraldry,[2] has written a work on Cockney London and has compiled *A Dictionary of Rhyming Slang*.

[1] See pages 4, 8, 26, 27. [2] Now published (our note).

'This combination of interests suggests that our member is the man to go to if a Pearly King is egged on by his bother-and-strife and gawd-ferbids to look into his family crime-and-mystery and discover whether he is entitled to fire-alarms and pants-and-vest. We have blazoning by the planets for royalty, and by the precious stones for noble-men. Why not another refinement, Cockney Blazon for those born within sound of Bow Bells?

'By this method the arms of the City of London would be:

Kiss-me-Sergeant, a pitch-and-toss, and in the first pint-of-porter a dartboard, football pools; and for pants-and-vest, on a race horse of the colours a water-wagon's main-spring charged with a pitch-and-toss as in the fire-alarms.

Press-reporters . . .

'Enough. Any intelligent nose-bleeder can work the rest out for himself.'

To those not learned in the figures of heraldry the following 'translation' of the blazon of arms for the Corporation of the City may be welcome:

Argent, [silver], a cross, and in the first quarter a sword, gules [red]; and for their crest, on a torse [twist] of the colours a dragon's wing charged with a cross as in the arms.

Supporters . . . (our own 'nose-bleeders' may like to be informed these are dragons).

## London Antiquary

F. W. Fairholt (1814–66) was an engraver and man of letters who wrote under the pseudonym of 'London Antiquary'. A body of opinion exists that Fairholt was the author of *The Slang Dictionary*. This opinion is not shared by the present writer who sees no need for it. The work was not beyond John Camden Hotten's own manifold abilities, and the first edition is by '*a* London Antiquary' which is clearly meant to be a descriptive term, not a pen-name.

Further, the subsequent edition, bearing Hotten's own name, was issued during the life-time of Fairholt and notwithstanding that the bookseller bought an author's manuscript outright and could do with it what he pleased, it did not pay him to pretend to authorship, and neither is Fairholt likely to have remained silent on the matter.

Finally, in the Catalogue of the British Museum the work is attributed to Hotten, not to Fairholt.